Contents

List of Tables, Figures and Maps

Tables

Figures

Maps

Acknowledgements

The spark for this book – as for more than one recent reassessment of the place of Europe in the world – was the US-led invasion of Iraq in March 2003. At the time I had been living in the United States for 16 years, and had long puzzled over the distinctions between European and American society. Indiana – where I live – is deep in the American heartland, a place that offers a perspective that is hard to find on the east coast or the west coast, where most American-based specialists in European studies live and work. From this vantage point, I have been deeply conscious of the contradictions in the US view of itself and of its place in the world, and repeatedly reminded of the failure of so many citizens of the 'world's last superpower' to understand the international system. At the same time, my regular return-trips to Britain and other parts of the EU have made me a strong believer in the idea that European integration is far more important and successful than most of the pessimists would have us believe. But the explanations for the changing balance in competing transatlantic views of the world had not yet fully resolved themselves in my mind. Then came the invasion, and many of the pieces of the jigsaw fell into place. The words and actions of the Bush administration not only shed new light on the nature of changes in the post-cold war world, but also clarified – to my mind – much of what Europe represented. And the outcry in the United States against the lack of support for the invasion from France and Germany made at least one new reality abundantly clear: the European Union finally mattered. After that, it was relatively easy to trace the outlines of the case for the EU as a superpower. All that was needed was to fill in the details, which is what this book sets out to do.

The bulk of the research was undertaken while I was on a sabbatical in 2005 from my home institution, and based at the Sussex European Institute at the University of Sussex. I owe a particular debt to Jörg Monar for setting up my visit to Falmer and for arranging access to all the resources I needed. My thanks also to the faculty and staff in the Institute – particularly Paul Taggart, Tim Bale, Aleks Szczerbiak, Adrian Treacher, Jo Amos, and my office neighbour David Evans – for their help, both conscious and uncon-scious. The Office for Professional Development at IUPUI gave me a Research Venture Award that helped ease the financial pain of living in today's extraordinarily expensive Britain. And Howard and Pella Mansell provided an inspiring country retreat near Piltdown where I was able to tap away on my laptop to the accompaniment of a background rural chorus, and to take breaks by walking the lanes and footpaths of the East Sussex countryside.

I also tested some of my ideas in presentations to audiences on both sides of the Atlantic. For being unwitting guinea pigs and sharing their thoughts, my thanks to those who attended my lectures during 2005–06 at the University of East Anglia, the University of Sussex, Manchester Metropolitan University, the College of Europe, the University of Miami, DePauw University, Ball State University, and IUPUI, and to Liki Koutrakou, Jim Rollo, Neill Nugent, Dieter Mahncke, Joaquín Roy, Bob Dewey and Gene Frankland for setting them up. My thanks also to participants in panels at two conferences where I presented some of my initial findings: the European Consortium on Political Research in Budapest, and the Midwest Political Science Association in Chicago. At IUPUI, my colleague Scott Pegg offered helpful thoughts and suggestions during conversations while the book was being written, and my research assistant Jon Brown – who knows far more about international relations theory than any other undergraduate I have known – pointed me in several useful directions. My thanks also to Richard Whitman for his feedback on a draft of Chapter 1, and to an anonymous reviewer for comments on the first five chapters.

My publisher Steven Kennedy brought his usual professionalism to the project and continued to show why he has become such a legend in the transatlantic publishing business. I appreciate his support for the project, and the conversations that we had at several lunches and dinners while the book was under development. My thanks also to Brian Morrison for his professional and remarkably fast work on the production side. My wife Leanne continued to take care of more than her fair share of domestic duties while I made myself scarce in my office or the library, and our sons Ian and Stuart provided frequent and welcome distractions. There are times when you can get too involved in your work, and it comes to dominate your waking (and sometimes sleeping) hours – and then there are times when your family can remind you what is really important in life. As with all my work, the book is dedicated to the three of them, with much love.

Introduction

Today's conventional wisdom holds that the United States is the world's last remaining superpower. In fact, it seems that no mention of the US as a superpower is any longer complete without the adjectives 'sole', 'only' or 'lone'. Since the collapse of the Soviet Union, mainstream thinking has argued that the old bipolar system of the cold war – in which Western ideas of democracy and capitalism were pitted against Soviet support for one-party government and central planning – has been replaced by a new unipolar era in which American military and economic power is so compelling and so dominant that none can hope to oppose it. For the former US national security advisor Zbigniew Brzezinski, the United States has become nothing less than the first, last and only global superpower.[1] For historian Paul Kennedy, it is 'the greatest superpower ever'.[2] In the opinion of political scientist Andrew Moravcsik, the United States can go it alone if it has to, and it is time 'to accept this fact and move on'.[3]

It is not hard to see why the lone superpower thesis is so seductive. The United States has the biggest military arsenal in history, and accounts for nearly half of annual global defence spending. The US military protects the biggest national economy in the world, which produces more than twice as much annually as the Japanese, and almost half as much again as the Germans, the British, the French and the Italians combined. Most of the world's biggest multinational corporations are American, and the American marketplace is widely acclaimed as the most inventive, dynamic and entrepreneurial in the world. The United States has diverse foreign policy interests, and its opinions on one issue after another attract international headlines. Foreign leaders pay homage to the president and Congress in much the same way as their predecessors once did to the Roman emperor and Senate. American popular culture can be found almost everywhere, whether in the form of American consumer products, or in the form of films and music produced by the American entertainment industry. And as if all this was not enough, the United States has the world's best universities, the greatest number of Nobel Prize winners, and the most advanced technology.

But not everyone bows to the weight of conventional wisdom. Some have conceded that US dominance cannot last forever, and a growing chorus points to the emerging challenge of the BRIC nations: Brazil, Russia, India and China.[4] A combination of rapid economic growth, large populations, and increased investments in military hardware suggests – to these observers, at least – that China certainly and perhaps also India pose short-term challenges to American dominance, and that the rise of Brazil and the promise of a revitalized Russia will later move us into an era of multipolarity. Japan, too, is sometimes described as a challenger to the United States, although with less conviction today than during the 1980s and 1990s, when the Japanese economy was in much better shape. Finally, there are those who argue that the European Union plays an important role in international relations, but this is still very much a minority view; majority thinking holds that the EU has too many internal problems – including divisions of political opinion, declining population growth, and enlargement fatigue – to stand up to the Americans on anything much more than economic matters.

This book challenges the conventional thinking. It rejects the traditional view that the greatest powers are states with large militaries that consciously pursue national interests, and argues instead that power can transcend states, can be expressed without resort to force, and can just as likely be latent and implied as it can be active and explicit. It also argues that globalization and interdependence have undermined old-style power politics and replaced it with a more complex and nuanced set of international relationships, in which ownership of the means of production is more important than ownership of the means of destruction, and cooperation is more effective than coercion. In this new post-modern environment, the qualities cultivated and projected by the European Union have made it a new breed of superpower.

The idea of Europe as a counterweight to American and Soviet power has been with us since peace settled on Europe in 1945. At first it was no more than a pipe-dream: the political and economic lifeblood of Europe had been drained by war, its treasuries emptied, its cities bombed, its infrastructure destroyed, and perhaps 30–40 million of its citizens had lost their lives. But this did not stop the dreamers from dreaming, and from elaborating the means by which Europe might rebuild, might stay at peace with itself, and might reassert itself in the post-war international system. They saw the new Europe not as an old-style military power – violence as a tool of statecraft had been severely discredited by two world wars – but as the champion of softer forms of influence, and of a new international system based around incentives, free markets, and peaceful negotiation.

So dominant was the power of the United States in the early cold war era that European opinion was barely heard. Many Americans saw their country as an exceptional state with a mission to export ideas and values that were claimed as essentially American, including democracy and capitalism. While Americans had focused until the late nineteenth century on imposing their values on North America, argues LaFeber, by the early twentieth century they had the power to extend and promote their values around the world, and – from the 1940s – to do so unilaterally if they wished.[5] Europe was not in the position to resist American leadership, being as dependent as it was upon American economic and security guarantees. But this did not stop Europeans from trying to withstand American influence, or from working to rebuild their troubled and divided continent so as to reassert the European voice in the world. The Atlantic Alliance is often acclaimed for its successful defence of the West against the Soviet threat, but behind the façade of cooperation lurked many differences of opinion, and the history of the Alliance is littered with crises, from Berlin to Suez, Vietnam, differences over détente, the collapse of Bretton Woods, the Arab–Israeli question, the Balkans, Iraq, and more.[6]

The end of the cold war encouraged triumphalists to hail the confirmation of the American way and the end of history, a view that seemed to be confirmed by the mixed record of the European Community, which lurched from one fumbled episode to another. But the visible expressions of American military, political and economic power drew attention away from a rather more complex set of developments. After many false starts and wrong turns, the Europeans had finally agreed what was needed to bring down the barriers to the free movement of people, money, goods and services, and had thereby created the world's biggest capitalist marketplace. European corporations were merging and offering more competition to their American and Japanese counterparts, reclaiming ground lost in the 1950s and 1960s. European governments worked together on international trade negotiations, agreed common policies in a host of different areas (some more effective than others), and Europe offered an irresistible magnetic attraction to prospective new members and to neighbouring states that wanted access to the European marketplace.

Their successes gave Europeans a new confidence, buoyed by their deliberate choice to eschew the old-style power politics still being pursued by cold warriors in Washington, and with particular vehemence by neo-conservatives determined to exploit American power to its fullest in order to promote American interests. Europeans took increasing comfort in their preference for non-military solutions to problems, in their support for multilateralism and international organizations, and in their penchant for soft power (economic incentives and diplomatic negotiation) over hard power (coercion, threats, and invasion). American critics of the European project were unconvinced, and were more than ready to accuse Europeans of using these channels because they lacked the option of military power, of appeasing dictators rather than standing up to them, and of criticizing US policy while always being ready to fall back on the military guarantees that only the United States could offer.

But changes in the character of the international system have challenged the old assumptions. The forces of globalization, interdependence and technology have altered international political and economic relationships. The magic ingredients for great power may once have been deliberate military options wielded by states, but we now live in a post-modern, post-national era in which military power has lost much of its credibility and effectiveness. Latent or unconscious power can be just as important to an understanding of international relations as visible and deliberate power, and global influence is expressed not just by states but by popular movements and by clusters of states that are working to integrate their economies and their public policies. And it is time to review the understatement of Europe's successes, while at the same time taking a closer look at the limitations of the American model of power.

The evidence of change can be found in three overlapping arenas. First, there have been developments internal to the EU that have given it greater strength and a sharper identity. With the single market programme all but complete, and expansion to 25 member states with a total population of 454 million, the EU has become the world's biggest economy. Most of its wealthiest members have adopted a single currency that threatens the dominant position of the US dollar. The EU has pursued a common commercial policy that has made it the colossus of international trade negotiations. The EU has adopted common policies in a wide variety of areas, and in spite of difficulties it has made progress on the development of a common foreign and security policy. There is also majority public support in almost every member state for the idea of the EU playing an assertive new international role and becoming independent of the US lead. Combined, these developments have not only encouraged the EU to become more assertive as a global actor, but have *allowed* it to become more assertive.

Second, there have been developments internal to the United States that have compromised and undermined its abilities to exploit its power. They include long-term domestic economic problems, the diversion of copious public spending into the military, internal social and political divisions, a breach in values between the United States and much of the rest of the liberal democratic world, and limits to the efficacy of the US military juggernaut. The US is without question a military, economic, political and cultural superpower, but the plaudits that are heaped on American achievements and capabilities must be seen alongside the handicaps that the United States has largely imposed upon itself, which have often frustrated its ability to achieve its foreign policy objectives, and have compromised America's leadership role in the world. Nothing generates so many searching questions about the old model of power as the remarkable failures of US foreign policy since

Map 0.1 *The European Union*

1. Albania
2. Belgium
3. Bosnia
4. Croatia
5. Kosovo
6. Luxembourg
7. Macedonia
8. Montenegro
9. Netherlands
10. Slovenia
11. Switzerland

EU member states

September 2001, a state of affairs which has led to a worldwide surge of anti-Americanism, has undermined America's claims to global leadership, and has enlarged the ranks of those standing behind non-military responses to international problems.

Finally, there have been developments in the international environment that have worked against the cold war realist model of power, with its emphasis on states and security. Prime among these has been the expansion of interdependence and globalization, which has reduced the significance of national borders and the powers of states. Meanwhile, the end of the cold war has reduced Western European dependence upon the American security umbrella, and has removed the barriers to cooperation and integration between the two halves of Europe that were divided during the cold war. Then there has been the replacement of the security challenges of the cold war with the more complex international challenges of the post-cold war era. At the same time, options pursued by its policymakers have left the United States increasingly isolated; it takes positions that regularly put it at odds with almost every other industrialized country, it has pursued unilateral initiatives in the face of a near-universal preference elsewhere for multilateral options, and it defines threats and their potential solutions on its own terms. It has been argued that the Americans use their military because they can, and that the Europeans prefer diplomacy because it is all they have.[7] But the reality is more complex: the EU has made a conscious decision to pursue non-military options, and the nature of the international system today is more suited to a new model of superpower, one that prefers to avoid military solutions to problems, that prefers to achieve its objectives through influence rather than coercion, and that prefers to lead by example.

These changes have combined to promote the long-standing desire of many Europeans to exert and express the European view of the world, and to act as a balance to the power of the United States. Along the way, Europe has also offered a new set of values and priorities that has resonated with many of those who worry about the costs and implications of American leadership. The result has been a resurgence of European global influence, which has had the effect of replacing the cold war bipolar system with a post-modern bipolar system. The cold war system was characterized by geopolitical and ideological competition between two superpowers that relied heavily on military options as their primary bargaining tools, that engaged in an arms race, that pursued intimidation and propaganda and assassination, and that developed networks of allies to act as both a source of support and a market for influence. In the post-modern system there is no prospect of war between the two superpowers, which instead compete for economic, political and cultural influence, and offer two distinctive sets of methods, values, and norms.

In this new system, the European Union is a superpower that relies upon soft power to express itself and to achieve its objectives, and that finds itself at a moral advantage in an international environment where violence as a means of achieving influence is increasingly detested and rejected, and at a strategic advantage because its methods and priorities fit more closely with the needs and consequences of globalization. The EU has become influential by promoting values, policies and goals that appeal to other states in a way that aggression and coercion cannot. In so doing, it has redefined our understanding of the meaning of power, as well as fundamentally and irrevocably changing the balance of influence in the international system.

Structure of the book

Chapter 1 reviews the changing nature of power in the international system. It argues that the age of the military superpower is over, and that influence in the era of globalization is best achieved by the use of diplomacy, the provision of economic opportunity and political incentives, and the exercise of soft power – all qualities that the EU has become adept at employing. The chapter challenges widely held assumptions about the unmatched global power of post-cold war America, argues that its exceptionalist and realist perspectives often hinder its interpretation of international trends and challenges, that its emphasis on military means is counterproductive and expensive, and that the declining credibility of American leadership – particularly since Iraq – has amplified the qualities and advantages that the European Union brings to the interpretation of global problems. It also argues that we must rethink our understanding of the term *superpower*; where it has in the past been associated with overwhelming military power, and with the deliberate actions of large states, superpower qualities in the new international system can be achieved without resort to war and coercion, can be latent and implied, and are not restricted to states.

Chapter 2 surveys the changing relationship between Europe and the United States since the end of World War II. It argues that while the Atlantic Alliance was a necessary and successful response to the Soviet threat, it was also a troubled marriage of convenience, involving partners who did not always agree either on goals or on methods. Europe was too weak and divided to offer much opposition to the United States, but with time it became more stable and more confident, and more willing to criticize and oppose American policy. The end of the cold war may have created a brief 'unipolar moment', during which the United States had no peer and Europe stumbled from one foreign policy embarrassment to another, but the EU was expanding and was using its economic power more effectively. Then came the rollercoaster of the Bush years, which took the Alliance from its moment of greatest agreement (following the September 2001 terrorist attacks) to its moment of greatest disagreement (over the March 2003 invasion of Iraq). Armed with strategic advantages and a closer fit with the realities of the new international system, and benefiting from the reduced credibility of American power, the EU found itself transformed as a global actor.

Chapter 3 surveys the changing character and value of military power in the post-modern system. Because military power is so much a part of claims that the United States is the world's only remaining superpower, the chapter begins with an assessment of the limitations on American military power: its mixed record on achieving political goals, the handicaps imposed by unilateralism, the practical limits faced by even the greatest armies, the diversion of valuable resources, the effects of inefficient spending, and questions about the value of war as a tool of policy. This is followed by an assessment of the progress that Europe has made on building a common security policy and the tools to back it up. Critics of Europe as a global actor will often quote the examples of the Balkans and the Gulf wars, but European military cooperation has allowed the EU to become a civilian power that is ready and willing to invest in and commit its military, but with a preference for multilateralism and for peacekeeping rather than for unilateralism and warmaking. The chapter concludes that Europe offers the world a new model for the political role of the military and the achievement of security, one in which troops and arms can be used to encourage and support rather than to coerce and threaten.

Chapter 4 makes the argument that whatever doubts there may be about Europe's global military power, there are few about its economic power. After assessing the remarkable achievements of the European single market, the chapter looks at three particular indicators of European economic power. First, there is the euro and its prospects for replacing – or taking its place alongside – the US dollar as the world's leading international currency. A combination of the success of the euro, the rise of the European marketplace and improvident US economic policies has boosted its prospects. Second, the EU has become the world's biggest trading power, and has used its common trade policy to take a more aggressive position on trade issues, actively using the dispute settlement system of the World Trade Organization. Third, the single market has been at the foundation of a boom in mergers and acquisitions, which has helped build European corporations that compete more vigorously with their American and Japanese counterparts. For doubters about Europe's economic prospects, demographic changes point to potential future problems. But if economic growth is the servant of quality of life, then Europeans – who work shorter hours but produce more with those hours – have the advantage.

Chapter 5 looks at the changing balance of political power in the world. It reviews Europe's learning curve on foreign policy, noting that while there were missteps and embarrassments along the way, Europe's role in the world has become both more confident and more distinctive. Policy cooperation has become habit-forming, Europe has exploited its advantages in the use of soft power and diplomacy, and there has been growing public support for greater cooperation and independence on foreign policy. Much has changed as a result of a sharpening of the identity of Europe, but much has also changed because of a reaction to US foreign policy leadership.

Particularly during the Bush administration, the US has adopted debatable interpretations of international problems and has pursued controversial policies. In many cases it has found itself alone or in a small minority. Meanwhile, the lure of the European model has strengthened, and Europe has exploited its economic advantages to become the most effective force in the world for the promotion of democracy and capitalism. Nowhere have its magnetic attractions been felt more strongly than among its neighbours, including those countries that may one day qualify for membership, and those that simply want access to the EU marketplace.

Chapter 6 compares and contrasts European and American values, arguing that the two actors now differ so greatly on so broad a range of social issues that they offer quite distinctive personalities to the rest of the world. It argues that brand image is central to notions of power, and that while the United States is still a cultural hegemon, the EU is catching up. Anti-Americanism has grown, taking multiple different forms, but there has been no corresponding rise of anti-Europeanism. Europeans and Americans see themselves – and are seen by others – in quite different ways, and offer distinctive interpretations about what they each represent. The chapter looks in detail at transatlantic contrasts in the role of religion, at competing social models, and at the manner in which Europe has begun to take the lead on addressing environmental problems. In the competition in the marketplace for ideas, European post-modern attitudes are building advantages over the values associated with American power.

Chapter 7 draws some conclusions by posing two questions. First, what does the European superpower represent, and how can we define Europeanism? While American power has led to strong – if not always consistent – views on what the United States represents, much less attention has been paid to the distinctive features of Europe. The chapter attempts to outline the values and preferences that give the European superpower its separate identity. Second, given the changed balance of power in the post-modern age, what prospects are there for the future of the Atlantic Alliance? The chapter argues that productive future cooperation is unlikely without changes on both sides of the Atlantic. The United States must realize that realist and exceptionalist interpretations of the world are no longer helpful or illuminating, that military solutions to problems can be costly and counterproductive, and that unilateralism (or, at worst, isolationism) is no longer either effective or viable. For their part, the Europeans must better understand and appreciate the possibilities of Europe, must understand and meet the obligations of their new global role, and must finally put nationalism to rest.

1

The Changing Nature of Power

During the cold war, we lived in a bipolar international system dominated by two superpowers, the United States and the Soviet Union. The one quality they had in common, and by which their power was mainly measured, was a large military that each was able and willing (if necessary) to project to all corners of the globe. When the cold war ended and the Soviet Union broke up, the United States was left without peer or competitor and was widely acclaimed as the world's only superpower. There may have been many middle-range aspirants for membership of the superpower club (notably China and India) and a small cluster of heretics might even have dared suggest that the European Union too could one day be a superpower. But according to standard definitions of power, the United States alone had the necessary combination of qualities to merit the title: it had superior firepower, a large and productive economy, a telling mixture of political and cultural influence, and an ability and willingness to pursue a wide range of policy goals on a global scale, with results that were both observable and measurable. And anyway, asked the cynics, how could the EU possibly become a superpower when it was not a state, but no more than a semi-integrated cluster of independent states that often seemed unable to read from the same script?

Such arguments may have appealed during the 1990s, but as cold war thinking has loosened its grip on the imagination of policymakers, so there is reason to review the way we understand power in the international system:

- We must question the historical link between political influence and military power. Those who belong to the realist school of international relations continue to insist that we live in an anarchic international system (that is, one that lacks a central authority), that security is the most important item on the agenda, and that force is an effective tool of statecraft. But the post-modern international system emphasizes markets, trade, and technology, all bound together in a new system of interdependence in which force has lost much of its utility, and may even be counterproductive: it not only sends a provocative message to potential

10

adversaries, but large militaries create more problems for their owners than they solve, not least because they divert resources away from more productive pursuits.

- We must question the old assumption that power (as Bertrand Russell put it) is 'the production of intended effects',[1] and that its exercise must be deliberate, must involve resistance, and must have measurable results.[2] In the era of mass and instant communication, and of economic and cultural globalization, latent power has achieved a new significance, and the value of example and attraction has superseded that of force and coercion. The most powerful actors in the new international environment will be those that create opportunities, not those that issue threats.
- We must question the link between power and statehood. Globalization has made national frontiers porous, undermining realist claims that states are the most important actors in the international system. Standing against this analysis is the view offered by the liberal school, which argues that states are not the only actors in the international system, that international organizations and institutions are also important, and that actors are interdependent and find that cooperation works in their interests. Ideas and popular movements also have power and influence. In short, statehood is no longer a prerequisite for power.

The European Union has been a progenitor – and the primary beneficiary – of these changes. As long ago as the late 1960s and early 1970s, there were suggestions that Europe might one day become a different species of global power. Whether because it had the potential to develop 'new kinds of society, new political ideas, [and] new philosophies',[3] or because the stalemates achieved by nuclear competition had 'devalued purely military power and given more scope to ... civilian forms of influence and action',[4] Europe offered the prospect of a new definition of great power. Europeans were unready and unprepared to face the challenges created by the end of the cold war, as shown by their confused response to the first Gulf crisis, their bungled ventures in the Balkans, and the political split over the 2003 invasion of Iraq. But as the deficiencies and dangers of cold war-style American military power became increasingly clear, as the EU learned from its mistakes and made progress on building common foreign and security policies, and as globalization gave new emphasis to the economic aspects of international relations,[5] so the rise of Europe took on a new meaning. The Gulf and the Balkans were not its finest hours, but along the way the EU had become the world's biggest capitalist marketplace and trading power, and in the new international system these qualities have become more important than the ownership of large military arsenals.

During the cold war, American and Soviet power had found its primary expression in an arms race, ideological competition, covert activities, surrogate wars, and the support of authoritarian client states. The Americans and the Soviets used their military might to threaten, bully, confront, contain, and restrain, driven mainly by the pursuit of national interests. But there was always a limit to how far the superpowers could exploit the military options, because there was always the danger of provoking a destructive response from the other side. Since the end of the cold war, US policymakers – particularly members of the Bush administration – have been encouraged to use military options more aggressively and more often. But this newly assertive militarism has done little more than further undermine the credibility of military force. Rather than furthering security, it has encouraged greater insecurity. It has also raised questions about American priorities, and has given clearer outlines to the new model of international relations offered by the European Union.

In place of the cold war era bipolar system, with its emphasis on military and ideological competition, we now have a new post-modern bipolar system that emphasizes economic and political competition. Contrasting with the US preference for coercion and unilateralism we now have the European preference for diplomacy, economic development, multilateral cooperation, and the politics of influence. Alongside the realist cold war model of power offered by the United States, we now have a liberal European superpower that represents a competing set of values that fits more closely with the needs and realities of the post-modern international system. The old US–Soviet bipolar system has been replaced by a new US–European system in which the Americans and the Europeans champion distinctive values, offer competing analyses of international problems, and pursue different approaches to dealing with those problems.

What is power?

Power is usually defined as the ability of one actor to encourage another to do something that it would not otherwise do.[6] Kenneth Waltz suggests that power in the international system can be understood as the capacity of a state to affect the behaviour of other states while resisting unwelcome influence from those states.[7] In the realm of international relations, power has traditionally been associated with military capacity, with deliberate behaviour, and – of course – with states. But its qualities are constantly changing, and there may be lessons to be learned here from evolutionary economics.

For 200 years, economic theory was based on the deterministic laws developed by physics,[8] the assumption being that economic change relied on external factors propelling the economic system from one state of equilibrium to another.[9] This idea was rejected by the Austrian economist Joseph Schumpeter, who argued instead that capitalism could never be stationary, because the capitalist engine was constantly in motion, responding to changing pressures and circumstances, destroying the old economic structure and creating a new one in its place. This process of 'creative destruction', he concluded, was the one essential fact about capitalism.[10] Much the same might be said about power in the international system: it is constantly in motion, the status of great powers challenged by new threats, problems, demands, understandings, and technologies. Conventional interpretations of problems are revisited, as are the potential answers to those problems, and in order to maintain their dominant position, great powers must either change in order to meet new circumstances or lose their share of the power market.

The most conspicuous change of the modern era has been the declining value of military power. Three conventional assumptions have been made about power. The first, in the traditional view of most scholars of international relations, has been that great powers must be able to wage war.[11] But critics of the state system have repeatedly pointed to the destructive association between states and violence, which reached a new nadir during the twentieth century when two world wars and a cold war showed how states seemed unable to guarantee the safety of their citizens except through the threat of aggression against other states. Since 1945 there has been more effort to build peace through cooperation rather than competition, a trend that has been reinforced more recently by globalization and by revolutions in communications and technology. The world has become smaller, and the dangers posed by military force have become both more immediate and more potentially destructive.

At no time in history has peaceful diplomacy been more preferred over the use of military force than in the modern age. Asking whether or not major war has become obsolete, Mandelbaum points to the striking increase in its human and physical price and the steep decline in its rewards.[12] Mueller argues that war has achieved a state of 'terminal disrepute because of its perceived repulsiveness and futility'. While nuclear weapons once drove the rhetoric of war and influenced defence budgets and planning, he suggests, they have not been necessary to deter major war, and the absence of such war – in the lives, most notably, of the French, the Germans and the Japanese since 1945 – has been more remarkable than its presence. Only two types of war remain: unconventional civil wars in the world's poorest countries, and policing wars launched by developed countries in order to impose order on civil conflicts or remove thuggish regimes from power.[13]

Military capability remains important, to be sure, but it has many limita-tions.[14] Most of today's most serious threats to international peace and security – including poverty, terrorism, environmental degradation, natural disasters, international crime, the drug trade, illegal immigration, forced labour, trade disputes, and public health crises such as the spread of HIV and AIDS – have sources that demand non-military solutions. The merits of military power are still championed by many American policymakers – particularly those realists who see a world full of threats – but Europeans have tired of violence and conflict, and have chosen instead to emphasize the economic, political, cultural, technological, and moral dimensions of power. For them, ownership of the means of production has become more important than ownership of the means of destruction. Real ongoing influ-ence in the post-modern world – say the Europeans – must be measured not in terms of the size and the firepower of a national defence force, but in terms of the role of corporations in the global trading system, the strength and influence of currencies and banking systems, the control of budget deficits and trade balances, and the availability of resources for foreign direct investment. As Rosecrance puts it, where states once had no choice but to pursue military power, they now have a choice; they may remain political-military states, or they may instead pursue economic power and become trading states.[15]

The second conventional assumption made about power – that it must involve deliberate action and resistance, and that it can be measured only when one actor changes the behaviour or the thinking of another against its wishes – also rests on increasingly unreliable foundations. In the early 1970s, Klaus Knorr noted the difference between influence that was coer-cive (actor B is affected by fear of sanctions or threats or restrictions by actor A) and influence that was non-coercive (B's choices are 'enriched rather than limited' by A). In a coercive situation, B loses or expects to lose while A gains; in a non-coercive situation, A and B both expect to gain.[16] The idea of non-coercive power is reflected in Joseph Nye's concept of 'soft power', which contrasts military and economic power based on a combina-tion of inducements and threats with persuasion based on less tangible inducements, such as shaping the preferences of others through values that others aspire to adopt. Soft power, Nye argues, is attractive power. If hard power rests on commands, or the ability to change what others do, then soft power is more cooptive.[17] If hard power rests on the use of military or economic resources to force or coerce an outcome, then soft power rests on a state working to achieve its goals through the appeal of its ideals. All states have elements of both, the mix depending upon a combination of the resources they have available and their political culture. Hard power is easier to identify than soft power, which Cooper sees as more elusive[18] and Nye as more widely dispersed.[19]

Most debates about power assume that it must be based on concrete behaviour, activity and intentional decisions, that states are rational actors that set out to acquire, keep and use power for narrow national interests, and even that conflict is needed in order to provide an experimental test of the capacity to exert power.[20] Other countries listen to the United States, runs the logic, because it has a large store of both sticks and carrots, and since World War II has been willing to wield them, to influence the international economic agenda, and to provide leadership on the most troubling security problems. Europe has none of these advantages, we are told, and even when it talks it is not always listened to. But Steven Lukes suggests that we should go beyond the study of observable behaviour and concrete decisions, and look also at latent or covert power, or the way in which an actor can influence, shape or determine the wants of another actor. In other words, strength, magnetism, wealth and diplomatic skills might provide an actor with power even when they are not deployed.[21] In contrast to the kind of explicit, active or manifest capacity that has been associated with great powers and superpowers in the past, we now have evidence – in the European case – of power by example. Militarily, the Europeans threaten no-one. This has been interpreted by realists as a sign of weakness (witness Europe's record in the two Gulf wars and the Balkans, they say), but it could as easily be interpreted as a sign of strength. Europe does not need to use force or the threat of force to encourage change; instead, it offers the incentive of opportunities.

The third conventional assumption made about power in the international system is that it is monopolized by states. States have power because they have a single government and are supported by a single body of voters and taxpayers. Powerful states have integrated militaries that answer to integrated command structures and pursue national security policies, and have integrated economies governed by a single set of national policies. But the European Union is a collection of sovereign states that frequently quarrel with each other, and often cannot agree on what position to take on the most troubling international problems. We do not even yet have a noun to describe the EU. It is less than a state but more than an international organization, so we are forced to use clumsy terms such as 'actor' or 'entity' or 'multilevel governance' in our attempts to pin down its character. And to make matters worse, it has a chameleon quality: sometimes it is 25 sovereign states that go their own way, sometimes it is two or more clusters of states that opt in or out of common policies, and sometimes it is a single seamless unit.

But while traditional discussions of power are based on an analysis of the kinds of attributes only states can have – including population, territory, natural resources, sovereignty, independence, and military strength – history offers many examples of non-state actors achieving influence and power, the most obvious being organized religion. Christianity was the primary driving force in European politics and culture for the best part of 1,500 years,[22] going so far as to define Europe in the face of external threats, and underpinning the logic of centuries of European colonialism. Similar arguments could be made about Confucianism and its impact on China, and Islam and its impact on the Middle East and North Africa.

Ideas, too, have power. In some cases, they have resulted in non-violent change: the Enlightenment, the Industrial Revolution, globalization, feminism, and environmentalism have all transformed politics, economics, technology, and culture without a single shot being fired. In other cases, ideas have been accompanied by violence: the American Revolution, the French Revolution, Marxism, Leninism, and decolonization all offer examples. More recently, al-Qaeda has been able to achieve change without statehood. With limited resources and a hazy identity, it has changed government policy and the routine of daily life throughout the world, launched the first foreign attack on the American mainland since 1812, prompted the biggest reorganization of the American bureaucracy in two generations, and is now so influential that even rumours of the *possibility* of action on its part are enough to draw a response from multiple governments.

In the new international system the power and significance of states has been reduced; as long ago as 1977, Keohane and Nye – and others – were arguing that the territorial state was being eclipsed by non-territorial actors such as multinational corporations and international organizations. They developed the concept of 'complex interdependence', suggesting that – in contrast to the realist emphasis on states – societies are connected by multiple channels (formal and informal), and that the international agenda contains many different issues with no clear ranking.[23] Globalization and interdependence have made international borders porous and permeable, and through them – as Gardels puts it – flow 'ideas, migrants, drugs, terrorists, money, merchandise, microbes, and pollution'.[24] It has become impossible for states to isolate themselves, leading to new demands for governance without government, and emphasizing the importance of collective action.[25] Power is no longer equated with population and territory but with control of trade, information and technology, a change that the EU is well placed to exploit.

Whitman argues that the EU has become a significant global actor without transforming itself into a nation-state, thanks to changes in the international environment that have enhanced the relative significance of the EU.[26]

Slaughter argues that we should review our perceptions of the way the world works, eschewing the focus on nation-states and their 'unitary' view in favour of a focus on complex global networks. She writes of states being 'disaggregated' and of relating to each other not only through formal governmental channels but through regulatory, judicial and legislative channels as well. It is not only national government officials who are involved, but regulators, judges, bankers, and bureaucrats as well, who exchange information and coordinate activity across national borders as they seek to address problems. The model for this new world order may be, she argues, the European Union.[27]

What is a superpower?

Until the Second World War, the most powerful states were commonly described as great powers, and were distinguished from other states mainly by the size and reach of their militaries. For Levy, a great power had four qualities:

- It had a high level of military capability and self-sufficiency in security issues, with the ability to project power beyond its borders and to conduct offensive as well as defensive operations.
- It had interests that were continental or global in scope rather than local or regional.
- It pursued a distinctive pattern of behaviour (including a willingness to defend its interests aggressively and with a broad set of tools).
- Its status was acknowledged by other powers.[28]

The great powers – which included Britain, France, Germany, and Russia – had the largest economies, the strongest positions in international trade, the deepest investments in the international system, and the most powerful militaries. But while their interests sometimes expanded and evolved from a regional base to a wider constituency, there were limits to what any one of them could achieve acting alone, or even in concert with others. Britain during the Victorian era came closest to achieving early superpower status, but large parts of the world – including Russia, most of Latin America, Japan and the United States – remained outside its direct sphere of influence, and its military power was not enough to save it from stalemates in Afghanistan, the Crimea, or in South Africa.

A superpower has resources and qualities of an altogether different scale. The term was a product of World War II, credit for its first use in a political sense being given to the American political theorist William T. R. Fox. Writing in 1944 he conferred the title on the three leading allied powers: the United States, the USSR, and Britain. He argued that a *super*power possessed more than just the straightforward attributes of military, economic and political power, but also had the ability and the willingness to project that power globally. It was a state with global rather than simply regional interests, and had a combination of 'great power plus great mobility of power'.[29] Spiegel later argued that material and military power are important to an understanding of superpower, but that motivation also enters the equation; without a willingness to exploit its resources, the ability of a superpower to influence international affairs will be greatly reduced.[30] Nijman agreed, suggesting that superpowers were defined not in terms of static factors such as wealth, population, natural resources and the size of their militaries, but by their behaviour, particularly their global involvement and influence.[31] This was certainly how Eugene McCarthy seemed to understand the idea as he ran against Lyndon Johnson in the 1968 US presidential race, and argued that the US had 'moved from a position of isolation and rejection of world responsibility to a position of isolated, almost singular responsibility for the whole world'.[32]

Fox was generous in describing Britain as a superpower, but while it was active in all major theatres of war, by the time of the 1945 Yalta conference (if not before) it was clear that the Americans and the Soviets dominated the war effort. When Britain began to dismantle its empire after the war, and the US and the USSR emerged as regional hegemons in post-war Europe, and then entered a nuclear arms race that gave them arsenals the size and scope of which had never been seen before, it became clear that there were only two superpowers. The new status of the United States was famously summed up by the British political theorist Harold Laski in 1947: 'America bestrides the world like a colossus; neither Rome at the height of its power nor Great Britain in the period of its economic supremacy enjoyed an influence so direct, so profound, or so pervasive.' The rhetorical flourish of his statement was more impressive than its factual substance, but it made the point about how international relations had changed, and about the emergence of this remarkable new breed of great power.

In short, a superpower is an actor that has the ability to project power globally, and that enjoys a high level of autonomy and self-sufficiency in international relations. More than was the case with the old great powers, a superpower has global interests,[33] and earns the prefix *super* through the extent of its ability to promote and protect those interests, whether directly or indirectly, whether actively or passively. A superpower may deliberately seek to influence policy or to impose its will, but it may also achieve its status by virtue of the resources that it controls, whether they are natural, economic, cultural or moral. Jönsson argues that there are two kinds of roles for a superpower: those that superpowers take for themselves, and those that are given by lesser powers.[34] There is also a third: the role that a superpower achieves by virtue of what it represents, whether that is economic opportunity, political influence, or moral credibility.

Until recently, only the Soviet Union and the United States had unquestionably earned the title of 'superpower'. The Soviet claim was based almost entirely on the size and the potential destructive power of its military. Soviet power was never about global economic influence; the Soviet economy was inefficient, inward-looking, geared towards the military rather than the consumer, and had little direct impact on the international economic system. And if the Soviets exerted any political, cultural or moral influence, it was only in a limited regional sense, impacting their satellites and their most ardent allies. It was only during the Brezhnev years that the USSR tried to reach strategic nuclear parity with the United States and to influence the politics of African and Latin American states, finally giving it qualities more like those of the American superpower. But the power resources of the USSR were narrower and more restricted than those of the United States, and the Soviets did not project their power as effectively on a global basis.[35] The USSR was an 'incomplete superpower', says Dibbs, because it lacked major global economic, technological or ideological influence.[36] By contrast, the United States was a 'complete superpower', because it could claim large measures of influence in all the major domains of power.[37] It was the multidimensional quality of American power that helped determine which side finally prevailed in the cold war.[38]

The vacuum created by the end of the cold war and the collapse of the Soviet Union led to an increase in the relative power of the United States, because it was no longer challenged or limited in the way that it had been during the cold war. But it was not long before suggestions began to emerge that other states had the potential to achieve superpower status. China is regarded as the prime candidate, mainly because it has a large population, a large army, and is wielding greater economic influence in the world.[39] But no matter how much we may be tempted to portray China as the emerging new threat to the West, it lacks many of the qualities that would give it well rounded superpower status: the state is still heavily involved in the marketplace, there is little prospect of the yuan becoming a major reserve currency (it is not convertible, as reserve currencies must be, and too little is known about China's financial institutions), it is a technological follower rather than a leader, it has little immediate prospect of achieving international cultural influence, and its political and moral power are undermined by its poor human rights record and its authoritarianism.

Miller notes that while China may have a large military, it is focused on threats from the near abroad, and does not appear to be developing the capacity for global power projection. On the economic front, it does not rank with the major trading powers, its foreign direct investment is negligible compared to that of the US and the EU, and its heavy reliance on exports makes it hostage to ups and downs in the international economy.[40] Rapid economic growth has turned in impressive results and brought new wealth to Chinese cities, but it has also created a gap between the rich and the poor, and between urban and rural areas, and nearly two out of three Chinese still live on incomes of less than $2 per day. Sutter argues that while it has potential as a global power, its leaders are – for now – too focused on domestic political, economic and social priorities, and prefer to deal with the world as it is rather than trying to exert Chinese influence.[41]

Other possible contenders for superpower status – including Japan, India, and Russia – all have their own sets of limitations. Japan may have the world's second largest national economy, and may be a technological leader, but it is not a military power, and it has not translated economic power into political influence. It also lacks cultural influence in the world, except indirectly through the promotion of new technology. For its part, India may have a population of more than one billion, and may be a nuclear power, but it is no more than a regional power with few short-term prospects of expanding its reach, and the majority of its people live in poverty. And Russia has been demoted since the end of the cold war to regional power status, too focused on domestic political and economic change to have much impact on broader international problems.

What, then, of the United States and the European Union? Opinions about US power are strong and well developed. Its status as a lone superpower is largely unquestioned, and the thesaurus has been picked dry of superlatives to describe its global dominance; champions of the lone superpower thesis insist that there is nothing more to be said, for now at least. But two opposing schools of thought offer alternative analyses. One points to evidence of American decline, whether relatively or absolutely. Another smaller school takes the more iconoclastic view that Europe has certainly achieved superpower status in the economic domain, and may have translated this into power in other domains as well.

The United States: Triumph or decline?

With the collapse of the bipolar system of the cold war in the early 1990s, Laski's vision of an American colossus was revived. So remarkable was the new standing of the United States, indeed, that even the term superpower had – for some – become inadequate. French foreign minister Hubert Védrine suggested that the United States had become a hyperpower, enjoying a level of global influence unprecedented in history.[42] Others spoke of a new American hegemony: the bipolar system of the cold war had been replaced by a unipolar system in which the United States had no real competitors. A hegemon emerges, says Wallerstein, when 'the ongoing rivalry between the great powers is so unbalanced that one power is truly *primus inter pares*; that is, one power can largely impose its rules and its wishes (at the very least by effective veto power) in the economic, political, military, diplomatic, and even cultural arenas'.[43] For Joffe, a hegemon has interests that extend throughout the entire system, and 'its sway over critical outcomes ... must exceed the capabilities of its rivals by a comfortable margin'. Only the United States, he argues, has this kind of power.[44]

A related school of opinion has even dared to talk of empire in connection with its analysis of the new global role of the United States,[45] the most popular analogy being with the power of Rome.[46] This is not an old-style imperialism based on territorial conquest so much as an informal hierarchical system of power relationships in which one power is clearly stronger than any other,[47] and may set up a permanent presence in other states, usually in the form of a military base. Opinion on the implications of American imperialism (assuming it exists) is divided. On the one hand, Johnson describes the United States as 'a military juggernaut intent on world domination',[48] Chomsky sees it as set on a 'quest for global dominance',[49] and Mann worries that American imperialism is little more than a new form of militarism, which contradicts the values that the US claims to promote, such as freedom, democracy, and capitalism.[50] On the other hand, Ferguson sees the United States as a liberal empire that underwrites the free international exchange of commodities, labour and capital, and creates the conditions without which markets cannot function, such as peace, order, the rule of law, stable fiscal and monetary policies, and infrastructure. The world, he believes, needs more American imperialism, not less.[51]

All these ideas – the lone superpower, the hyperpower, the hegemon, and the new empire – are reflected in much of today's debate about the global role of the United States. The declaration of American triumph was made even before the cold war was over. In a 1990 lecture, American commentator Charles Krauthammer proclaimed the arrival of the 'unipolar moment', arguing that while there was no lack of second-rank powers in the world, 'there is but one first-rate power and no prospect in the immediate future of any power to rival it'.[52] By 2002, he was chiding himself for the modesty of his original claims, and arguing that the 'unipolar moment' had become 'the unipolar era'. US dominance, he said, was 'unlike anything ever seen … Its navy, air force and space power are unrivalled. Its technology is irresistible. It is dominant by every measure: military, economic, technological, diplomatic, [and] cultural.' He even claimed that the spread of English was an indication of the linguistic power of the United States.[53]

Many others have echoed this triumphalist view, and most make roughly the same arguments based on roughly the same logic:

- 'We live in a one-superpower world', claims John Ikenberry, 'and there is no serious competitor in sight'.[54] On the economic front, the US predominates in part because Western Europe has 'turned inward'.[55]
- No state is likely for decades 'to be in a position to take on the United States in any of the underlying elements of power', argues William Wohlforth,[56] and there are no signs of attempts from other actors to counterbalance the United States.[57]
- The US faces 'neither an existential enemy nor the threat of encirclement as far as the eye can see', says Josef Joffe.[58]
- For Samuel Huntington, the US is the only state with 'pre-eminence in every domain of power … [and] with the reach and capabilities to promote its interests in virtually every part of the world'.[59]
- 'Almost everyone concedes today that US power will be nearly impossible to match for decades,' claims Robert Kagan.[60]
- American primacy is robust and unlikely to be challenged in the near future, argues Robert Lieber. With the possible exception of China, he concludes, 'no other country or group of countries is likely to emerge as an effective global competitor in the coming decades'.[61]
- Robert Hunter, former US ambassador to NATO, argues that the US has been 'steadily amassing, relatively and absolutely, more incipient military, economic, political, and even cultural power than any other country in centuries'.[62]
- There is no longer a balance of power in the international system, concludes Richard Haass, but – thanks to the dramatic American advantage – 'a decided *imbalance* of power'.[63]

These claims of American triumph are the logical outcome of a long strand of thinking – dating back to colonial days – which argues that the United States is an exceptional society, exempt from all our usual assumptions about states and what they stand for.[64] It has no feudal past, it has traditions of individualism and freedom of opportunity, and Americans believe in small government, features that – it is held – set the US apart from others. For Shafer, American exceptionalism means that 'the United States was created differently, developed differently, and thus has to be *understood* differently – essentially on its own terms and within its own context', and that there exists 'a sense of critical distinctiveness in political, economic, religious, or cultural life'.[65] The United States is not only unusual, runs the argument, but its distinctive political, economic, and social values offer unusual opportunities for the rest of humanity, and it may even have a mission to change the world in its image; certainly, claims of exceptionalism have been used to interpret and justify the actions of the United States.

American exceptionalism was reflected in Ronald Reagan's attempts to revitalize the national psyche post-Vietnam and post-Watergate, which included a reassertion of the ideas and values that he believed made the United States great and unique.[66] For Bill Clinton, the United States was 'the indispensable nation', and the only country that could make the difference between war and peace, between freedom and repression, and between hope and fear.[67] The exceptionalist view has been aggressively revived by the present Bush administration, perhaps because it fits well with the neo-conservative view that the United States should exploit its power to the fullest. The US was targeted on 9/11, Bush said following the attacks, because 'we are the brightest beacon for freedom and opportunity in the world'. At the Republican National Convention in September 2004 he argued that the United States was 'the greatest force for good on this earth', and that 'like generations before us, we have a calling from beyond the stars to stand for freedom'.

But not everyone is quite so ready to support the transcendence of America. Another school of thought, active as long ago as Vietnam, suggests that US power may be in a state of decline, whether relatively or absolutely. The logic of declinism is rooted in five main lines of thinking:

- US power is not what it once was, and indeed may never have been as great as we are led to believe.
- Claims of the wisdom of US global leadership are misplaced, and while many admire much of what the US has to offer (the promotion of economic opportunity and competition, technological leadership, educational opportunities, and the attractions of American culture, for example), US foreign policy has been controversial and has suffered from declining credibility.
- According to balance of power theory, it was inevitable that the dominance of the United States would encourage other powers to rise up in order to provide balance. As Kenneth Waltz puts it, 'overwhelming power repels and leads other states to balance against it'.[68] Thus the EU, China and other powers can be expected to balance against the US.

- The US is more vulnerable than its leaders and people are prepared to admit, whether to terrorism, rogue states, drugs, budget deficits, an addiction to oil, or internal economic and social divisions.
- The US is suffering from the 'Lippmann gap', the difference between its ambitions and its resources. A leader, warned Walter Lippmann in 1943, 'must bring his ends and means into balance. If he does not, he will follow a course that leads to disaster.'[69]

Suggestions that American power is in decline are built on a history of debate about the nature of power in the international system, where opinions differ about how and why great powers emerge.[70] Do states actively try to build power, is power thrust upon them by changes in the nature of the system, or do they inherit a new prominence as a result of the decline of existing powers? One of the best known proponents of the idea of American decline was Paul Kennedy, whose book *The Rise and Fall of the Great Powers* was published in 1987.[71] Looking at the changing positions over time in the role of the world's leading powers, Kennedy concluded that Europe, China and Japan were in the ascendant, that the United States and Russia were in relative economic decline, and that the bipolar system of US–Soviet military competition had been replaced by a multipolar system. He argued that the United States faced the problem of 'imperial overstretch', because its interests and obligations were larger than its abilities to defend them all simultaneously.[72]

Many have taken issue with this thesis. Huntington argues that America may have gone through several waves of decline and renewal, but that its 'self-renewing genius' has ultimately prevailed.[73] Kennedy himself has changed his mind, arguing in 2002 that a combination of the collapse of the USSR, the stalling of the Japanese economy, and a reaction within the United States to talk of decline had led to a rebirth of American power. He was now of the view that nothing in history could compare to the overwhelming global influence of the United States, with only China being able one day – perhaps – to mount a serious challenge.[74]

In 1993, Christopher Layne was applying the 'unipolar moment' analysis in a different vein from Krauthammer when he argued that American hegemony was no more than an interlude that would quickly give way to multipolarity. In part, he argued, this would be because of the prediction of balance of power theory.[75] Meanwhile, Richard Haass felt that the ability of the United States to have its way would diminish because of the unavoidable emergence of competing centres of power, and because of the likely weakening of the American will and ability to be a world power.[76] Charles Kupchan agreed, noting that America's will to underwrite international order would not last indefinitely, and that its global influence would decline as other large powers became 'less enamored of following America's lead'.[77] Elsewhere, Haass argues that the proper goal of US foreign policy should be 'to encourage a multipolarity characterized by cooperation and concert rather than competition and conflict'.[78] He criticizes the philosophy of imposing democracy unilaterally and at gunpoint, and argues that the United States has been relying too much on military power, and wasting its opportunity to work multilaterally and to integrate itself politically with the rest of the world.[79]

Even before George W. Bush came into office, there was a growing chorus of concern among American commentators about the nature of US foreign policy and the character of American leadership. Historian Garry Wills warned in 1999 that the United States had become the 'bully of the free world', that it was failing to lead by persuasion, and that it was instead using covert action, sabotage, and threats to get its way. The US, he felt, would have to learn to acknowledge the outside world, to listen to the opinions of others, and to act in partnership with other countries rather than browbeating them.[80] Not long after Bush came into office, the chorus rose to a crescendo. John Ikenberry, so much a supporter of the idea of American pre-eminence in the world, argued that the Bush administration's war on terrorism was the basis of 'a neo-imperial vision' in which the US had decided to give itself the role of setting standards, defining threats, and using force. This, he conceded, 'threatens to rend the fabric' of international partnerships at a time when they are urgently needed. 'It is an approach fraught with peril and likely to fail,' he argued. 'It is not only politically unsustainable but diplomatically harmful. And if history is a guide, it will trigger antagonism and resistance that will leave America in a more hostile and divided world.'[81]

The on-going association between political and military power is clear in the arguments of both the triumphalists and the declinists. For the former, the US dominates because no-one else can match the vast American military establishment. For the latter, it has been mainly the failures of the United States to capitalize on its military capabilities, and an international reaction against American militarism, that has fed the decline of American power. So just how effective is American military power? The United States certainly has the biggest and the most technologically advanced military in the world, its personnel are professional and dedicated, and its annual military budget is more than twice as big as that of the entire European Union. But none of this necessarily means that it can always achieve its political objectives. Indeed, as Vietnam and Iraq have shown, even massive firepower may not always be enough to demoralize and defeat a motivated enemy, no matter how poorly armed it may be. And both Vietnam and Iraq have shown conclusively that even so great a power as the United States cannot always achieve its objectives without the support of allies.

As if this was not enough, the massive military spending that is routinely quoted as evidence of US power may in truth be an indication of weakness, because while Americans are investing so much in weapons, Europeans are investing much more in education, healthcare, and infrastructure. And the United States has only been able to absorb high levels of military spending because of its economic growth; should that growth slow, then the weight of military spending will descend with greater weight upon the shoulders of taxpayers. American military power has become its own rival and its own worst enemy. One study of the United States after the end of the cold war, which looked at the increased complexity of international problems, nuclear proliferation, the US national debt, and a host of issues that the US could no longer solve unilaterally, concluded that America had become 'vincible'.[82] And if the limitations on its military power are not enough, there are at least three additional reasons to question the ability of the United States to translate its power into influence.

First, the United States faces a troubling array of domestic economic problems, not least of which are the twin deficits, on the budget and trade. In 1998, after decades of deficit spending, it was able to achieve a budget surplus of nearly $70 billion, rising to nearly $240 billion in 2000. But a combination of tax cuts and increased defence spending by the Bush administration had by 2005 turned a surplus into a record deficit of more than $400 billion. Furthermore, there was no end in sight to this deficit spending, and by 2006 the US had accumulated a national debt of more than $8 trillion (eight times the figure in 1980). The debt has undermined faith in the dollar, and also obliges the US federal government to spend nearly one-fifth of its revenues on interest payments. As for the trade deficit, this has been in place since the late 1970s (reaching a record of more than $600 billion in 2005), driven by the enormous US dependence on imported oil, which accounts for about half its oil consumption, holds its economic welfare hostage to the international price of oil, pushes the security of oil supplies to the top of the US foreign policy agenda, and gives the Middle East a skewed significance in US foreign and security policy. The budget and trade deficits are illustrative of the Lippmann gap with which the US currently struggles.

Second, the United States is deeply split within itself. The famous red and blue states of the 2004 presidential election (the Republican and Democrat states) were symptomatic of broader and deeper divisions, which raise questions about whether there really is an 'American' view of the world, or even a truly 'American' foreign policy. Americans are divided in ideological terms, and are marking out increasingly uncompromising positions on a variety of social issues, from capital punishment to abortion, prayer in schools, and same-sex marriage. They are also divided on racial lines, with the old black–white divide being further complicated by the rapid growth of Latino and Asian-American minorities. They are also divided on economic lines, with a large and growing gap in wealth and opportunity between the rich and the poor. And all of this means that they are divided on foreign policy priorities and on the place of the US in the world.

Third, the ability of the US to lead is undermined by the growing breach between Americans and non-Americans on political norms and social values, undermining the moral influence once enjoyed by the United States. Americans are increasingly driven by a different set of values, goals and priorities from those that drive politics in most other liberal democracies, and even in emerging states. In the political field, the differences are exemplified by contrasting views over terrorism, the Middle East, Cuba, the International Criminal Court, the land mines treaty, support for the United Nations, and global environmental issues (see Chapter 5). In the social field, they are exemplified by differences over welfare, core values, and the place of religion in public life (see Chapter 6). Huntington argued in 1999 that 'on issue after issue, the United States has found itself increasingly alone, with one or a few partners, opposing most of the rest of the world's states and peoples'.[83] Kingdon politely describes his homeland as 'America the unusual',[84] but Prestowitz describes it as a 'rogue nation', notes the inconsistencies in US policy, and sees his country as one that is inclined to take a unilateral approach to dealing with many such problems, that cares little about the views of other countries, whose self-righteousness makes it unwilling to listen to competing analyses or to consider alternative solutions, and that has alienated its allies and enraged its enemies.[85]

The rise of post-modern Europe

If one school of thought supports the idea of American triumph, and another of American decline, a third now holds that the European Union has achieved a new presence on the international stage, and has begun to look and act much like a superpower itself. Supporters of this argument place less emphasis on military power and more on Europe's post-modern attitudes to government, society, and economic structures. There was an early hint of this idea when Community leaders, in launching European Political Cooperation in 1970, noted the potential of a united Europe to promote international relations 'on a basis of trust'.[86] It was explored in more depth in 1972 by François Duchêne, when he argued that the lack of military power was not the handicap that it once was, and that Western Europe might become the world's first civilian centre of power, 'the first major area of the Old World where the age-old process of war and indirect violence could be translated into something more in tune with the twentieth-century citizen's notion of civilized politics'. As a civilian power that was 'long on economic power and relatively short on military force', he argued, Western Europe would be 'free of a load of military power which could give it great influence' in the world. Years before Francis Fukuyama, Duchêne even concluded that the change might represent 'the end of history'.[87]

In 1973, Johan Galtung wrote of the European Community as a superpower in the making. He argued that the common market was more than a market, but was also a struggle for power and an effort to make the world Eurocentric 'with an explicit peace philosophy, with a *pax bruxellana* in mind'.[88] When David Buchan described Europe in 1993 as 'a strange superpower', he agreed that it had many of the 'physical potentials of a superpower' and was without question a major trading power. But a combination of historical and political divisions among its member states, and a division of powers between the member state and EU institutions, and within EU institutions, ensured that there was 'no prospect of the United States of America being mirrored in Europe'.[89]

Ever since its creation in the 1950s, pessimists have relished the difficulties experienced first by the European Community and then by the European Union, and have repeatedly predicted its demise. It has become almost unfashionable to talk of Europe's successes,[90] and almost heretical to suggest that Europe can be a serious global player. Rather than standing tall on the international political and economic stage, argue its critics, Europe is mired in squabbles over budgets, lost votes on treaties, midnight crisis negotiations, over-regulation and over-expansion, unaccountable bureaucrats in Brussels, and failed foreign policy ventures.[91] Galtung noticed even in 1973 that the Community's failures were better publicized than its achievements; 'journalism', he argued, 'focuses on drama rather than permanence'.[92] Zielonka has written of 'euro-paralysis', suggesting that explanations for the EU's problems fall into one of five categories: a reversion to old-style national power games, a divergence of national interests, confusion on how to deal with the post-cold war world, structural crises within European democracies, and the weakness of European institutions.[93] Debates about Europe's elitism, its democratic deficit, differences of opinion about European foreign policy, and Europe's uneven record in defining and achieving its goals tend to crowd out sober assessments of its achievements.

In 1993, Stanley Hoffman argued that the signing of the Maastricht treaty had 'marked the beginning of a serious crisis' for Europe and had led to a new wave of pessimism about its future. Every Western European economy was stagnant, he declared, European governments had turned inward, the democratic deficit was causing resentment, troubling questions were being asked about the relationship between the EU and its member states, there was little progress on the single currency, Italian politics faced an 'apocalyptic crisis', Britain was still in decline, Yugoslavia had been a 'disastrous tragedy', and Europe's ambitious plans were 'now falling apart'. Perhaps it was time – he suggested – to say 'goodbye to a united Europe'.[94] A few years later, economist Martin Feldstein, while conceding that a unified Europe might pose challenges to the global role of the United States, also hinted that Europe's economic and monetary union did not preclude the possibility of conflict and even war within Europe.[95]

More recently, American neo-conservative Irving Kristol has rejected any possibility of Europe competing with US power, arguing that it 'has no ambitions beyond preserving its welfare state as best it can', describing its state of military preparedness as 'pitiable', and dismissing it as 'a quasi-autonomous protectorate of the United States'.[96] The historian Paul Johnson dismisses the EU as 'bureaucratic, anti-democratic and illiberal', predicts that it is heading for 'economic bankruptcy and political implosion', and further predicts that by 2050 the US share of global production could be three times that of the European Union.[97] NATO secretary-general Jaap de Hoop Scheffer dismisses the idea that Europe could ever rival the United States as 'politically impossible, militarily unrealistic, and financially unaffordable'.[98] John Hulsman and William Schirano of the Heritage Foundation interpreted the 2005 votes against the EU constitution as signs that the EU was 'dead', that the European system simply was not working, and that 'ever closer union is now a matter of history'.[99] The failure of the EU to confront the issue of how to take decisions, argue Salmon and Shepherd, means that while the EU will become a regional player, 'in this generation it will not become a superpower'.[100] And any number of British eurosceptics would willingly offer a host of reasons for suggesting that Europe has ideas above its station.[101]

The rejection of the Europe-as-superpower thesis is based on a variety of arguments.[102] The EU lacks that essential quality of (enough) military power, and the willingness or ability to use it. Europe is not a state, and so the EU is not in a position to be able to exploit its potential. Europe also faces a host of institutional, economic and even demographic problems, including the fatigue caused by eastern enlargement, the elitist nature of the EU decision-making structure, the persistence of high unemployment, an aging population, and a slower population growth than the United States. Finally, European integration has been a history of one crisis after another, interfering with the ability of the EU to exert itself; Europeans are too busy squabbling, it seems, to make much of a mark on the rest of the world.

But while there have undoubtedly been crises, the EU has survived and indeed has prospered. And while some find it easy and tempting to amplify the significance of the crises, others take the longer view and argue that the EU is proclaiming itself in a rather different way than that which we associate with conventional great powers. For Rummel, the EU is 'a silent global player' rather than an openly assertive one.[103] For Padoa-Schioppa, the EU is a 'gentle power' that emphasizes the rule of law and democracy over the violence of military and police instruments, that unites without conquering, and that organizes without subjugating.[104] For Moravcsik, the EU is a 'quiet superpower' that does not rely on guns and bombs but focuses instead on the promotion of peace and democracy through economic opportunity, trade, peacekeeping, and foreign aid.[105] For the Party of European Socialists, the EU can use the soft foreign policy instruments it has at its disposal to act as a 'rational counterweight' to those who rely excessively on military force. The EU, they argue, is in a unique position to be able to offer a broad range of crisis management instruments, although it should also possess a 'credible military option' – albeit a limited one – and not leave hard security options to the United States.[106]

We also find hints that the global influence of the EU has for too long been underestimated, and that the global influence of the US has for too long been overestimated. In 1998, William Wallace and Jan Zielonka warned that the United States should not be so sanguine about its powers and abilities, and in particular that US policymakers misunderstood the potential of Europe. 'Smug assumptions of American supremacy are wildly overdone,' they argued, in part because of the robustness of European economies and the increasingly productive patterns of cooperation in Europe, and in part because of the inconsistencies of US foreign policy. They also suggested that some of the anti-Europeanism then being heard in Washington DC was based on fear and ignorance: American policymakers were concerned about the potential for the EU to become a global rival, but there had been a reduction in the amount of information and expertise on Europe that was available to American policymakers and public opinion.[107]

Ironically, much of the support for the idea of European global power comes from American analysts. Samuel Huntington, while criticizing talk of American decline in the late 1980s, admitted that the most probable challenge to predictions of continued American dominance would come from a united Europe. With political cohesion, he argued, it 'would have the population, resources, economic wealth, technology and actual and potential military strength to be the pre-eminent power of the 21st century'. It might even have an 'ideological appeal' comparable to that of the United States.[108] In 1990, Ronald Steel predicted the rise of the European superpower based on the rise of European economic power, the growth of European nationalism, the need to find a place for a unified Germany in Europe, and the erosion of Atlanticism.[109] More recently, Charles Kupchan has written of 'the end of the American era' and argues that the next challenge to the United States might come not from an ascendant China or from the Islamic world but from a rising Europe emerging as a counterweight to the United States.[110]

Jeremy Rifkin contrasts the American emphasis on economic growth, personal wealth, individual self-interest, and the use of military power with the European emphasis on sustainable development, quality of life, community, and political cooperation, and concludes that Europe is developing a new social and political model better suited to the needs of the globalizing world of the new century.[111] The journalist T. R. Reid offers an economic perspective on the rise of the EU, arguing that the emergence of Europe has meant the end of American global supremacy.[112] Rockwell Schnabel, former US ambassador to the EU, offers his support to the idea of Europe using its soft power to influence world events, and warns of the challenge it poses to the United States.[113] And from the other side the Atlantic, Stephen Haseler has looked at developments intrinsic to the EU – including monetary union, an integrated legal system, trade, and common diplomacy – and has written of 'Europe's hour', arguing that the EU is already 'well along the road to becoming the world's second superpower'.[114] Mark Leonard argues that Europe will 'run the 21st century', and writes of the 'invisible hand' of Europe exerting a new kind of influence based less on military power than on offering a long-term model of economic and political transformation. The end of the American era is nigh, he concludes.[115]

Political leaders, too, have added their voices to the debate. Well known is the long-held dream of French presidents – from de Gaulle to Chirac – for greater European foreign policy independence. De Gaulle's hope was 'to make this European organization one of three world powers, and, if need be, one day, the arbiter between the two camps, the Soviet and the Anglo-Saxon'.[116] Much later, European Commission president Romano Prodi spoke of the mission of the EU to become a 'global civil power at the service of sustainable global development'.[117] As the prospect of a second term for George W. Bush became stronger in November 2004, Jacques Chirac commented that it was clear 'that Europe, now more than ever, has the need, the necessity, to strengthen its dynamism and unity when faced with this great world power'. In the campaign leading up to the failed May 2005 French vote on the EU constitution, he often spoke of the constitution in terms of its importance as a means to unify Europe, to make it stronger, and to establish its superpower credentials.

Tony Blair, too, has been a supporter of European power. In a speech in Warsaw in October 2000, he suggested that the member states of the EU could work together on core policy areas, including foreign policy, and that in its economic and political strength, it could be 'a superpower, not a super-state'. In an interview with T. R. Reid, he said: 'We are building a new world superpower. The European Union is about the projection of collective power, wealth and influence. That collective strength makes individual nations more powerful – and it will make the EU as a whole a global power.'[118] Meanwhile, Spanish prime minister José Luis Zapatero was arguing in 2004 that 'Europe must have faith in the prospect of becoming the most important global power in 20 years, because it has the best opportunities to do so.'[119]

If there is one point on which almost everyone can agree, it is that the EU will never be a global actor along the old cold war-style military lines of the United States and the Soviet Union. But the age of the military superpower is over. Instead, the EU has rejected realist interpretations of the international system, and has emerged as a post-modern superpower. There is a close association between modernism, militarism, and environmental devastation;[120] the European post-modern view, by contrast, is better suited to the rise of the global economy, new levels of personal mobility, the increasing irrelevance of borders, the shift from manufacturing to service economies, new attitudes towards the role of science, the anti-war movement, a preference for social spending over military spending, mass communications, multiculturalism, the emergence of a new global culture, sustainable development, and a concern for the environment. For 'post-modern', we could as easily insert 'post-national' or 'post-material' – these are all related concepts. While the European Union is adapting to the new international system – indeed, even shaping that system – American policymakers are having difficulty leaving behind their realist, statist cold war thinking.

Richard Cooper writes of a world divided into three zones: a pre-modern zone of chaos (mainly Africa and Asia) where the rule of law has failed and which acts as a source of modern terrorism; a modern zone with an emphasis on national interests and national security, and a belief in force as a means of protecting them (he includes in this group the United States, China, and India); and a post-modern zone (including the EU and Japan) that has the luxury of abhorring war and the use of force as a primary instrument of policy.[121] In a related argument, Mary Kaldor argues that while the United States still holds to realist views of the world, the European Union has moved away from a desire to impose its will, and has instead embraced what she calls 'cosmopolitanism': a mix of idealism and multilateralism, a belief in containment through political and legal means, and a commitment to a liberal world economy and global social justice. There is a role in this view for military means, but mainly for the protection of civilians, the arrest of war criminals, and the achievement of humanitarian goals, and always with the authorization of appropriate multilateral procedures.[122]

In the post-modern era, the kind of economic and political influence that the EU enjoys is more pertinent to the resolution of the most urgent international problems than the military options so often pursued by the United States. This is not to say that the military option will not always be necessary, and that it should not at least be kept in reserve, but it is of little value – and may even be counterproductive – when governments are faced with problems to which there is no military solution. In short, the changing nature of power has allowed the EU to become a new kind of superpower, exerting influence based not on its military firepower, but on its economic, political, and diplomatic influence. Out of a combination of its intrinsic advantages, the disadvantages of the cold war model of American power, and changes in the international system, the EU has emerged as a post-modern superpower. The bipolar system of the cold war era – where Americans and Soviets competed on ideological grounds using military tools – has been replaced with the bipolar system of the post-modern era – where Europeans and Americans offer competing sets of values, competing definitions of global problems, and competing sets of prescriptions for addressing those problems.

2

The Emergence of Europe

The European Union was the most successful product of the post-war era of generalized peace and economic change guaranteed and promoted by the United States. Europeans owe a great deal to Americans for underwriting the post-war international system, within whose structures European governments were able to achieve a new durability, and European economies were able to build new wealth and competitiveness. It is all the more ironic, then, that US policy should have paved the way for the development of a postmodern European Union that has so pointedly and effectively illustrated the declining relevance of the American model of great power politics, and that is itself now taking the lead in redefining the international system.

At the heart of the cold war international system was the Atlantic Alliance, often described as the most successful international alliance in history. For more than two generations it not only squared up to the cold war Soviet threat, but it also promoted the formal interests of its members and projected to the wider world their common values: democracy, capitalism, human rights, social justice and – later – globalization. The benefits of the Alliance worked both ways: Americans needed a stable Europe as a buffer to Soviet aspirations and as a market for American business, and Western Europe needed American investment and security guarantees. These guarantees were to act as an incubator for the European Union. They provided economic nourishment and military protection at a critical juncture in the history of Western Europe, and at a time when it could as easily have fallen sway to extremism as to democratic stability.

But the Alliance also promoted European integration in another, reactive, sense: US foreign policy helped Europeans redefine themselves by offering a set of positions against which Europeans could more clearly understand what they stood for, and against which they could better define their strengths and weaknesses. What they found was that they differed with the Americans as often as they agreed. If Europeans worried about the threat of nuclear weapons during the cold war, Americans were more ready to see them as trump cards in the struggle against the Soviet threat. If Europeans saw the state as an essential actor in the domestic economy and social welfare as a moral obligation, Americans were unapologetic champions of the free market, the profit motive, and self-reliance. And if Europeans preferred to use the rules and institutions of the international system, Americans were prepared to ignore or even break those rules.

Behind the outward impression of solidarity, the two sides quarrelled so often that the history of the Alliance is a story of one crisis after another. To the Europeans, the Americans sometimes seemed to have a narrow and naïve interpretation of the character of the international system, and were too ready to follow their own path and to pursue national interests rather then trying to reach a consensus with their European 'partners'. To the Americans, the Europeans often seemed to be weak, vacillating, and parochial, too ready to appease or excuse many of those who posed threats to international security, and too ready to criticize US policy while lurking behind the cover of the US security shield.

During the 1940s and 1950s, the Alliance was patently one-sided: the Americans rarely felt the need to justify themselves to the Europeans, and the Europeans were too divided, too busy rebuilding, and too conscious of their dependence on the United States to offer much opposition. But as Western Europe regained its confidence, so it asserted itself by more actively promoting its own analyses of international problems, and the idea of Europe acting as a Third Force in international relations was never far below the surface.[1] By the 1970s and 1980s, West Europeans had been buoyed by the early successes of economic integration, and by the rise of the Community as a trading power. Membership of the Community doubled between 1973 and 1986, and after a brief spell of worried introspection, the idea of 'Europe' was relaunched in 1986 with the passage of the Single European Act. The institutional lines of the Community achieved new clarity, member states agreed a longer list of common policies, and the Community developed an irresistible magnetic attraction, both for aspirant members and for governments and corporations vying for access to the European marketplace. Instead of a collection of independently minded governments, Europe was now a club whose members increasingly thought along the same lines (even if they also occasionally disagreed among themselves), and whose economic and trading power could not be ignored.

With the end of the cold war, the fault lines in the Alliance became more visible. Much like a couple in a long and troubled marriage, whose children had left home and taken with them the one joint project that kept the family together, the partners in the Alliance began to bicker more openly. American conservatives declared that the cold war had been 'won', and quickly claimed that the bipolar international system had been replaced by a unipolar moment, and then by a unipolar era in which American military domination was unchallenged. But others argued that the prospects of European self-determination had become more evident:[2] European economic and security reliance on the United States had declined, the identity of Europe had achieved a sharper focus, and transatlantic points of disagreement had become easier to find than points of agreement. The first Gulf war and the Balkans may have caught Europeans wrong-footed on security policy, but they were encouraged to address their weaknesses. Europe used the new World Trade Organization to pursue its commercial advantages over the Americans, and to remind everyone of its new role as a trading behemoth. Europeans became more willing to publicly disagree with the Americans on policy instead of keeping their discomfort to themselves. Then came the US-led invasion of Iraq in 2003, which was to prove a watershed like no other.

Today's Atlantic Alliance is a beast of a different stripe. No longer does the United States have so clear an advantage on economic and political matters, and its military power is no longer so convincing or so politically effective as it once was. Meanwhile, Europe has become the biggest capitalist marketplace in the world, its moral authority has grown, its political influence has spread as the reach of its economy has expanded, its foreign policies are achieving new consistency, and it is building a modest common military and the foundations of a common security policy. In short, Europe's aspirations to become a global power have been achieved, and the old, realist cold war order has been replaced by a new post-modern arrangement in which a resurgent Europe offers policies and priorities that leave it standing in clear distinction from that of the United States, to which it owes so much but with which it no longer always agrees.

The Americans take the lead

Until December 1941, international relations were dominated by rivalries among the great European powers. The United States was not seen to have essential interests in Europe, beyond trade and investment, and European governments were more interested in keeping the United States involved in European affairs than vice versa. But once Pearl Harbour had pulled the US into the war, American foreign policy was transformed. Roosevelt wanted to make sure that the US took centre-stage in designing a post-war settlement that would ensure the removal of the potential causes of future conflict. By the time of the D-Day landings in June 1944, the Americans dominated the allied war effort. At wartime summits, Roosevelt was the senior partner in discussions with Churchill, who was increasingly sidelined as the American leader switched his attention to Stalin.

The United States emerged from the war with superiority in four critical power domains:

- *The military domain*   Before the war, the US had been both pacifist and isolationist, its military aspirations so limited that its defence forces ranked twentieth in the world in size, behind those of the Netherlands.[3] By 1945, it had the world's first atomic bombs and the biggest air force and navy, and it was to account for about one half of global military spending for many years after the war. In the face of the post-war Soviet threat, only the Americans had the resources to be able to protect Western Europe. And there was much goodwill in the minds of many Western Europeans towards the Americans, and gratitude for the wartime sacrifices made by what NBC anchorman Tom Brokaw was later to call 'the greatest generation'.[4]
- *The economic domain*   The US economy had done well out of the war. About 400,000 Americans had died in the war, it was true, but there was no physical damage to the American mainland, giving the US an economic advantage over its European competitors. US industries were producing about as much as those of the rest of world combined, and major US corporations such as Standard Oil, General Motors and Lockheed were on the rise. US investments in Europe surged, and US companies acquired large slices of the European corporate pie.[5]
- *The political domain*   The Americans were able to translate their military and economic advantages into global political influence. Before the war, the leading figures in international relations had been mainly European, but now American presidents and their secretaries of state captured the headlines.
- *The cultural domain*   Hollywood was in its stride, American culture continued its steady insinuation into the global consciousness, and the icons of the changing international marketplace – from Coca-Cola to Mickey Mouse and blue jeans – were almost all American.

As the lines of the cold war became better defined, so the superpower credentials of the United States and the Soviet Union became more clear. Europe was weak and divided, its major states transformed into supporting actors in the confrontation between capitalism and communism. Western Europe was drawn into a dependence upon the American security shield, was nudged out of the driving seat of the global economy, and had to worry about both internal and external threats. For the United States, world leadership fitted naturally with its view of itself as an exceptional and morally superior power that should ensure the promotion of its ideals of democracy and free trade; however, it was to be torn between a resentment of the cost of power, and a welcoming of the influence it brought.[6] The Alliance was premised on American leadership, a US commitment to the defence of Western Europe, and an expectation by Europeans that Americans would play an active role in their affairs.[7] The lines of this new arrangement were confirmed by five critical developments between 1944 and 1952.

The first came in July 1944 at Bretton Woods, New Hampshire, when representatives from 44 countries met to plan the peacetime global economy, along lines suggested mainly by the Americans.[8] The priorities were free trade, non-discrimination, and stable rates of exchange, underpinned by the creation of the General Agreement on Tariffs and Trade (GATT), the International Monetary Fund (IMF), and the World Bank.[9] As the world's biggest economy, the United States became the driving force behind all three organizations, the IMF and the World Bank were headquartered in Washington DC, and the Bretton Woods system went on to promote stable monetary relations, expanded trade and economic growth, and the emergence of the US dollar as the new lynchpin of the international financial system.

The second came in 1947, when an economically exhausted Britain ended its financial aid to Greece and Turkey, and President Truman concluded that the United States – which had been pulling its troops out of Europe – had no choice but to step into the vacuum in order to curb communist influence. Arguing that the world faced a choice between freedom and totalitarianism, he charged that it must be US policy 'to support free peoples who are resisting attempted subjugation by armed minorities or by outside pressures'.[10] The short-lived post-war policy of American disengagement from Europe ended, and the Truman Doctrine confirmed US interest in European reconstruction as a means of containing the Soviets and discouraging the growth of communist parties in Western Europe.[11]

The third came in 1948, when – having realized that it had underestimated the extent of wartime economic destruction in Europe – the United States offered financial assistance. It had already provided over $10 billion in loans and aid during the period 1945–47,[12] but something more was needed. Although driven both by political motives (a strong Europe would be less likely to fall to extremism, and would be a buffer to Soviet expansionism) and by economic considerations (the US needed new peacetime export markets), the plan outlined by Secretary of State George Marshall was couched in humanitarian terms, emphasising the need to address 'hunger, poverty, desperation and chaos'. The Marshall Plan provided just over $12.5 billion in aid between 1948 and 1951,[13] and – because Europeans themselves had to decide how the aid was dispersed – helped lay the foundations for European integration.

The fourth came in 1949 with the creation of the North Atlantic Treaty Organization (NATO). The 1948 Berlin blockade had made it clear that all hope of East–West cooperation after the war had gone, and there were now fears that Stalin planned an expansion of Soviet influence in Europe, and that the Nazi threat had simply been replaced by a new Soviet threat. But despite the consensus among NATO members on the need to contain communism, despite the guarantees NATO offered, and despite the fact that most Western European governments felt that they had no choice but to rely on the United States for their security, European opinion on American motives was mixed. Analyses of the international situation and of the most useful action to take continued to differ,[14] the split pushing some Europeans (notably Britain) into the US camp and others (notably France) toward greater European cooperation.

Then, in 1950, came the fifth critical development, the launch of the endeavour that would eventually become the European Union. Europeans had been pondering the question of how they could best help themselves in the post-war world, and protect themselves from each other. The key challenge was to allow Germany to rebuild in such a way that it would pose no threat to France or its other neighbours. The solution proposed by Jean Monnet and Robert Schuman, and announced in May 1950, was to integrate European economies, thus making war less likely. The first modest step was taken with the 1951 Treaty of Paris, which created the European Coal and Steel Community (ECSC) in 1952, with six members: France, West Germany, Italy, and the Benelux countries. If there was some initial scepticism in the American business and political communities about a united Europe, and concerns that the ECSC would amount to a cartel, by the end of the Truman administration it had become official US policy to be supportive.[15] Ten years later, John F. Kennedy was announcing that the US looked on 'this vast new enterprise with hope and admiration', and that it viewed Europe not as a rival but as 'a partner with whom we can deal on a basis of full equality'.[16]

By 1952, then, the lines of the post-war international system were achieving a new clarity. The pre-war multipolar system centred on Europe had been replaced by a new bipolar system whose reference points lay outside Europe, in the hands of the United States and the Soviet Union. The lines of the cold war had divided Europe into belligerent Eastern and Western sectors, but the Western sector had taken the first steps in a process designed to transform itself into an integrated single economy, with the prospect of political integration further down the line. The Americans supported European integration, hoped that a united Europe would be better able to share US burdens, and assumed that Western Europe would be a loyal partner in tackling the problems of the world.[17] But these were no more than ideals; the reality was to be rather more complex.

From Korea to Suez

While West Germany had few illusions about its post-war status, being divided into four zones of occupation and enjoying little say in the matter, many in Britain and France continued to believe that their nations were still great powers. Britain believed in the special relationship with the United States, even though it had been cut out of the development of nuclear weapons, had been excluded from the redevelopment of post-war Japan, and was now under American pressure to dismantle its empire. But the British did not always agree with the Americans: even in the face of US disapproval, they recognized communist China in 1950. Meanwhile, the French were more openly wary of the Alliance, more deeply invested in 'Europe', and more concerned about American influence in Europe and about the US cold war agenda.[18]

The state of the Alliance was quickly unsettled by events in the Korean peninsula.[19] The June 1950 invasion of the South by the communist-dominated North prompted a US-led response, endorsed by the United Nations and including small contingents of European troops. European leaders initially took heart from the US response, which allayed fears of a new American isolationism, and proved that the US was willing to use the multilateral channels offered by the UN. But when the United States expelled the invaders and invaded the North, setting off an intervention by China and threatening to generate Soviet hostility, European confidence turned to alarm. Concerns were heightened by the emerging hysteria of McCarthyism, and by suggestions from American military leaders that the US might use nuclear weapons to resolve the Korean issue. Europeans now worried about American strategic over-extension and the threat to NATO's security. They wondered whether the US was a reliable partner, fearing both entrapment (being pulled into wider conflicts by the US) and abandonment.[20] Their fears were allayed somewhat by the election of Dwight D. Eisenhower, the resolution of the Korean problem, the death of Joseph Stalin, and the 1955 East–West summit in Geneva. But then the Alliance was to be shaken and the international system permanently transformed by events in Indochina and at Suez.

The French had regained Indochina in 1945 after its brief Japanese wartime occupation, but immediately faced nationalist demands for independence and an uprising in the north by the Vietminh under Ho Chi Minh.

Even as the end of the European colonial era was being signalled by the independence of India in 1947, and the Dutch withdrawal from Indonesia in 1949, the French engaged in an increasingly bitter war that ended in April 1954 with the surrender of 11,000 French troops near Dien Bien Phu. The loss dealt a severe blow to French national pride, and left the French feeling betrayed first by the lack of American support, and then by the manner in which the US replaced France as the key external power in the region.

If Dien Bien Phu had been the first strike against French hopes of maintaining global influence, the fatal blow was delivered at Suez in 1956.[21] Seeking to build a dam at Aswan on the Upper Nile, and having seen the initial offers of British and American financial support withdrawn, Egypt nationalized the Suez Canal, still under a 99-year concession to a company in which the British government and French investors had interests. Secret meetings were held among the British, French and Israelis, as a result of which Israel attacked the Canal Zone, and the British and French responded with a staged demand for an Israeli and Egyptian troop withdrawal. When the demand was ignored, British and French paratroopers were dropped into the Canal Zone in October.[22]

Coincidentally, the government of Imre Nagy in Hungary had announced the end of one-party rule, the evacuation of Russian troops, and Hungary's withdrawal from the Warsaw Pact. The Soviets responded with force, just as Britain and France were invading Egypt to retake the Suez Canal. The United States wanted to criticize the Soviet action and thereby boast of the moral superiority of the West to the emerging Third World, but it could not do so while British and French paratroopers occupied the Suez Canal. The Soviet Union was strongly critical of the invasion, there was a run on the pound that the Americans refused to offset, Britain and France were ostracized in the UN Security Council, and the US demanded the withdrawal of all three armies from the Canal Zone. They were finally pulled out in March 1957 and replaced by a UN peacekeeping force.

The consequences of Suez were tumultuous. In addition to its immediate political effects – the resignation of British Prime Minister Anthony Eden and its contribution to the collapse of the troubled French Fourth Republic in 1958 – the crisis confirmed the end of Britain and France as great powers, showing that they did not have the capacity to sustain significant military operations far from home. Suez also confirmed what almost everyone already knew, even if they were not always willing to admit it: the United States was a military and political superpower, and the senior partner in the Atlantic Alliance.

The British decided that they should never again find themselves at odds with the United States,[23] but the French – resentful of the unequal status accorded by the Americans to the British during the early years of NATO,[24] and still smarting from the effects of American policy in Indochina – drew the opposite conclusion, and were now more doubtful than ever about American trustworthiness, and more convinced of the importance of European policy independence.[25] Suez was one of the sparks that encouraged France to embark on the production of its own nuclear weapons,[26] and it also encouraged the British to begin (or to continue; opinion is divided) their slow turn towards Europe.[27] For Walter Hallstein, later president of the European Commission, Suez also helped encourage greater European unity;[28] it was no coincidence that in 1957 the Treaty of Rome was signed, creating the European Economic Community (EEC), and committing its six founding members (France, West Germany, Italy, and the Benelux countries) to the creation of a common market, a common Community external tariff, and a reduction in the barriers to the free movement of people, goods, services and capital.

The nuclear element

Meanwhile, feelings had begun to run high in West Germany about US influence on European defence issues, the new role of nuclear weapons, and the prospects of being used as a cold war battlefield. Many West Germans preferred the development of conventional weapons and felt that a strong national army would reduce the need for a nuclear defence strategy. West German public opinion changed somewhat after events in Hungary in 1956 and the 1957 launch of Sputnik, followed by a massive build-up of US nuclear warheads in Europe. But instead of guaranteeing Western European security, this build-up encouraged the Soviets to respond with their own nuclear build-up.

Concerned over the way in which it had been marginalized by the Americans in the development of the atom bomb, and interpreting this as a sign of new US isolationism, Britain had developed its own bomb, carrying out its first test in 1952. But this added to concerns about the nuclear threat, which in turn spawned a vocal anti-nuclear movement in Britain, spearheaded by the Campaign for Nuclear Disarmament (CND). Although British public opinion largely favoured the Alliance and CND represented the views of only a minority, its activities were symbolic of a growing rift within the Alliance. France in particular was unsettled, being initially undecided about whether or not to develop its own bomb, but then moving ahead as part of its search for new respectability, prompted by doubts about US reliability. De Gaulle had become president of France in 1958, and was obsessed with the issue of French pride and independence. The world, he felt, had been divided into Anglo-Saxon and Soviet spheres, with the French playing an inferior role.[29] This was certainly clear in the halls of NATO, which was commanded by a US general with a British deputy. France carried out its first atomic test in 1960, and de Gaulle ruled that no nuclear weapons would be based on French soil unless they were under the control of France. He felt that Europe under French leadership could now take over some of the functions carried out by the United States in NATO.

More strains in the Alliance surfaced in 1961 with the construction of the Berlin wall, cutting off the Soviet-controlled East from the US-British-French zones in the West. The absence of a strong American response, and President Kennedy's seeming acceptance of the wall as a *fait accompli*, was a disappointment to the Europeans. Then in 1962, responding to criticism of the 'massive retaliation' policy tied to its nuclear arsenal, the Kennedy administration adopted a 'flexible response' philosophy that gave the US stronger prospects of being able to use conventional forces to deal with a Soviet threat. But the Europeans were anxious to avoid a conventional war at all costs, and preferred the deterrent value of the nuclear option.[30] Then came the Cuban missile crisis in late 1962. Kennedy kept the British and the French informed of developments, but it was clear that US strategic interests were centre-stage and that European and NATO interests were marginalized. There was now a fear that Europeans might face 'annihilation without representation'.[31]

French concerns about Anglo-Saxon influence in Europe were reflected in de Gaulle's decision to twice veto British membership of the European Economic Community (in 1963 and 1967), for fear that Britain was an American Trojan horse. In 1966 de Gaulle sent his most dramatic signal to the Alliance by withdrawing France from the military structure of NATO – it remained a member, but withdrew its forces from the joint NATO command. Although de Gaulle was the instigator of these actions, they were symbolic of a broader unease within continental Western Europe about the American role in its security matters. Western Europe had become divided between an American-led Atlanticism and a Gaullist-inspired Europeanism,[32] or between those supporting an Atlantic Europe within which NATO members could try to influence US policy, and those supporting a more independent Europe with greater freedom of manoeuvre.[33]

From Vietnam to *Ostpolitik*

In spite of its differences with the Americans over policy, Western Europe benefited greatly from the Alliance. Calleo argues that NATO provided it with a shelter behind which it could focus on economic development and integration, as well as removing the need for Europeans to compete among themselves for military hegemony. The competition offered by US corporations helped encourage European business to restructure and to become more productive. Internal divisions made Germany a manageable partner for France, and the East–West continental split removed a traditional source of discord. The Alliance also meant participation in an open world economy, which in Calleo's view – 'more than compensated for the loss of colonial empires'.[34]

But the Faustian nature of the transatlantic pact was given new significance by developments in the 1960s. With an uneasy balance apparently achieved with the Soviets in Europe, John F. Kennedy proclaimed that the arena of the cold war had now shifted to Asia, Africa and Latin America.[35] A particular problem emerged in Vietnam, which had been partitioned – like Korea – into a communist North and a capitalist South. This was unacceptable to the communists under Ho Chi Minh, and war almost immediately broke out between the two Vietnams. When the North seemed to be gaining, the United States was drawn in, first with military advisors committed by Kennedy, and then – between 1962 and 1968 – with a massive US military build-up that included the transfer of 66,000 US troops from their bases in Western Europe.

Where European public opposition to US policy in the 1940s and 1950s had been muted and limited, it was made both louder and broader by Vietnam; anti-war demonstrations were held in many countries, and a 1967 poll found 80 per cent of those asked critical of US policy.[36] If the public was opposed to the war itself, European leaders worried about the potential impact on US security commitments to Europe. American leaders had their own set of worries: Lyndon Johnson sought the support of US allies, fearing that the United States was becoming morally isolated. But while European leaders were careful not to publicly criticize US policy, and were concerned that a refusal to help out in America's hour of need could lead to a reaction by Americans questioning the merits of continuing to defend Europe, they were forthcoming with neither military nor political assistance. Over the longer term, Vietnam was to have at least four critical effects:

- Questions were asked more openly than ever before about the confluence of US and European foreign policy, and about the extent to which the two sides could agree on their interpretations of international problems, and on the appropriate responses. The Watergate scandal was later to add troubling questions about American moral integrity, reliability and responsibility.[37]

- It was revealing that the world's pre-eminent military and economic power seemed unable to fight and win a war against a less well trained and armed guerrilla movement.
- Opinion in the American military and political establishments turned critical of European attitudes, wondering whether the US should continue to maintain large troop commitments to Western Europe.
- The United States entered several years of foreign policy introspection during which the value of military force was closely examined. It did not emerge from its 'post-Vietnam inhibition' until the invasion of Grenada in October 1983.[38]

To the strains on the security front were now added strains on the economic front. The Bretton Woods system had helped achieve a fixed exchange rate system by the end of the 1950s, but the US balance of payments deficit had raised concerns about its viability.[39] In 1970, the Nixon administration unilaterally suspended the convertibility of the dollar against gold, blaming the problems of Bretton Woods largely on the protectionism of the Community and its unwillingness to take more responsibility for the costs of defence (while in reality the inflationary effects on the US economy of the war in Vietnam were chiefly to blame[40]). On 15 August 1971, Nixon cut the link altogether, again with no reference to the Europeans. This prompted accelerated discussions on British membership of the EEC, and caused even pro-American European leaders such as Edward Heath and Willy Brandt to argue that Europe needed to unite in order to protect its interests.[41] When exchange rates were allowed to float in 1973, it meant the end of Bretton Woods.

Over Cuba, Vietnam and Bretton Woods the Americans had pursued their own definition of pressing strategic problems. It now fell to the Western Europeans – particularly the West Germans – to reciprocate. Although the idea of détente had been on the political agenda since the 1950s, it achieved a new significance during the 1960s. The US and the Soviets had reached approximate nuclear parity, leading to agreement that both sides should control the growth of their strategic nuclear arsenals; thus the opening in 1969 of the Strategic Arms Limitation Talks (SALT). A reduction in nuclear tensions was to be welcomed, but SALT also created concerns in Europe, because it was a bilateral series of negotiations from which Europeans were excluded, suggesting that the Americans gave precedence to their relationship with the Soviets over their concerns for the cohesion of the Alliance.[42]

The 1969 victory of the Social Democrats in West Germany brought to power Willy Brandt, former mayor of West Berlin. Brandt's *Ostpolitik*

(Eastern Policy), recognizing that Germany was the most likely site of any conventional war with the Soviets, sought to reduce cold war tensions by looking to the East rather than to the West alone. In return for concessions (including recognition of East Germany's borders with Poland and closer trading relations with the East), the Soviets recognized special West German links with West Berlin, and more contacts were allowed across the iron curtain. Just as the US was becoming bogged down in Vietnam, *Ostpolitik* was indicative of a new European self-assurance and sense of self-reliance.[43]

More problems in the Middle East

At a meeting in The Hague in 1969 Community leaders spoke grandly of 'paving the way for a United Europe capable of assuming its responsibilities in the world of tomorrow', and described the Community as 'an exceptional seat' of development, progress and culture.[44] During the 1970s this new attitude was reflected in the aspirations of the Western Europeans (notably to take a more active role in dealings with Eastern Europe) and in American concerns that the Community could evolve into a protectionist trading block from which it would be permanently excluded.[45] European confidence was in part a reflection of American angst: the US had lost a war for the first time in its history, faith in the institution of the presidency was shaken by Watergate, the energy crises of the 1970s emphasized American economic vulnerability, and when the Iranian hostage crisis came in 1979, it put the cap on a decade in which the United States seemed to be in decline.[46] Symptomatic of these developments was the emergence of yet another strain in the Alliance; within months of a declaration from US Secretary of State Henry Kissinger that 1973 should be the 'Year of Europe' and a celebration of the need for members of the Alliance to have a 'shared view of the world we seek to build', they had fallen out over the Middle East, in a dispute that for some was to be a 'Suez in reverse'.[47]

Israel may have been a child of Europe, but Europe had long equivocated over its attitudes to the Jewish state. While the United States had been quick to recognize Israel, for example, and France had been its major supplier of arms in the 1950s, it was not until the 1980s that Greece and Spain sent ambassadors to Israel. With the outbreak of the 1967 Six-Day War, France had branded Israel the aggressor for firing the first shots, and the Community had supported (as did the United States) UN Security Council Resolution 242 calling on Israel to return to its pre-war borders. But the United States adopted an 'Israel First' policy that was to result in a tradition of almost unqualified US support for Israel, in the face of European criticism of Israeli policy in the occupied territories.[48] The differences came to a head over the October 1973 Yom Kippur war, when the United States quickly and predictably came to the aid of Israel, but most European governments kept their distance, fearing a disruption of oil supplies from Arab producers.

When the Americans tried to resupply Israel, all their NATO partners except Portugal denied them access to airbases and airspace. West Germany blocked the loading of US weapons onto Israeli ships in German harbours, France continued to ship tanks to Libya and Saudi Arabia, and Britain and France refused to support a US proposal for a ceasefire resolution in the UN General Assembly. The Community also issued a joint statement in November (the Copenhagen Declaration) that was consciously designed to outline a position distinct from that of the US: a lasting peace would need to take account of the rights of Palestinians, and the UN should play a role in brokering a settlement. The Europeans railed against what they saw as American arrogance,[49] while across the Atlantic an aggrieved Henry Kissinger concluded that 'For two weeks, while the US had to make significant decisions, the Europeans acted as though the Alliance did not exist.'[50]

But the Americans were to reciprocate in kind. When the Soviets threatened to intervene in the dispute, the Nixon administration moved US forces around the world to DefConIII, the highest state of readiness in peacetime. The Europeans were not informed in advance, supposedly because the US did not want to risk the danger of the news being leaked, and thus of its impact being diminished. NATO officials were angered by the US move, observing that it was a reminder that the US and the Soviets often dealt with problems over the heads of the Europeans. It was also a reminder that Europeans were justifiably nervous of the prospects of superpower confrontation, particularly if Nixon continued to link détente to Soviet regional behaviour.[51]

The significant point here was that the Community had for the first time agreed and issued a foreign policy position that was distinct from that of the US.[52] On the Middle East, the Community continued to pursue policies that were at odds with those of the Americans: it invited the Palestine Liberation Organization (PLO) to the Euro–Arab Dialogue meetings in 1975, promoted the status of the Palestinians as participants in peace negotiations, looked to the stability of the eastern Mediterranean broadly defined (in contrast to US interests in the security of Israel), and refused to endorse the 1978 Camp David Peace Accords, instead insisting that Middle East peace had to include arrangements for a Palestinian homeland.[53] The effect, however, was to fundamentally undermine the credibility of the Community in the eyes of Israel, and to emphasize its inability to influence policy in the face of American support for Israel.

The late 1970s brought yet another transatlantic disagreement, but this time one that was symptomatic as much of European confidence as of American weakness. Following the December 1979 Soviet invasion of Afghanistan, and in an effort to reassert American leadership and prestige, the Carter administration tried to orchestrate an international political and economic response, including sanctions and the symbolic gesture of a boycott of the 1980 Olympics in Moscow. But the Germans and the French became alarmed about the threats thus posed to their efforts to achieve détente in Europe, and were keen to insulate these efforts from developments elsewhere. The differences reflected the contrasting priorities of the American global superpower and the European regional powers, the former taking a more global view than the latter. While Carter described the invasion as the 'greatest threat to world peace since World War Two', the Europeans were more doubtful about its implications.[54] The proposed boycott of the Olympics turned into a farce: more than 60 countries joined in, but they included only one Community member state, West Germany. Britain supported the boycott but allowed its athletes to make the final decision. Along with France, they sent a reduced delegation, had their athletes march in the opening ceremony under the Olympic flag, and had the Olympic anthem played at medal ceremonies.

Enter Reagan, stage right

If Western European opinion about US foreign policy had sometimes equiv-ocated during the early decades of the cold war, it was to achieve a new focus in light of the actions of the Reagan administration. For a new generation of Europeans born after the war, Ronald Reagan was to provide the first clear illustration of just how different were the worldviews of the partners in the Alliance. His term in office was to witness an America more willing to use its power to achieve its policy objectives, by fair means or foul, and to nurture a right-wing reaction to the hesitancy of the post-Vietnam years that was to reach a new apogee during the administration of George W. Bush. It was also to fertilize the seeds of doubt about the Alliance then germinating in the minds of that new European generation.

Entering office in January 1981, Reagan promised to clear away the murk of Vietnam, Watergate, two energy crises, slow economic growth, high infla-tion, and the 1979–81 Iranian hostage crisis. He cheerily announced that it was 'morning in America', promising economic revival and a reassertion of

American global leadership. As well as facing up to the Soviets, he argued that there should be no questions about American leadership in Western Europe. He increased US defence spending, made clear that he was not much interested in arms control, spoke of the need to negotiate from a position of strength, and announced his plans to provide a protective shield for the United States with his Strategic Defence Initiative (SDI), quickly dubbed Star Wars by the media.

Many Western Europeans had been frustrated by the vacillation of the Carter years, had recently returned right-wing governments to office, and so were at first buoyed by Reagan's policies. But hope turned to dismay as they realized how far he was prepared to go to sacrifice Alliance opinion on the altar of US interests. Despite Reagan's claims that the US was regaining the respect of its allies and adversaries alike,[55] assertive and even belligerent new policies followed in quick order. He continued backing the Afghan *mujahidin* (taking up where Carter had left off), supported Unita rebels ranged against the Soviet- and Cuban-backed MPLA government in Angola, and provided covert aid to right-wing Contras in their struggle against the left-wing Sandinista government in Nicaragua. Not only did several Western European governments adopt opposing positions – France, Spain and the Netherlands gave the Sandinistas diplomatic and financial aid, and France sold them weapons – but most Europeans held that providing military assistance to forces trying to overthrow governments ran counter to international law.[56] Critics of the Reagan Doctrine charged that it would lead to 'blowback', or retaliation by developing countries upset by US involvement in the affairs of their neighbours; Osama bin Laden is often portrayed as just such a product of blowback.[57]

Reagan famously dismissed the USSR as an 'evil empire', and saw its influence in the 1981 attempt on the life of Pope John Paul II, and in the 1983 shooting down of a South Korean airliner that had strayed into Soviet air space. In 1984 he mined harbours in Nicaragua and in 1986 ignored a ruling by the International Court of Justice that this was illegal and that the US should pay restitution, claiming that the Court was not competent to make the judgement. He supported the centre-right government of El Salvador in its struggle against left-wing insurgents, failed to criticize the Pinochet regime in Chile, and tried to sustain a pro-Western regime in Lebanon (only to have 241 US Marines die in a bomb attack in 1983). He also raised the ire of anti-apartheid campaigners by his failure to criticize the South African government, a position that prompted Nobel laureate Bishop Desmond Tutu to describe Reagan policy as 'immoral, evil and totally un-Christian', and to charge that it was 'giving democracy a bad name'.[58] All of this was to be but a prelude to the two most worrying incidents of the Reagan years: the INF episode, and Iran-Contra.

In the 1970s the Soviets had threatened to upset the cold war military balance by deploying mobile SS-20 missiles capable of reaching Western Europe. Soon after moving into the White House, Reagan proposed a 'zero option' by which all Soviet intermediate nuclear missiles would be removed, and no American missiles would be deployed. By doing so, he went against previously agreed NATO policy on the need to deploy new cruise and Pershing missiles in Western Europe. When negotiations on Intermediate Nuclear Forces (INF) broke down in 1983, the US responded by deploying its new missiles. There was strong opposition in the Belgian, Dutch and West German legislatures, and the anti-nuclear movement was revived in several countries, including Britain and Italy. The new French government of François Mitterrand was in favour of American deployment, being concerned that the US might otherwise pull out of Western Europe altogether, but the German Social Democrats were opposed, falling out with their coalition partners the Free Democrats, who formed a new coalition with Helmut Kohl and the Christian Democrats.[59]

In October 1986, Reagan met in Reykjavik with Mikhail Gorbachev, in what was billed as a pre-summit summit. But Reagan came close to agreeing a double-zero option: deep short-term cuts in all long-range nuclear weapons, and their eventual elimination by 1996 along with all intermediate-range nuclear weapons. Reagan discussed these proposals with none of his European allies, who were not only shocked by how little Reagan seemed to care about European security interests, but, supporting a NATO strategy based on nuclear deterrence, worried that a removal of nuclear weapons raised the possibility of a decoupling of US and European interests. Reagan insisted that the United States be allowed to continue to develop SDI, which the Soviets found impossible to accept, and so the proposals failed. Had they succeeded, they would have caused much embarrassment.[60] Western European leaders were now encouraged to more openly talk about greater European security cooperation. Reagan, concludes Michael Howard, may have done more for the defence of Western Europe than any of his more NATO-minded predecessors.[61]

Meanwhile Reagan had become mired in the Iran-Contra affair (1985–87), which combined an attempt to achieve the release of US hostages in the Middle East (while claiming that the US would not deal with terrorists) with the sale of weapons to Iran, the funds raised being used to arm and fund the Contra rebels in Nicaragua, bypassing the US Congress. Although Reagan claimed not to know what was happening, he later back-pedalled, and a 1987 Congressional report declared that he bore 'ultimate responsibility' and that his administration had exhibited 'secrecy, deception, and disdain for the law'.[62] Watergate had horrified European opinion, but it had been a primarily domestic affair. Iran-Contra had international implications, and for what it said about the kind of people making US foreign policy, and the manner in which they acted, it struck a blow to the reputation of the United States as a reliable partner.[63]

As if these difficulties were not enough, questions were raised once again about American economic leadership. In spite of recovery in the mid-1980s, and in spite of Reagan's optimistic arguments that the US was a 'shining city on a hill' whose citizens had 'the right to dream heroic dreams', his attempts to both reduce taxes and increase defence spending led inevitably to large budget deficits, a growth in the national debt, and the neglect both of social services and of the needs of the underclass. During his two terms in office, the federal budget deficit doubled and the national debt tripled.[64] Americans were also saving less, there was insufficient investment in infrastructure, and economic divisions between the rich and the poor had grown. The Reagan years also made Europeans aware, more clearly than ever before, of their differences with Americans on social values. The religious right had played a large role in Reagan's election, and he was criticized for his slow response to the AIDS/HIV crisis that emerged during his administration, and for his stance against abortion.

Tellingly, Reagan's policies could even raise the hackles of his closest European ally and supporter, Margaret Thatcher. When the US in October 1983 launched an attack on Grenada, claiming that Cuba was helping it build an international airport that could be used to trans-ship Cuban and Soviet weapons to Central American insurgent groups, Thatcher warned Reagan that it would be seen as interference in Grenada's internal affairs,[65] and suggested that the invasion be cancelled. When Reagan tried to impose economic sanctions on Poland – and then on the USSR – in response to martial law imposed by General Jaruzelski following the rise of the Solidarity trade union, Thatcher urged caution (most European governments felt that martial law was preferable to a Soviet invasion[66]). And it was Thatcher who met with Reagan following the Reykjavik episode in order to elicit an explanation on behalf of Reagan's European NATO allies.[67]

In spite of claims that Reagan's pressure on the Soviets helped bring about the end of the cold war (it was Thatcher who famously suggested at Reagan's funeral that he had won it 'without firing a shot'[68]), the policies of the Reagan years were to sully the reputation of US global leadership in the eyes of many Western Europeans. Where Reagan is admired by most Americans, and his death in June 2004 resulted in a month of official and unofficial mourning, combined with active attempts to rewrite the history of the Reagan years and thus to polish up his legacy, he was seen by most Western Europeans as too emotional, too divisive, and too casual, and as representing the worst elements of American international leadership; it was revealing that many of them looked more favourably upon Gorbachev than upon Reagan.

The end of the cold war and the rise of Europe

Throughout the cold war, the power potential of Europe had been subverted by a combination of its own weaknesses and divisions, and by relative American strength in the face of the Soviet threat. But despite Reagan's claims to the contrary, American influence and leadership declined during his administration, helped by Western Europe's doubts about his policies, the diminution of the Soviet threat, and the revival of the European project. Now, just as the end of World War II had redefined the international system, so too the end of the cold war brought another adjustment. Bipolarity began to decay as the Soviet Union collapsed and the relationship between the Americans and the Europeans underwent a fundamental shift. The cold war division of Europe began to dissolve, the security threat posed by the USSR lifted, and the integration of the European economy accelerated. The United States may have been the last remaining military superpower, but it faced new political resistance from a Europe that was no longer quite so worried about maintaining US security guarantees or quite so willing to keep its concerns about US foreign policy under its hat.

There was little evidence of these changes on show during the 1990–91 Gulf war.[69] Community members provided political and military support for the US-led response to Saddam Hussein's invasion and annexation of Kuwait, but at very different levels, and significantly below those committed by the United States. Britain and France provided the most military support, but Belgium, Portugal and Spain were all unwilling to become too actively involved, and Ireland protected its neutrality. For Luxembourg foreign minister Jacques Poos the Community's response symbolized 'the political insignificance of Europe'. For the Belgian foreign minister, it showed that the EC was 'an economic giant, a political dwarf, and a military worm'.[70] While the member states had taken a firm line against Iraq on sanctions, recorded Commission President Jacques Delors, once it became obvious that the situation would have to be resolved by force, the Community realized that it had neither the institutional machinery nor the military force to allow it to act in unison.[71] Margaret Thatcher felt that only Britain and

France had 'done more than the bare minimum' and that it was sad that Europe had 'not fully measured up to expectations'.[72]

The signature of the Maastricht treaty in 1992 gave the Community (now the European Union) a common foreign and security policy, but it was no more than a framework, and the absence of details was reflected in the weak and divided European response to developments in the Balkans. When the Yugoslav federal army invaded Slovenia two days after the latter had declared independence in June 1991, the Community had a clear need and desire to intervene. Early developments held promise, with a Community-brokered peace conference in September, but when the Community recognized Croatia and Slovenia in January 1992, its credibility as a neutral arbiter disappeared. Talks continued, sponsored by the Community and the UN, but the Community was once again divided over how to proceed, and lacked the capability to intervene militarily. Peace in Bosnia was ultimately achieved under US leadership, and it was NATO – again under US leadership – which was to respond to the 1997–98 crisis in Kosovo, sparked by the aggression with which the Milosevic regime met attempts by ethnic Albanians to break away from Serb-dominated Yugoslavia. When the NATO bombing came in March 1999, it was to provide a catalyst that would finally encourage the EU to take action on building a military capability.[73]

The cold war was barely over before suggestions began to surface that the end of the bipolar international system would lead to a decline of the Atlantic Alliance. The idea was anticipated in structuralist realist theories of international relations, which suggest that alliances are partnerships of convenience, and that once the power of the adversary has gone, the forces that tie an alliance decrease. John Mearsheimer was predicting in 1990 that because 'the distribution and character of military power are the root causes of war and peace', and because the departure of the superpowers would remove the 'pacifying' effect of nuclear weapons, the 45 years following the end of the cold war 'would probably be substantially more prone to violence than the past 45 years'.[74] But globalization had changed the nature of the international system, and the old assumptions no longer held.

Following each other in short order, the events of the 1990s transformed perceptions about the Alliance, and about the relative global roles of the European Union and the United States. The one joint US–European project of the cold war – dealing with the Soviet threat – was gone. Freed of their dependence upon American security guarantees, Europeans were in a stronger position to purse policies independent of the Americans. The days when Western Europe had to rely on the United States for investment and for economic support were also gone, the near completion of the European single market had transformed the Community into a marketplace that was almost as big as that of the United States, agreement was approaching on the new single currency, and the identity of Europe was being redefined as the cold war divisions of Berlin, Germany and Europe faded into history. The result was a necessary adjustment of the way Europeans and Americans saw themselves, each other, and the international system.

Nowhere was European confidence more clear than on the issue of trade.[75] In 1986, the European Economic Community had 12 member states, which among them accounted for one-fifth of global GDP, and about a quarter of global exports and imports. By 1995, membership had risen to 15 countries, and Europe's share of economic wealth and trade increased accordingly. The Europeans and the Americans had tussled over trade before (for example, over European agricultural subsidies), but the growing value of their bilateral trade combined with the new size and confidence of the European market and the new dispute settlement system that came with the creation in 1995 of the World Trade Organization to generate a string of bruising trade disputes: these included the issue of sanctions imposed by the US on foreign firms dealing with Iran, Libya and Cuba, and the disputes over genetically modified foods, government subsidies to Airbus, and tariffs imposed on steel imports in 2002 by the Bush administration (see Chapter 4). The security concerns of the cold war, pitting the Americans and the Soviets against each other, were now being replaced by the economic concerns of the post-modern era, pitting Europeans and Americans against each other.

The return of the neo-conservatives

If the policies of the Reagan administration had prompted European frustration in the face of American strength, they were to prove but a preview of the impact of the policies of the second Bush administration. In 1997, a project named the New American Century had been launched by two conservatives, William Kristol and Robert Kagan. Several of its sympathizers – including Paul Wolfowitz and John Bolton – were later to become key members of the Bush administration. In their manifesto *Rebuilding America's Defenses*, they spoke of the need to 'promote American global leadership' through a strong military and 'a foreign policy that boldly and purposefully promotes American interests'.[76] This was a view that was to be heartily embraced by George W. Bush. Elected to office in November 2000 in a disputed vote, and claiming to be both a 'compassionate conservative' and a 'uniter, not a divider', he quickly became the most doctrinaire, divisive and disliked president the Europeans had ever had to deal with. At the heart of the problem was his support for the neo-conservative view: an aggressive approach to foreign policy, a rejection of pragmatism, robust support for Israel, criticism of the United Nations, a rejection of multilateralism, and a belief in exploiting American power to its fullest.[77] It was a grand strategy, argues Schwenninger, of 'muscular dominance'.[78]

Bush gave an early taste of his approach to international relations with the manner in which he dismissed the 1997 Kyoto protocol on climate change, angering the EU as much for the decision as for the abrupt and unilateral manner in which it was announced. Bush claimed that Kyoto was flawed, in large part because China and India had been exempted, but his critics commented on the fact that Bush was a former oilman, and was surrounded by officials with links to the oil industry. Bush raised further suspicions when he did nothing to encourage energy conservation until the international price for oil began to reach record levels in 2005–06, the impact on the US worsened by the impact of hurricane Katrina on domestic refining capacity.

Kyoto was quickly pushed aside, however, when the September 2001 terrorist attacks in New York and Washington DC injected an entirely new element into the character of international relations. The nature of security issues had already been transformed by changes in both the causes of conflict and in the technology and intelligence available to respond, but the attacks raised a problem of an entirely new order. The initial European reaction was an outpouring of political and public sympathy for the United States, and – for the first time – diplomats invoked NATO's Article 5 (dealing with mutual defence). Many European leaders hoped that the tragedy would usher in a new era in US foreign policy, emphasizing multilateralism and diplomacy. Indeed, in the hands of a statesman it might even have been an opportunity for a reassertion of American leadership in the world.

Initially, things went well. Having identified the Taliban regime in Afghanistan as a supporter and protector of terrorists, and with political and public support from the EU, the United States orchestrated an attack on Afghanistan in October 2001. Once the Taliban had been removed from power, contingents from multiple EU countries took part in peacekeeping and reconstruction. But European support for US policy evaporated as the Bush Doctrine took on aggressively unilateralist features. Bush claimed the right to an independent American definition of the sources and the nature of terrorism, and warned that he would judge allies according to their position ('You're with us or against us,' he declared during a press conference in November 2001), and would consider all options, including the use of nuclear weapons on rogue states. In all this, the opinions of the EU, the United Nations, and NATO were largely ignored. When Bush referred to an 'axis of evil' consisting of Iran, Iraq, and North Korea,[79] he raised concerns among European allies that he was planning to open new fronts in the war on terrorism. French foreign minister Dominique de Villepin dismissed the remarks as 'simplistic', EU external affairs commissioner Chris Patten dismissed US unilateralism as 'ultimately ineffective and self-defeating', and it became clear that the Europeans were reacting as much to the US reaction to terrorism as they were to terrorism itself.[80]

When Bush began clearing the way for an invasion of Iraq, accusing Saddam Hussein of possessing weapons of mass destruction, planning to build nuclear weapons, and posing a threat to US interests, the Europeans finally woke up. Governments were divided, with the British, the Italians, the Spanish and much of Eastern Europe in support of US policy, while France and Germany led the opposition. For many, and particularly for Europe's American critics, these divisions were another sign of the weaknesses of the EU and of the hollowness of European foreign policy aspirations. But outside the political divisions there was a remarkable unity of public opinion. Polls found 70–90 per cent opposition in almost every European country (see Figure 2.1), massive anti-war demonstrations were held in most European capitals, and several pro-war governments faced political difficulties. The Vatican came out against the war, Pope John Paul II arguing that 'Violence and arms can never resolve the problems of man.' Even Ireland slipped off the fence. It had declared a day of national mourning following the 9/11 attacks, but after Iraq, the US was widely portrayed as a bully, an estimated 100,000 people took part in an anti-war demonstration in Dublin, and demands were made that US forces on their way to the Middle East be denied access to Shannon airport. A June 2003 poll found reduced European faith in American global leadership, with less than half of those questioned wanting to see a strong global US presence. President Bush's European approval rating – already a modest 36 per cent in 2002 – had fallen to 16 per cent by 2003.[81] Most remarkably, an October 2003 survey found that 53 per cent of Europeans viewed the United States as a threat to world peace on a par with North Korea and Iran.[82]

Most have chosen to interpret the divided European political response as a sign of crisis or of weakness, but it might better be seen as a reflection of Europe's new confidence and of declining faith in American leadership. Never before had the governments of France and Germany been so vocal and open in their opposition to US policy. During the cold war, they would have sent careful diplomatic signals of concern, but here were their respective leaders going public with their criticism. As his public approval reached new highs, and there was talk of nominating him for the Nobel Peace prize, Jacques Chirac charged that the invasion of Iraq was illegal,

Figure 2.1   *European public opposition to the invasion of Iraq, 2003*

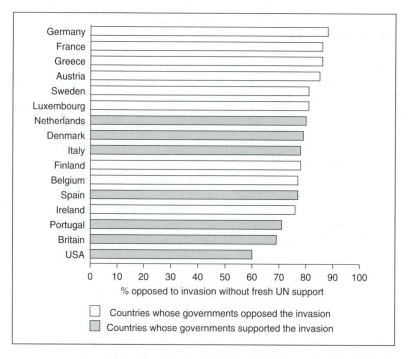

Note: The governments of all eight prospective Eastern European member states of the EU – the Czech Republic, Estonia, Hungary, Latvia, Lithuania, Poland, Slovakia and Slovenia – also supported the invasion.

Sources: EOS Gallup poll, January 2003. US figure is average of polls taken by CNN/*USA Today*, *Los Angeles Times*, and Fox News.

and that a resolution could have been achieved by peaceful means, not military means.[83] Gerhard Schroeder, having snatched victory from the jaws of defeat in the September 2002 German election with his criticism of Bush, became the first post-war German leader formally to announce the opposition of his country to US policy.[84]

And while most Americans had largely shrugged off or ignored earlier instances of European opposition to US foreign policy, they were both keenly aware of and deeply affected by the European reaction to Iraq. But while they might have learned something, many were prompted to respond to heightened anti-Americanism with new levels of anti-Europeanism, focusing particularly on France.[85] Calls were made for a boycott of French imports, France was criticized for not supporting the US despite the deaths of so many US soldiers during the World War II liberation of France, and two Republican members of Congress earned plaudits for taking international relations to new lows by supporting a move to rename French fries and French toast as 'freedom fries' and 'freedom toast'. By themselves minor, together these developments reflected a new sense that the opinions of Europe mattered to Americans, and that there was a new insecurity in the United States about the health of the Alliance.

At one level, the dispute over Iraq could be dismissed as just another of the many that have plagued the Alliance since 1945. It might even be argued that the dispute was more reflective of the short-term goals and values of the Bush administration than of long-term US policy. Surely Europe and America would eventually patch up their differences, as they had so many times before? But the depth of European public opposition to US policy in 2003–04 was remarkable, as was the division among the leaders of the EU's four major powers: Germany, Britain, France and Italy. Furthermore, the character of the Alliance was now quite different. For most of the cold war, Europe had been economically, politically and militarily disadvantaged in its relationship with the United States. It did not publicly disagree with US policy, and even where it had expressed itself, the United States could afford to ignore European opinion. By 2003, the picture was quite different. The threat of the Soviet Union was long gone, Europe was economically resurgent and well on the path to reunification, the United States was deeply divided and facing multiple economic challenges, and Europeans were becoming increasingly aware of just how many points of disagreement there were between the two cold war partners.

3

Europe's Civilian Power

Power in the international system is so closely linked with military capability that the two have become almost synonymous; Mao's dictum that all power comes out of the barrel of a gun must, it seems, be taken to heart. The other dimensions of power – economic, political, cultural, technological and moral – are important, to be sure, but claims that the United States is the world's last remaining superpower rest almost entirely on its military credentials; these are what make it truly unique. And when claims that the EU is also a superpower are denied, it is usually on the basis of its lack of a large common military. Risse argues that while the EU matches the US in economic power, it lacks the willingness to match it in military power.[1] Stanley Hoffman wonders whether recent changes on the European security front will make the EU a 'complete' power, promoting it from 'merely' a civilian power.[2] For Alfred van Staden, the 'undeniable attribute' of full power status for Europe must be a common army.[3]

The raw statistics of American military power are certainly impressive. The United States has a bigger annual defence budget than the next ten countries combined,[4] spending more than twice as much as the European Union and accounting for nearly half of global military spending. Its military arsenal is the biggest the world has ever seen, with nearly 6,000 nuclear warheads, 18 nuclear submarines, 12 aircraft carriers, nearly 6,000 combat aircraft (including more than 220 long-range bombers), and more than 1.4 million military personnel.[5] No other state has such an array of advanced military technology, whether in the form of stealth fighters and bombers or in 'smart' bombs that can be aimed at the enemy with remarkable accuracy. The US military in 2006 was active in more than 50 countries. And unlike the European military, which has few unifying policy objectives and many separate command structures, the US military answers to a single set of policies and a single command structure. In size, firepower, and unity of purpose, the United States has no military peer.

Military capacity will probably always be needed in some form for defence and deterrence if not for compliance,[6] but size is not everything. American military power helped bring lasting change in Germany and Japan, and ensured a nervous balance of peace during the cold war, but its limits were revealed in Vietnam, Haiti, Somalia, and Lebanon, and continue to be clear in Iraq today. Americans may seek comfort in the security provided by so much firepower, but it may in fact be leaving them less secure: it sends questionable messages about the priorities of US foreign policy, encourages many to think of the United States as a threat to world peace rather than as its guardian, feeds into growing anti-Americanism, compromises US economic power by diverting valuable resources from other economic and social sectors, and may no longer be relevant to helping us solve the most troubling international problems. Instead of being seen as a benevolent economic and political power in the word, the United States has become infamous in the minds of many for its association with militarism and state-sponsored violence.[7] In short, US military power – rather than promoting security and stability – may make the world more dangerous and unstable.

During the cold war, the United States was – by virtue of its overwhelming military and economic power – the clear leader in the Atlantic Alliance, no matter what reservations European political leaders and their publics may have sometimes had about the details of US foreign policy. But much has since changed.[8] The Soviet threat to international security has gone, its place taken by problems to which a military response is not always appropriate. And in those cases where a military response is appropriate, it is typically of a different scale and nature than the scenarios for which NATO prepared itself during the cold war. Finally, since the collapse of the USSR, the Europeans have been freed from their reliance on American security, and have become more willing and able to promote their own distinctive, non-military, interpretations of international problems and solutions.

Kagan tells us that while the United States believes that security and defence still depend on the possession and use of military power, Europe has moved into a world of laws, rules, and international cooperation. While Europeans see a complex global system, and prefer to negotiate and persuade rather than to coerce, the United States is less patient with diplomacy, and sees the world as divided between good and evil, and between friends and enemies. The differences, Kagan concludes, are a reflection of the relative positions of the two actors in the world. When European states were great powers in the eighteenth and nineteenth centuries, they were more ready to use violence to achieve their goals. Americans, by contrast, appealed to rules and laws as a means of resolving disagreements, when it suited them. Now that Europeans and Americans have traded places, they have also traded perspectives.[9]

The differences can be seen in the contrasting roles that the military plays in American and European culture. Americans tend to laud and lionize the military, perhaps because it is the most visible expression of American power. In the American national psyche, the flag, patriotism, military service, and national identity are all but indistinguishable. American leadership in military technology is proudly projected as proof of American economic might and inventiveness, more so today than ever. Veterans are honoured and rewarded for their public service, military experience is almost *de rigueur* for any serious candidate for the US presidency, and questions about the quality of that experience (or lack thereof) can be enough to derail a campaign.[10] In Europe, by contrast, military service is so understated as to be almost invisible. War has unpleasant associations with nationalism, and has been decoupled from definitions of national identity. And while veterans are honoured annually at remembrance ceremonies, the link between military service and public service is minimal. Indeed, to run for office in Europe on a background of military experience can be a positive handicap.

The United States and the EU now offer two distinctive models of the role of military power in international relations. While the former is more ready to opt for a military response to terrorism, for example, and to talk of a 'war' on terrorism, the latter prefers to examine and address the problems that have led to the rise of terrorism, and to approach the matter as a question of law enforcement. While the Bush administration has refused to rule out the option of force against 'rogue states' such as Iran, the European Union prefers to explore non-military solutions. While Americans are more willing to act alone, refusing even to allow their soldiers to wear the blue helmets of the UN, Europeans prefer multilateral approaches to security problems backed by UN resolutions. Kagan is wrong when he argues that this is largely down to capability, and that those who have the weapons will be inclined to use them. On the contrary, Europe has identified a new approach to international relations which relies less on military power,[11] and in so doing has become a civilian superpower.

The limits to American military power

If we go by size and resources alone, the United States is without question the world's dominant military power. Ronald Steel boasts that America's 'fleets and air squadrons roam the world unimpeded by any rival force. No nation has the means to challenge us. We can exert overwhelming power virtually anywhere we choose and in whatever cause we see fit.'[12] Larry Diamond concludes that 'not only is the United States without peer among potential military challengers, but there is no conceivable coalition of nations that could challenge the military might of the United States today or at any time in the foreseeable years to come'.[13] Increased military spending and independence, argued Andrew Moravcsik shortly after the outbreak of hostilities in Iraq in 2003, allowed the United States to 'wage war confident of quick victory, low casualties, and little domestic fallout'. In his view, it had been 'demonstrated in Iraq that military force can be remarkably effective'.[14]

But such confident declarations tend to overlook the many examples of American military failure. Ferguson asks, 'What is power?', and gives us the quick answer 'America'.[15] But if we ask, 'What symbolizes the limits on power?', then the quick answer is surely 'Vietnam'. Even the richest country in the world, with the biggest defence budget and the largest and most technologically advanced military, was unable to overcome a deadly triple cocktail: a war fought almost alone, against a backdrop of divided public opinion at home and abroad, and against an enemy willing to fight to the death. The US invested billions of dollars in Vietnam, and at its peak committed more than half a million personnel to the war. It could carpet bomb acres of jungle with squadrons of massive B-52 bombers that each carried up to 70,000 pounds of ordnance. It could pound North Vietnamese cities and factories with near impunity. And yet, after eight years of war, and after the deaths of 58,000 American military personnel, about 1.1 million North Vietnamese military personnel, as many as 300,000 Cambodians, and as many as 2 million Vietnamese civilians, the United States withdrew in 1973, its core objectives unmet.

Apologists for Vietnam will usually argue that not enough resources were committed to the war, and that the necessary political will was missing. But history tells us that military Goliaths are often laid low by Davids (in what is known technically as 'asymmetric warfare'). The Greeks held off superior numbers of Persians at Thermopylae in 480 BC, Hannibal prevailed over the Romans in 218–216 BC, the French crumbled at the sharp end of English longbows at Agincourt in 1415, the Americans defeated the British during the revolutionary war, the French left Indochina and Algeria with mud on their faces, and the Afghan *mujahadin* (albeit with Western aid) held off the invading Soviets. Most recently, the Americans have found in Iraq that massive military spending and advanced technology cannot always bring order and stability. Moravcsik's quick victory has failed to materialize, casualties have been high, domestic fallout has grown, and – once again – the limitations of great force have been clearly illustrated. There are many reasons why claims that overwhelming American military power is peerless do not always hold up in the field.

First, military action alone is not always enough. The United States has an enviable reputation for confronting and dealing with conventional foes in the open field, and for fighting and winning wars in days or weeks with minimal losses; the first Gulf War was over in 42 days with less than 150 battle-related casualties, the war in Kosovo was won with no coalition fatalities, and the 2001 invasion of Afghanistan was completed in a matter of weeks with less than 120 battle-related casualties. But the US also has a regrettable record of overlooking plans for post-war peace and stability. As Winston Churchill once quipped, 'America is very powerful but very clumsy.' In Iraq, despite all their abilities and resources, American soldiers have been unable to make Iraq the beacon of democracy that George W. Bush has so often said they could, in part because of failure to predict and plan for post-invasion problems, and in part because US policy has surrendered the moral high ground. Claims by Bush that the US has sought only to promote democracy have been tarnished by the pre-emptive strike, by disregard for allies and international organizations, by the scandalous treatment of prisoners at Guantanamo Bay and at Abu Ghraib, and by rumours of secret CIA flights taking prisoners to third countries where they could be tortured. The United States – rather than being acclaimed as a purveyor of ideas – is widely seen by its critics as a purveyor of violence. It has overlooked the advice of the *Financial Times*: 'to win the peace ... the US will have to show as much skill in exercising soft power as it has in using hard power to win the war'.[16]

American policymakers have routinely used the defence of freedom and democracy as an explanation for their military interventions since World War II, but the record of success has been surprisingly modest. A recent Carnegie Endowment study found that of 16 nation-building efforts in which the United States engaged militarily during the twentieth century, only four were successful in that democracy remained ten years after the departure of US forces: these were Germany and Japan (enormous achievements, to be sure), and Grenada and Panama. In cases where the US engaged alone, not a single American-supported surrogate regime made the transition to democracy. The study concluded that the odds of success would only be raised in future if the US supported a multilateral reconstruction strategy under UN auspices.[17]

Another study – looking at more than 35 post-World War II US interventions, including those in Grenada, Haiti, Lebanon, Nicaragua, Panama and Thailand – found that in only one case (the war on drugs in Colombia from 1989) did the intervention result within ten years in a full-fledged democracy with limits on executive power, universal adult suffrage and competitive elections. Such failures are not unique to the US: Britain and France have shown no better average returns in their military interventions, and countries neighbouring those in which interventions have occurred have often shown more progress towards democracy than the target countries. Why so? The authors of the study blame US, British and French policy, which they argue 'has been motivated less by a desire to establish democracy or reduce human suffering than to alter some aspect of the target state's policy'. Despite official claims, promoting democracy is rarely the most important goal.[18]

A second problem with military power is that there is a limit to how much it can achieve within a vacuum of international political support. The contrast between the first and second Gulf wars is clear. George H. W. Bush went into Kuwait in 1991 with the backing of the UN Security Council and the participation of a 34-nation coalition, and succeeded in his aims: Iraq was expelled. Ten years later, his son successfully pulled together a multinational coalition for the 2001 attack on Afghanistan, but when faced with resistance to his plans for Iraq, petulantly declared that he would attack with or without support from the UN or other countries. Once committed, it not only became clear that the United States needed access to bases and airfields in some of those countries in order to launch a substantial military operation, but widespread international opposition to the war hobbled American efforts. The Bush administration later failed to encourage other countries to forgive their debt to Iraq, and to encourage NATO partners to commit troops to Iraq in more than a reconstructive or peacekeeping role.

Bush might have learned from Joseph Nye's assertion that – thanks largely to the technological revolution in information and communications – there are limits to what the United States can do alone.[19] He might also have learned from the wistful recollections of former US Secretary of Defense Robert S. McNamara in the 2003 documentary *The Fog of War*:

> We are the strongest nation in the world today, [but] I do not believe we should ever apply that economic, political or military power unilaterally. If we'd followed that rule in Vietnam, we wouldn't have been there. None of our allies supported us. If we can't persuade nations with comparable values of the merit of our cause, we'd better re-examine our reasoning.

And finally, Bush might have heeded the words of the new NATO secretary-general Jaap de Hoop Scheffer when he argued during his first visit to the United States in 2004 that events in Iraq had shown that the idea that the United States could and should act alone on security issues was a 'dangerous illusion'.[20]

A third problem with military power is that even the biggest military establishment finds itself coming up against practical limits. At the height of activities in the Middle East in 2004, there were 135,000 American troops in Iraq and 15,000 in Afghanistan. This was only about 10 per cent of the total US military establishment, but in order to sustain this presence while preserving those in other parts of the world, tours of duty were being extended and more reinforcements were being pulled in from the National Guard. Recruitment to the armed services was also falling as public opinion in the United States turned against the war in Iraq. And when hurricane Katrina devastated the coasts of Alabama, Mississippi and Louisiana in August 2005, it became clear that the United States did not have enough National Guard units nearby to respond quickly to the subsequent break-down in law and order, and that it would have to go deeper into debt in order to meet the costs of the clean-up. (Undeterred, Bush was asking Congress in February 2006 for another $120 billion to commit to the conflicts in Afghanistan and Iraq.) Questions were meanwhile asked throughout the Iraqi conflict about the ability of the United States to commit troops to trouble spots in other parts of the world. Unless it could withdraw militarily from Iraq, the Pentagon would have been unable to respond to another serious international crisis.

A fourth problem is posed by the effects of large military spending on the foundations of the American state. Ferguson argues that the 'revolution in military affairs' in the 1990s was possible because rapid American economic growth made increases in defence spending seem insignificant in relative terms, and because the US federal government was able to convince taxpayers to continue contributing 15 cents in every dollar to its military.[21] But this is shaky economic logic. The remarkable level of US defence spending – projected to grow from nearly $400 billion in 2003 to nearly $440 billion in 2007[22] – has not only contributed to record federal budget deficits and a massive national debt, but also diverts resources away from schools, hospitals, transport networks, scientific research, anti-poverty programmes, and new infrastructure (including levees in New Orleans). The US also has less to invest abroad in economic and social development, undermining its ability to compete in the global economy, and reducing its political and economic influence. There are those who argue the sustainability of defence spending, claiming that there is no plausible challenger to American economic leadership, and that US economic health is underpinned by technological dynamism, flexibility, and openness to trade.[23] But how does this square with the persistence of domestic poverty, declining educational standards, the national debt quagmire, decaying infrastructure, and a looming social security and national health crisis?

A fifth reason for questioning American military advantages lies in the misleading impression conveyed by the budget figures: they look less impressive when waste, inefficiency, redundancy and duplication are taken into account. (This dilemma also plagues the Europeans, but on a smaller scale.[24]) Just how many nuclear warheads does the United States need to deter potential enemies – assuming, that is, that by launching even a limited nuclear strike it would not at least destroy the last shreds of its moral advantage, and at worst invite a counterstrike that would lead to massive loss of life and widespread radioactive fallout? On the conventional front, the US Air Force flies many more models of aircraft (30) than it really needs, and has been so anxious to stay ahead of potential enemies on technology that there are large airfields in Arizona full of not-very-old planes that were little used and may never fly again. Meanwhile, dozens of ships built for the US Navy have been mothballed because they are surplus to needs.[25]

The budget figures are driven up by the extraordinary US investment in advanced military technology, which does not always offer advantages. Advanced weapons systems were not enough to defeat the guerrillas of Vietnam or the warlords of Somalia, and have had only a mixed record in controlling the insurgents of Iraq. Advanced technology also faces significant handicaps when dealing with an enemy that cannot always be identified or located, and indeed the use of such technology may actually bring out the weaknesses in American military power rather than its strengths; consider, for example, the ineffectual cruise missile strikes on Sudan and Afghanistan in 1998.[26] And the obsession with technology runs the danger of making new weapons too sophisticated to work properly: witness the experience of the Apache attack helicopters deployed in Afghanistan in 2000–01, more than 80 per cent of which were badly damaged by ground fire. The NATO bombing campaign against Kosovo in 1999 revealed many of the holes in 'advanced' technology: stealth aircraft occasionally showed up on radar during wet weather (and one was shot down), radar beams sometimes reflected off hard surfaces and caused confusion to precision-guided missiles (PGMs), simple decoys were used by the Serbians to confuse heat-seeking missiles and infrared sensors, NATO wasted expensive missiles on dummy targets (allowing a surprising number of Serbian tanks and military aircraft to survive the campaign), and the cloudy Balkan weather sometimes blocked laser guidance beams and cancelled out the value of PGMs.[27] And then in 2004 there was the embarrassment caused to Defense Secretary Donald Rumsfeld when American soldiers in the field in Iraq complained that they were cannibalising wrecked vehicles for parts, and that their Humvees did not have enough armour to withstand roadside bomb blasts.

America's addiction to technology has made many of its weapons enormously expensive, the budgets for their development and construction often inflated by cost over-runs. A single B-2 Spirit stealth bomber costs over $1 billion (more than the entire annual defence budget of Ireland in 2004), an F-117 Nighthawk stealth fighter costs $45 million (the US Air Force has 55 of them), and the US Navy's newest aircraft carrier – the nuclear-powered USS *Ronald Reagan*, commissioned in 2003 – cost $5 billion. To further inflate the defence budget, spending is often subject to pork barrel politics: large spending bills are passed by Congress and legislators compete with each other to make sure that as much of the money as possible is spent in their home districts, regardless of need. And military installations are often kept running even when surplus to needs: when a plan was announced in May 2005 to close down or consolidate more than 60 military bases across the United States, the local outcry and resistance was immediate, and political pressure resulted in many of those bases quickly being removed from the list. Meanwhile, accusations flew that the Pentagon was adding to the defence budget by giving large contracts to corporations such as Bechtel and Halliburton on a 'no-bid' (non-competitive) basis.

The final problem facing the American military behemoth is the declining relevance of war as a tool of policy. Wars were once fought between states that confronted each other on the field of battle with a foreseeable end to hostilities.[28] Combatants fought each other for power, land, influence, or resources, or over ideological differences. The causes of war were relatively easy to identify, and conflict typically ended in a tightly defined (if not always permanent) resolution of the problem. But Samuel Huntington warned in 1996 that wars of the future would be fought over cultural issues, leading to a 'clash of civilizations'.[29] Is the conflict between al-Qaeda and the West an example of a modern cultural war? Even if it is not, the nature of conflict today is much different from the days of the cold war, and non-military means of dealing with conflict are increasingly vital. Not all US policymakers yet seem to have understood this. The Pentagon is still full of cold warriors geared up to fighting large wars, unilaterally if necessary, and who are slow to appreciate the merits of the multilateral and multifunctional approach taken by the Europeans.

Former US Assistant Secretary of State Chester Crocker argues that while it was understandable for US policymakers to seize upon the 9/11 attacks to declare the beginning of a new era and to try and 'restore foreign policy … to its erstwhile primacy in American national politics, the "war on terror" has been a dubious template for that policy because it oversimplifies the challenges we face, exaggerates the effectiveness of force as the primary response, and denigrates alliances and the non-military dimensions of statecraft'.[30] In a related set of arguments, Jeffrey Record suggests that while US conventional military primacy is unprecedented, it is becoming its own worst enemy because its disadvantages are accumulating: it has encouraged the enemy to invest increasingly in irregular warfare and the development of weapons of mass destruction; it appears to reduce the cost of going to war and promotes a 'strategic hubris' that encourages the unnecessary use of force by the United States; and it isolates war from politics, encouraging US policymakers to overlook the difficulties of converting easy military victories into lasting political successes.[31]

In short, then, we should treat claims of American military power with care. When the political, strategic, tactical, technological and budgetary handicaps created by the association between US foreign policy and force are taken into account, it becomes clear that all is not as it seems. Americans often wonder about the gap between their military power and their international political standing. Why is it that the country that fought and won the cold war is so widely criticized by so many of those who benefited by the end of that war? And why, in spite of American investments in military power, do the threats not appreciably recede? Part of the answer may lie in the very association between US foreign policy and military power, and in fears of the threat that the US seems to pose. In this regard, the European Union has a moral advantage by virtue of the fact that it invests less in the capacity to destroy than in the capacity to produce. Furthermore, the diversion of capital and investment away from welfare, public services and infrastructure in the United States leaves the European Union – which invests a greater percentage of its wealth in human capital – at an advantage. It has been able to employ its economic and diplomatic tools in such a way as to offset its lack of a unified military. Having said all this, though, Europe has made more progress in the direction if building its military options than most people realize.

Europe's military aspirations

Critics of the Europe-as-superpower thesis are quick to argue that the EU lacks the military credentials needed to earn the title. In moving a resolution on NATO enlargement in 1998, US senator Jesse Helms derisively charged that 'the European Union could not fight its way out of a wet paper bag'.[32] When France and Germany opposed the 2003 invasion of Iraq, they were dismissed by American critics as being too ready to appease dictators. When the cartoon show *The Simpsons* described the French as 'cheese-eating surrender monkeys', American conservatives adopted the term with glee. In the view of former US Secretary of State Alexander Haig, Franco-German policy proved that 'passives' such as Europe were 'afraid to use military force' in response to terrorism.[33] And for Robert Hunter, former US ambassador to NATO, Europe still depends too much 'on US power, influence, engagement, and leadership to be fully assured of its own independence, security, long-term prosperity, and in some places even domestic tranquillity'.[34]

Throughout the cold war, three realities were indisputable: Western Europe was part of NATO, NATO was dominated by the United States, and while several European members of NATO had large militaries, Western Europe as a whole was not a significant actor on international security issues. Unlike almost every other policy area on which the Europeans cooperated, security and defence policies were subsumed under the Atlantic Alliance.[35] NATO was a cheap and effective security alliance which not only kept the US engaged and interested in European affairs, but also gave Europeans the luxury of being able to limit their defence budgets and invest instead in economic development; given Europe's aging population and extensive social security programmes, it could not anyway have afforded increased defence budgets.[36]

Today's realities are rather different. NATO may have more European members than ever before (up from 13 in 1990 to 23 today), and the US still dominates in firepower, but Europe's role has changed. Its faltering evolution was once described as a 'journey to an unknown destination',[37] but its global identity is now quite different from what it was during the cold war. For many, it has been transformed into a 'civilian power'. There has been a small but vigorous debate over the meaning of this term dating back now for the best part of 30 years,[38] even finding its way into the sentiments of political leaders.[39] As noted in Chapter 1, it was François Duchêne who first made the link between Europe and civilian power in 1972. Writing against a background of détente, problems for the Americans in Vietnam, and a general sense that power politics was in decline, he made five related arguments:[40]

- There was no point in trying to build a European superpower, because it would need to be a nuclear, centralized state with a strong sense of collective nationalism. Europe's influence should not be wielded along traditional lines.
- There was not much point in trying to build a European army because there was more scope for civilian forms of action and influence, and the lack of military power could actually be an advantage because it removed suspicions about Europe's intentions and allowed it to act as an unbiased moderator. Military power should not be ignored, but Europe should avoid trying to achieve military dominance.
- Europe should try to act as a model or example of a new kind of interstate relationship that could overcome war, intimidation, and violence.

- Europe should remain true to its core characteristics of civilian means and ends. It should be a force for the diffusion of civilian and democratic standards, otherwise it would itself become the victim of power politics run by stronger powers.
- Europe could only succeed if it became a cohesive international actor with purpose – it should acquire a 'sense of its corporate capacity to act'.

The concept of civilian power was taken up in 1976 by Kenneth Twitchett, who argued that the Community's impact on the international system had been via trade and diplomatic influence rather than via 'traditional' military strength, although he conceded that it was not wholly improbable that there might be some future collaboration on defence policy.[41] But then Hedley Bull – as we saw in Chapter 1 – dismissed the idea of civilian power as a contradiction in terms, and argued that the capabilities of great powers were likely to be defined indefinitely by their military resources. His advice to the Community was to become more self-sufficient in defence and security by, among other things, improving its conventional forces, giving West Germany a greater role, encouraging a change of policy in Britain, and pursuing careful coexistence with the Soviets and the Americans.[42]

In his study of Germany and Japan, Hanns Maull defined a civilian power as one that concentrates on non-military and mainly economic means to achieve national goals, leaving the military as a residual safeguard, and emphasizing the importance of cooperation (rather than conflict) and of developing supranational structures to deal with critical international problems.[43] For Karen Smith, there are four elements to civilian power:

- Means: using non-military instruments – such as economic, diplomatic and cultural – to achieve objectives.
- Ends: a preference for international cooperation, solidarity, and strengthening the rule of law.
- The use of persuasion.
- Democratic civilian control over foreign and defence policymaking.

She concedes the fuzziness between civilian and military power, pointing out that while soldiers can be used for peacekeeping operations, they are still soldiers who have been trained to kill.[44] In general, a civilian power will have a preference for the kind of soft power described by Nye, while a military power will have the ability to use large-scale violence and force. But it is important to note that civilian power need not be taken literally; as much as anything it is about a difference of attitude. The EU can still be a civilian power, even if it develops a common army, so long as it emphasizes non-military tools in its foreign policy, and promotes the military as a peace-keeper rather than a peacemaker.

In terms of weaponry and manpower, the EU is better armed and equipped than most people appreciate. Through Britain and France it has a significant nuclear capability, and the armed forces of its member states bring together substantial firepower: it has more active service military personnel than the United States, backed up by 12,000 artillery pieces, 3,430 combat aircraft, more than 150 surface naval vessels (including five aircraft carriers), and 82 submarines (including eight tactical nuclear submarines).[45] If there were a single European military, with a unified budget, all weapons and personnel pooled under a single command system, and governed by a single security policy, the EU would be the second biggest military power in the world (see Table 3.1). And this is not a military that stays at home – Britain and France have been engaged in multiple conflicts since 1945, and almost all EU member states have committed

Table 3.1   *Military resources compared, 2004–05*

Resource	United States	European Union	China	Russia	India	Japan
Defence budget* ($ billion)	420	186.4	25.0	14.2	19.1	45.1
Active personnel (thousand)	1,430	1,860	2,250	960	1,330	240
Nuclear warheads	5,968	523**	252	4,978	–	–
Aircraft carriers	12	5	–	1	1	–
Nuclear submarines	18	8	1	14	–	–
Non-nuclear submarines	54	74	68	37	16	16
Surface combat vessels***	106	154	63	26	24	54
Combat aircraft	5,991	3,430	2,600	2,002	714	360

Notes:
European Union figures are for the EU-25.
* FY 2004
** France 338, Britain 185
*** Destroyers, frigates and others

Source: Calculated from data in International Institute for Strategic Studies, *The Military Balance 2004–2005* (Oxford: Oxford University Press, 2004).

troops to peacekeeping operations. Finally, more progress has also been made on developing a common European security policy than most people realize. When Kagan argued in 2003 that efforts to build a European security policy had been 'an embarrassment', and that the EU was 'no closer to fielding an independent force, even a small one, than it was three years ago',[46] he was quite wrong.

The story did not begin well, it is true. Security was at the heart of the justification for integrating Europe: security from the Soviets, and a desire to protect Europe from itself, particularly by encouraging the peaceful integration of Germany into the post-war system. But the collapse in 1954 of a proposed European Defence Community reflected the lack of political readiness for a European security policy, which in turn was a result mainly of narrow national interests and concerns.[47] And little progress was made thereafter, thanks to a complex combination of factors: the early decision to focus on economic integration while sidelining the security dimension of European cooperation, a lack of political will to move more actively on the security front, opposition to the diversion of resources away from social services, a focus on national defence policies, the absence of the necessary institutional apparatus, and – perhaps most importantly – the confusion caused by Europe's obligations to and/or reliance upon NATO. Throughout the cold war, NATO not only protected Western Europe from the Soviet menace, but also gave Western Europeans the bonus of being able to spend less on defence and more on welfare, education, and healthcare. But the commitment to NATO retarded the development of a European defence capability, even when the cold war ended and the organization seemed to reinvent itself as a pan-European security actor.[48] And it also encouraged Europeans to become used to conceding their independence on security matters to the Americans.

An early prospect for a common security structure was offered by the Western European Union (WEU),[49] founded in 1948 in response to concerns about Soviet intentions in Central Europe, and with the intention of helping bring the United States into NATO,[50] which was founded the following year. While NATO obliged its members to respond to an attack on another member only with 'such actions as it deems necessary', the WEU obliged each member to provide 'all the military and other aid and assistance in their power' to any member that was attacked. But this was no more than a symbolic gesture given the modest capacities of Western European fighting forces, and the scale of the threat posed by the Soviet Union. NATO (in effect the United States) continued to be the dominating actor in European defence policy throughout the cold war, and the Western Europeans focused instead (with mixed results) on the non-military aspects of foreign policy.

The WEU was resuscitated in 1984, but although it helped coordinate the operations of its member states in the 1990–91 Gulf war, it was stretched beyond its limits.

The Gulf war triggered a sequence of events that was to result in a change of direction that would lead to the construction of the security structure that the EU has today. The time was ripe, for at least two reasons. First, the implementation of the 1986 Single European Act meant that the Community was coming close to meeting the original economic goals that it had set for itself in the 1950s. And second, the Americans had begun a major withdrawal of troops from Western Europe – numbers fell from 350,000 in 1989 to 150,000 in 1994.[51] Then came the Gulf war itself, which was significant not only for the jumbled positions taken by the governments of the 12 Community member states, but also for the way in which their national military units operated in isolation rather than as part of a joint European contribution. Also in 1991, civil war broke out in Somalia, and – despite the history of British, French and Italian colonialism in Somaliland – it fell to the United States to take the leadership in the UN humanitarian response.

A debate was meanwhile under way about the future of the WEU, which was seen by some (notably the British) as a potential European wing of NATO, and by others (notably the French) as a vehicle for the transfer of defence functions from NATO to the Community. The Germans and the French meanwhile took the bull by the horns and set up an experimental army brigade outside Community and NATO structures, which was converted in May 1992 into the 50,000-member Eurocorps. Declared operational in November 1995, it has since been joined by contingents from Belgium, Luxembourg, and Spain, and has sent missions to Bosnia (1998), Kosovo (2000), and Afghanistan (2004).

In agreeing the terms of the Maastricht treaty in 1991, European leaders set out to develop a limited Common Foreign and Security Policy (CFSP), which included 'the eventual framing of a common defence policy which might in time lead to a common defence'. Then in 1992, a meeting of WEU foreign and defence ministers at Petersberg, near Bonn, agreed to make the WEU responsible for the so-called 'Petersberg tasks': humanitarian, rescue, peacekeeping, and other crisis management operations, including peacemaking. It was meanwhile agreed that the WEU should be developed as the defence component of the Community and as a means of strengthening the European pillar of the Atlantic Alliance.

But events in the Balkans during the 1990s showed that there was a yawning gap between the capabilities of the EU to act on security matters, and the expectations of Western European governments.[52] There was also a perception gap between the Europeans, who looked to the US for leadership, and the Americans, who made it clear that they wanted the EU to take the lead.[53] Sparked by the unilateral declarations of independence in June 1991 by Slovenia and Croatia, the crisis initially seemed to find the Community ready to act quickly: ceasefires were negotiated within days under Community auspices, and a peace conference was convened in September in The Hague. The Luxembourg foreign minister Jacques Poos confidently asserted that 'This is the hour of Europe, not of the United States.'[54] Commission president Jacques Delors warned that 'We do not interfere in American affairs; we trust that America will not interfere in European affairs.'[55] But the Community could not agree on how to proceed: its security was not threatened, there were no major economic or political interests at stake, and the member states had their own individual interests and goals.[56] It also lacked the common command structures needed to mount a significant joint military operation. The Community initially favoured Yugoslav unity, but it was soon clear that Germany was heading in another direction, and the collapse of the peace conference was followed by Germany's unilateral recognition of Croatian independence.

To be fair, the WEU had developed four different scenarios for European intervention in Croatia, but they were vetoed by Britain, the Netherlands and Portugal, which felt that intervention should be a NATO matter, even though the US thought it was a European matter. By 1992, the UN had replaced the Community in taking the leadership role in the Balkans, and it was the United States that eventually brokered the December 1995 Dayton peace accords. The outcome not only confirmed the impotence of the Community's foreign and security policy aspirations, but also confirmed the new inequalities in the transatlantic relationship: the United States was more dominant than it had been during the cold war, but also had less immediate interest in the security of Europe. The idea of a rebalancing of the transatlantic relationship now became more evident, and the development of the CFSP achieved a new urgency.

In 1991, Community leaders at their summit in Rome had endorsed the idea of a 'European security identity and defence role', clearing the way in 1994 for a European Security and Defence Identity (ESDI) within NATO. When the 1997 Amsterdam treaty incorporated the Petersberg tasks into the EU treaties, argues Treacher, 'the Union finally became a military actor'.[57] That same year, Tony Blair – freshly installed in Downing Street, dismayed at finding how limited were Europe's abilities to respond militarily to an emergency, and keen to see Europe pulling its weight on military matters – expressed his willingness to see Britain play a more central role in EU defence matters. After a December 1998 meeting in St Malo, France, he and French president Jacques Chirac declared that the EU should have the capacity for autonomous military action, and suggested the creation of a European Rapid Reaction Force. German Chancellor Gerhard Schroeder later endorsed this idea.[58]

In 1998–99 it was decided to merge the WEU into the European Union, and in 1999 agreement was reached at the European Council (EU heads of state or government) meeting in Cologne to launch the European Security and Defence Policy (ESDP). Reflecting the Blair–Chirac agreement, it declared that 'The Union must have the capacity for autonomous action, backed up by credible military forces, the means to decide to use them, and a readiness to do so, in order to respond to international crises.' The ESDP had two key components: the Petersberg tasks, and a 60,000-member Rapid Reaction Force (RRF) that could be deployed at 60 days' notice, be sustained for at least a year, and carry out those tasks. Championed mainly by Britain and France, the Force was not intended to be a standing army, was designed to complement rather than compete with NATO, and could act only when NATO decided not to be involved in a crisis. It was designed in particular to intervene with emerging crises, filling a gap before UN peace-keepers could move in.

The potential value of the ESDP approach was emphasised by events in Kosovo. A low-intensity guerrilla war that began in 1996 quickly flared up into a full-scale conflict between the Serbian government and Kosovar separatists. Britain, France, Germany and Italy participated in a six-nation contact group set up in January 1997 to coordinate the international response, but were able to achieve little. When refugee Albanians began to flee into neighbouring Macedonia, raising the possibility of a civil war that might spill over into neighbouring countries, including EU member Greece, it became clear that the EU had a direct security interest in the conflict. But when peace talks in early 1999 failed, it was NATO that took the lead in the bombing campaign against Serbia in March–June 1999, with the United States once again the dominant partner.

In the wake of the serial embarrassments of the Balkans, the EU security identity has taken on a quite different character and there have been more European military ventures, whether by the British or the French acting alone, or under the aegis of the EU.[59] In April 2003, the EU began its first military operation – Operation Concordia – when it deployed 300 troops in Macedonia for nine months, taking over from NATO the responsibility for protecting a peace signed between the Macedonian government and ethnic Albanian rebels in August 2001. Small it may have been, but it was symbolic, and bigger operations were anticipated. In June 2003 the EU launched its first mission outside Europe, when – under Operation Artemis – 1,800 troops were sent to the Democratic Republic of Congo at the request of the UN, filling an important gap pending the eventual arrival of a UN peacekeeping force. In December 2004 the EU launched its biggest peace-keeping mission when 7,000 troops (many coming from outside the EU, it is true) took over from NATO in Bosnia. In 2003–04 the EU was contributing 50 per cent of peacekeeping forces in Bosnia, 60 per cent of the forces in Afghanistan, and 70 per cent of the forces in Kosovo. Twelve EU states also had 19,000 troops in Iraq.[60] And national military interventions must not be forgotten, such as Britain's operation in Sierra Leone in 2001 (establishing order after a much bigger UN force had failed) and France's operation in Côte d'Ivoire in 2002.

Meanwhile, EU defence ministers formally agreed to the creation of the RRF in November 2003, and in December the European Council adopted the European Security Strategy, the first ever declaration by EU member states of their strategic vision. In May 2004, EU defence ministers agreed on the formation of several 'battle groups' that could be deployed more quickly and for shorter periods than the RRF, and that were designed for anything up to full-scale combat situations. Based on the model used in Operation Artemis, the plan was for groups of 1,500 troops each that could be on the ground in 15 days, and could be sustainable for between 30 and 120 days. Like the RRF, the battle groups are designed to be used very much in the service of UN operations; there is no sign here of a desire to develop a unilateral European military capability. It is also important to note that these developments have taken place against a background of majority public support; about three-quarters of Europeans favour a common defence and security policy (see Figure 3.1).

Those who dismiss the case for European global power tend to focus on the weaknesses in the case for a distinctive European security identity and capability. The Europeans, they point out, come nowhere close to the Americans in being able to quickly commit massive firepower and large invasion forces. The Europeans are far from being able to claim the agreement of a common security policy, as the dissension over Iraq made only too clear. The Europeans may now have a better grasp on how to deal with geographically and politically limited problems such as the Balkans, or their former African colonies, but they still have only a marginal impact on events in the Middle East, where US influence – albeit controversial – reigns supreme. The US still has a critical advantage over the EU in that it can take a two-pronged approach to international problems (civilian and military), while the Europeans have a cellar full of carrots, but very few sticks. And it has even been argued that the ESDP poses a threat to transatlantic relations and to the EU–NATO partnership.[61]

But there has been a clear trend since the 1990s toward the EU giving

Figure 3.1 *Public support for a common European security policy, 2005*

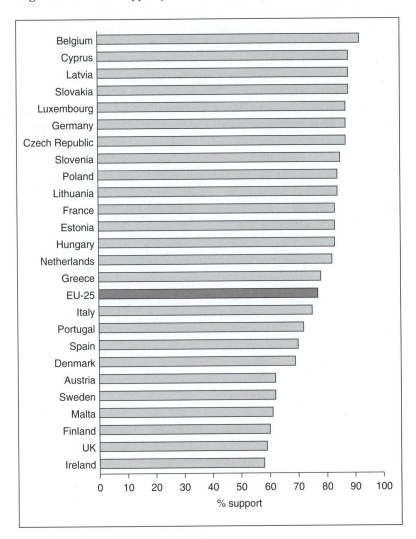

Note: Figures reflect public support for a common defence and security policy among the EU member states.

Source: European Commission, *Eurobarometer* 64, Autumn 2005.

more definition to its policy goals, and building the resources needed to shoulder a greater share of defence and security burdens. The political will for Europe to take more of the responsibility for dealing with security threats is stronger than it was even a decade ago, given a boost by events in the Balkans, and by growing concerns for the implications of allowing the United States to define both the problems and the responses. The Balkans underlined one kind of problem (the inability of Europe to deal with problems in its own backyard), and the 2003 invasion of Iraq underlined another (the willingness of the United States to take pre-emptive unilateral action). A strengthened European defence capacity helps address both these problems, as well as giving the EU more well rounded claims to global power.

Opinion on the implications is divided. Atlanticists such as Denmark, Britain, the Netherlands and Portugal continue to feel nervous about undermining the US commitment to Europe, despite questions about just how much longer that commitment may last. Tony Blair has said that he is committed to European defence, but has been careful to couch his views in the context of the Petersberg tasks. For their part, Europeanists such as Belgium, France, Luxembourg and Spain continue to want to develop an independent EU capability; hence Jacques Chirac's suggestion in October 2003 that 'there cannot be a Europe without its own defence system'.[62] Meanwhile, the United States is content to see the Europeans taking responsibility for those tasks from which NATO should best keep its distance, but insists that there should be no overlap or rivalry in the event of the creation of a separate European institution.

Europe's distinctive security role

What does all this mean for the identity of Europe? Is the EU still a civilian power, or is it a proto-military power, or is it something in between? Can it be understood and defined only in relationship to the United States (America fights, Europe funds, the UN feeds[63]), or is it something more distinctive, the model of a new kind of international actor? Some argue that it is now too late for the EU to be a civilian power. After all, it has the makings of a common security policy, it has the Eurocorps, it has a growing record of military engagements, and it has the Rapid Reaction Force and multiple battle groups in the pipeline.[64] And European public opinion is changing against a background of growing concerns about post-9/11 American militarism. Even so, Europe's move away from a purely civilian role in the world has taken many by surprise; European governments collectively have doubled the number of troops deployed abroad with little national or European debate on the implications.[65]

Others hold on to the civilian thesis, arguing that the EU could use military tools and still be regarded as a civilian power, just so long as non-military means are put first and the military is only used as a safeguard of last resort; the critical issue is the question of the ends that are pursued. So Maull, for example, argues that even though Germany used its military force outside the NATO area during the 1990s, and took part in the 1999 bombing of Serbia, it is still a civilian power.[66] Jørgensen argues that the EU has retained its civilian qualities because questions of defence and nuclear capability remain with NATO.[67] Stavridis argues that thanks to its militarization, the EU might finally act as a real civilian power: an international force for the promotion of democratic principles. In other words, the EU is in the position to become a civilian power 'by design' rather than a mere civilian presence 'by default', as he believes is now the case.[68]

But perhaps we should be tossing out the old civilian vs military debate and looking instead at how the European Union has broken the mould of traditional conceptions of great power politics. Most political and economic rivalries until the twentieth century were maintained or resolved by military power. Then two great global conflicts took tens of millions of lives and raised elemental questions about the value and morality of war. The cold war may have been a competition over ideas, without direct military confrontation between its major protagonists, but the balance was maintained by the threat of war, and of mutually assured destruction. Wars continue to blot the international landscape even today,[69] and military spending makes up a large part of the budgetary calculations of most national governments. But the nature of international rivalry and cooperation is changing, and there is a rising chorus that points to the declining utility of force, the new importance of economic interdependence, and the strategic advantage of trading states over political-military states. Consider also the evidence provided by the rise of international organizations and law, the globalization of trade, investment, immigration, education, technology, and culture, the revolutions in international travel and communication, and the internationalization of policy problems as diverse as poverty, drugs, and environmental decay. They all point to the growing irrelevance of war, and the increased need to understand and exploit economic and diplomatic tools as a means to resolving differences. In terms of international relations, perhaps the EU is the shape of things to come.

Andrew Moravcsik has dismissed the idea of a large, independent European military as 'incoherent'. The logic of the view that Europe should build a large military may be seductive to the public and politicians alike, he says, but it would incur the kind of budgetary costs that European public opinion would not tolerate. And it would be an ineffective response to US unilateralism, because it would encourage just the kind of withdrawal from Europe advocated by American policy hawks. Rather than criticizing US military power or hankering after it or competing with it, Moravcsik believes, Europe would be better advised to complement US military power and to invest its political and budgetary capital in exploiting its comparative advantages as a 'civilian and quasi-military power'. Those advantages, he believes, include the attractions of EU membership, the EU's leadership in providing development aid, its skills in peacekeeping and monitoring, and its greater abilities in the effective deployment of civilian power.[70]

This is no new argument. NATO itself recognized the changing environment as long ago as 1956, when it acknowledged that security was much more than a military matter: 'The strengthening of political consultation and economic cooperation, the development of resources, progress in education and public understanding, all these can be as important, or even more important, for the protection of the security of a nation, or an alliance, as the building of a battleship or the equipping of an army.'[71] Duke argued in 1994 that the EU had an important role to play in promoting awareness of the non-military aspects of security, particularly those with an economic bias.[72] Bailes has since argued that with the weakening of the exclusive nature of US–European ties since the end of the cold war, Europe has strategic values of its own, such as a multilateral and multifunctional approach to global problems, a preference for minimizing and legitimizing the use of force, and a readiness to absorb past enemies. The new strategy makes the EU a more self-conscious and ambitious actor, which will mean a deepening of its effect on transatlantic relations.[73]

The differences in European and American philosophies and values are illustrated by their contrasting approaches to international terrorism. Few dispute that this is the primary security threat facing the world today, but unlike the terrorism of earlier ages, that was limited in its reach and restricted in both its targets and in the tools it had available, terrorism today has a global reach, a wider diversity of targets, and greater abilities to wreak havoc and destruction. Europeans and Americans agree on the overlapping threats posed by terrorism, weapons of mass destruction, cross-border crime and failed states, but they take quite different views on how to respond: where the US emphasizes military solutions, the EU places more emphasis on dealing with the causes of conflict.[74] An early example of the philosophical breach was offered by the European response to attacks on Rome and Vienna airports in late 1985, in which Libya was implicated; the Europeans refused even to impose trade sanctions on the Ghaddafi regime. Just a few months later, the United States bombed Libya after another terrorist incident, eliciting criticism from West Germany and in particular from Chancellor Helmut Kohl, who quipped that 'Force is not a promising way of dealing with things.'[75] More recently, French foreign minister Dominique de Villepin summed up the majority European view: 'There is no military solution to terrorism. You need to have a political strategy.'[76]

Transatlantic differences have been reviewed in the comparative studies of the US National Security Strategy (2002) and the European Security Strategy (2003). Duke concludes that while they agree on identifying the threats posed by terrorism and weapons of mass destruction, and both pay lip service to multilateralism and the importance of the transatlantic relationship, the American document is notable for its emphasis on pre-emptive action, and for playing up the distinct American view of the world, which allows it to act alone if needed.[77] A 2004 report by the Party of European Socialists in the European Parliament summarizes the differences as follows:

> Where the Europeans speak of preventive engagement and effective multilateralism, the US government underlines the possibility of pre-emptive (unilateral) military action and the ambition to remain the only military superpower. While the US mentions the national interest as the guiding principle very often, the EU devotes much more attention to the need to promote justice at the international level in whatever form. And when the EU defines the UN system as essential to international security, the US states that the mission defines the coalition. These contradictions within transatlantic relations are at the core of the security debate.[78]

Europe will not match the United States in military power any time soon. This is not because it lacks the resources, but because it lacks a common security policy and a unified command and control structure. More importantly, it also has a different attitude towards the use of the military in international affairs, and many qualities that the United States either lacks, or chooses not to use. The Americans have the firepower, but they lack the political follow-through. The Europeans lack the firepower, but they can bring political skills and economic pressures to the table. The Europeans have enormous influence over international trade and investment, and they also account for more than half of the world's overseas development assistance (see Chapter 5). They are building experience in the field of peacekeeping, their troops helped by a credibility advantage over their American counterparts; while European soldiers are associated with peace, American soldiers are associated (rightly or wrongly) with war.

If we reject the idea of power resting on military capability, then it can be argued that Europe could be a superpower without a large military. And even though it lacks that unified army, this does not mean that it has no military capability, or – more importantly – *enough* military capability. How much is enough? Clearly, the United States – which has the power to destroy civilization – has more than enough. For the EU, 'enough' may be simply the necessary quantity and ability to achieve its political and economic ends. Woken from its lethargy in the 1990s, it has quickly built a new presence in the international system. Just since 1997 it has outlined a security and defence policy, a security strategy, and a series of tasks for which it believes its forces are best suited, and the framework for a Rapid Reaction Force and battle groups. Even outside formal structures, troops from the EU have been involved in several peacekeeping operations; in 2006, 24 out of the 25 EU member states had uniformed personnel active in the field (Luxembourg – which has no army – was the only exception).[79]

In the immediate aftermath of the end of the cold war, the break-up of the Soviet Union, and the remarkable changes in Eastern Europe, many questions were raised about the future of European security. There were doubts about the priorities of the United States and about the extent to which Europe could continue to rely on the American security shield. There were worries about the new set of threats posed to European security, and about how best to address them. And many questions were asked about which institution was best placed to deal with Europe's security interests, and whether the emphasis should be transatlantic (NATO), internal to the EU (the Western European Union), or pan-European (the Organization for Security and Cooperation in Europe, whose 55 members include Russia and the US). Europe was described as a ship without a rudder.[80]

Large question marks now hang over the future of NATO. Its *raison d'être* – defence against the Soviet threat – has gone, and with it a common transatlantic view of when it should be mobilized. The EU has made progress in building the foundations of a common security policy. Iraq confirmed that the United States is now willing to use pre-emptive strikes, to go it alone in the face of opposition from the EU and the UN, and to allow the mission to decide the coalition. Cameron argues that NATO will never fight another war, and that while the EU may never develop the same power-projection capabilities as the US (because it does not need to), it cannot avoid developing a full range of security capabilities. Thus – he believes – the EU, not NATO, is the future.[81]

Duchêne was remarkably prescient in his assessment of Europe's future role. As he suggested, there is more scope today for civilian forms of action and influence. Europe's inability (or unwillingness) to use the kind of military force that the Americans have at their disposal has worked in its favour. Europe has not ignored military power, but neither does it aspire to achieve military parity with the Americans. Europe is acting as a model of a new kind of interstate relationship that holds strong prospects for overcoming war, intimidation, and violence. It is remaining true to its core characteristics of civilian means and ends, developing its credentials as a force for the diffusion of civilian and democratic standards. In the process, it has developed a model of a superpower that is distinctive from its American and Soviet predecessors.

4

The European Economic Colossus

If there are questions about the EU's military credentials, there can be few remaining doubts about its economic power. It is the world's biggest capitalist marketplace, the world's biggest trading power, and the world's biggest magnet for – and source of – foreign direct investment.[1] It is one of the world's biggest markets for mergers and acquisitions, and 12 of its member states now have the euro, which threatens to depose the US dollar as the world's leading reserve currency. And if quantity alone is not a mark of power, then the EU also enjoys a qualitative advantage – it drives a hard bargain in trade negotiations, European corporations compete aggressively with their American and Japanese counterparts, every multinational worth its salt wants access to the European market, and their new wealth is helping Europeans live longer and healthier lives.

The remarkable growth of the European economy has been a direct result of the near-completion of the European single market. Since its relaunch in the mid-1980s, it has encouraged the removal of almost every significant barrier to the free movement of people, money, goods, and services within Europe.[2] There are still some limitations,[3] and Europeans do not yet find it as easy to move around their new hinterland as Americans find it to move around the United States, but most of the border checks that were once the bane of travellers and corporations have gone, and there has been a surge in cross-border trade, cross-border investments, and corporate mergers and acquisitions. Cheap travel and open borders have contributed to an explosion of tourism, helping Europeans learn more about their neighbours, and making cross-border travel almost routine. So many Europeans have moved to new jobs or to retirement homes in other EU member states that governments have all but stopped trying to count the numbers.

External factors, too, have played into Europe's hands, with a downturn in economic prospects for the United States and Japan. The US still has the world's biggest national economy, the biggest multinationals, the favourite currency, the best universities, the most Nobel Prize winners, and the most rapid technological advances, but all is not well in the temple of capitalism.

It suffers an addiction to deficit spending, a growing national debt, a widening trade deficit, spiralling defence spending, falling personal savings rates, growing personal bankruptcy rates, a heavy reliance on increasingly expensive foreign oil, and growing pressures on social security and healthcare. Majority opinion still holds that the Americans have the advantage, their vibrant and robust economy being able to address whatever the Europeans throw at them. One analyst suggests that thanks to different rates of population and economic growth, the US economy by 2020 will be at least 20 per cent bigger than that of the EU.[4] Another suggests that continental Europe may need a new Marshall Plan to rescue its declining economies.[5] Two more hold that because the US is continually extending its lead in innovation and the application of new technology, its economic hegemony is 'solidly grounded'.[6] But not everyone is so sanguine; an opposing analysis suggests that a combination of enlargement, low defence spending, the growing number of women in the workplace, higher personal savings rates, low current account deficits, and accelerated integration of IT into business could all work in favour of the EU.[7]

As for Japan, after turning in remarkable growth rates during the 1970s and 1980s, there has been little but bad news since the mid-1990s; Japan's global position has been undermined by a falling rate of growth in GDP, record unemployment, declining share prices, a falling trade surplus, record numbers of bankruptcies, a growing national debt, and a banking system in trouble. The underlying causes have been hard to identify, mainly because of the difficulty of drawing a clear line between business and politics.[8] Public policy still reflects the preferences not so much of voters as of 'Japan Inc.', a nickname for the close association between Japanese government, bureaucracy, and big business. Problems have also been exacerbated by secrecy within the political system, offering little accountability, making it difficult to know whom to blame for policy failures, and giving policymakers little motivation to change.

Meanwhile, the removal of Europe's internal trade barriers has helped spark a revival of entrepreneurial innovation and corporate ambition. From its original base in six member states with a population of 160 million, the European marketplace has expanded to absorb 25 member states with a population of more than 450 million. In spite of fears that the EU's decisionmaking system could not keep up with the addition of new member states, it has managed remarkably well. Europe has played a critical role in helping push aside Eastern European state socialism, replacing the stagnation of central planning with the openness and creativity of capitalism. The most obvious changes have come in the eight former iron curtain countries that are now members of the EU, and whose entry in 2004 expanded the

European market by nearly 75 million consumers. But the gravitational pull of the EU has also been felt in more than 30 neighbouring states that are home to nearly 600 million additional consumers (see Chapter 5), as well as in the many other countries that have developed economic and trade ties with the EU.

Throughout the cold war, the United States was an economic behemoth without equal. Its economy was several times bigger than its nearest competitor, its corporations dominated almost every field of business activity, its consumers had the most disposable income, its presence in global trade was unrivalled, and it had the world's pre-eminent currency. But the rise of Europe has changed everything. It is now a massive economic presence on the world stage, building on the foundations of its home market, its wealthy (and healthy) consumers, its trading clout, and its single currency. It has survived the forecasts of the dismal economists who see the glass as half empty rather than half full, and has taken maximum advantage of the new opportunities offered by globalization. In economic terms, at least, we are now clearly living in a bipolar world.

The rise of the European marketplace

During the 1940s and 1950s, the American and Western European economies prospered, but the Americans had the clear advantage: while they took over leadership of the international financial and trading system, Eastern Europeans suffered the stultifying influence of state socialism, and Western Europeans were too focused on reconstruction to provide much of a contest. There was progress on the European common market and a common trade policy, but the strength of the original EEC-6 depended heavily on the West German 'economic miracle': its economy grew by 290 per cent between 1946 and 1960, while the combined economies of the other five EEC states grew by just 130 per cent. The waters were further muddied by the emergence of Japan, whose economy grew by more than 800 per cent between 1946 and 1970,[9] and whose investment in research and development transformed the label 'Made in Japan' from code for cheap and disposable consumer products into a signature for reliability and innovation.

By the 1970s, Western Europe was in trouble: it was unable to adjust quickly enough to the effects of enlargement, it suffered from oil price rises and the instability of currency markets following the collapse of the Bretton Woods system (which undermined the first attempts to create a single European currency), progress on the development of common policies was slow, European corporations were handicapped by the persistence of cross-border controls, inflation and unemployment were worsening, and progress on the single market had stalled. In short, eurosclerosis had set in. Concerns about poor economic performance now combined with changes in leadership and a supportive corporate environment to prompt a 'relaunching' of Europe. This meant a new approach to completing the single market (outlined in a 1985 European Commission white paper[10]), and new efforts to establish a single currency. In 1986, the Single European Act gave the EU five years to complete the single market, and so concentrated the minds of EU businesses and governments that by 1993 the EU-15 had become a bigger importer and exporter of commercial services, and a bigger exporter of merchandise, than the United States. European foreign direct investment grew, and just as multinational corporations had found it essential since World War II to sell to the US market, so they now found it increasingly important to seek a foothold in the European market.

In 1989, European Commission president Jacques Delors outlined a three-stage plan to achieve the single currency. This demanded the establishment of free capital movement, greater intra-European monetary and macroeconomic cooperation, greater cooperation among central banks, coordination of the monetary policies of member states, and the eventual fixing of exchange rates.[11] In November 1993 the Maastricht treaty on European union came into force, setting a timetable for the creation of a single currency, which in 1995 was named the euro. In June 1998 the new European Central Bank became responsible for monetary policy in the euro zone, in January 1999 participating states fixed their currency exchange rates relative to each other and to the euro, and in January 2002 the final switch was made in the 12 participating euro states when their currencies were replaced with euro coins and banknotes.

At the time, eurodoubters made much of the practical and political difficulties involved in completing the single market and building the single currency, but in retrospect it is remarkable just how much progress was made once the right combination of political support and economic opportunity came along. In the space of eight years – from the publication of the 1985 Commission white paper on the single market to the setting of the timetable for the single currency under the terms of Maastricht in 1993 – the European project had been transformed. Where once there had been a heavily nationalist approach to economic policy, now the European Union stood on the brink of full economic union, and quickly began to use the new opportunities it had created for itself to convert its potential economic influence into real economic power.

American policymakers were taken by surprise. They had long been of the view that domestic change was more important to the health of the US economy than international trade,[12] and persisted in thinking of Europe as a cluster of individual states. But anyone looking in the right direction would have seen that the European marketplace was growing in tandem with that of the United States (see Figure 4.1), and that Europe was a trading force to be reckoned with. While the value of global and EU exports grew by 96 per cent between 1993 and 2003, the value of US exports grew by only 60 per cent. While the US share of exports fell from 13 per cent to 11 per cent in the same

Figure 4.1   *Comparative economic growth, 1950–2004*

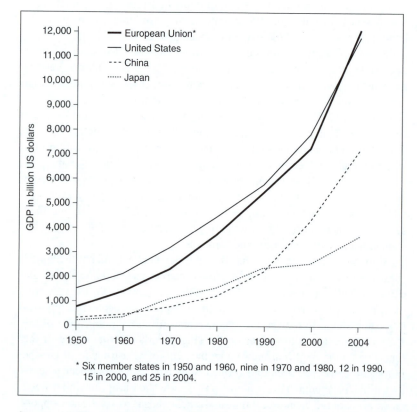

* Six member states in 1950 and 1960, nine in 1970 and 1980, 12 in 1990, 15 in 2000, and 25 in 2004.

Sources: All figures calculated from OECD, *The World Economy: Historical Statistics* (Paris: OECD Development Centre, 2003) except 2004, which come from World Bank (2006), www.worldbank.org. Latter figure is US dollars adjusted for purchasing power parity.

period, the EU share held steady at 40 per cent.[13] By the late 1990s the EU was matching the United States on most trade fronts, and was flexing its muscles in the hallways of the new World Trade Organization. And corporate Europe was on the rise as well: in 2002, just 36 of the 100 biggest corporations in the world – and only two of the ten biggest – were European. By 2005, 48 of those corporations were from the EU, and the top 10 included BP, Royal Dutch/Shell, DaimlerChrysler, and Total.

With the 2004 enlargement into Eastern Europe, the EU overtook the US to become the biggest and richest capitalist marketplace in the world, accounting for nearly one-third of the world's gross domestic product and nearly half the industrialized world's consumer population. It is today by far the world's biggest trading power, accounting for about 42 per cent of trade in merchandise and about half of all trade in commercial services (see Figure 4.2). And the wealthiest EU members have a single currency that is now used (officially) by more consumers than the US dollar: 310 million versus 291 million. True, not all is entirely well with the EU – economies always have their problems, and the EU still faces the challenge of dealing with high unemployment in Germany, France, Italy, Spain and Poland, and with sometimes over-regulated labour markets. But we have only to look at the prospects for the euro, at Europe's high-profile trade policies, and at the rebirth of the European multinational to see that the original core economic goals of the founders of European integration have been more than met.

Will the euro replace the dollar?

Since the 1950s, one of the defining features of the international economic system has been the dominance of the US dollar. At its height, the dollar was the preferred official reserve asset of most governments, was involved in about 90 per cent of the world's foreign exchange transactions, was the primary currency for business between banks, and was used for the invoicing of almost all international trade in commodities. The dominance of the dollar was underpinned by the strength of the US industrial base, the productivity and efficiency of its economy, and by its gold reserves, which were the largest in the world. In the 1970s and 1980s, the Europeans made several attempts to launch a single currency, but their failures did little more than fulfil the warnings of the deepest of eurosceptics, as well as confirming the supremacy of the dollar.

Well into the 1990s, little credence was attached to the prospects for a single European currency: some doubted that its creation would make much

Figure 4.2   *Shares of the economic pie, 2004*

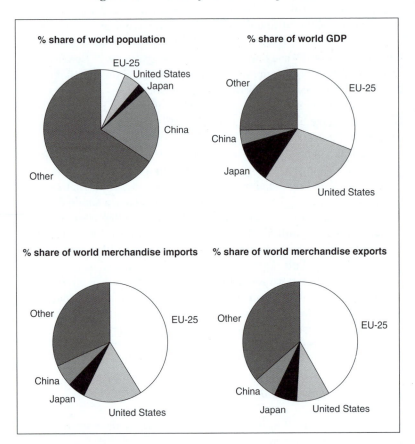

Sources: Population and GDP figures from World Bank (2006), www.worldbank.org. Trade figures from World Trade Organization (2006), www.wto.org.

difference, while others doubted that it would ever actually become a currency. Writing in 1995, Berkeley economist and soon-to-be Clinton advisor Jeffrey Frankel felt that there was 'little likelihood' of another currency supplanting the dollar by 2020, because there was 'simply no plausible alternative' to the dollar's occupation of the top position.[14] Two years later, Deputy Treasury Secretary Lawrence Summers argued that the dollar would 'remain the primary reserve currency for the foreseeable future' and that the impact of the euro would be 'quite limited initially and [would] occur only gradually'.[15]

On 1 January 1999, 12 EU states – representing two-thirds of the population and three-quarters of the GDP of the EU-15 – made the switch to the euro, and finally replaced coins and banknotes in early 2002. Public opinion in the euro zone was mixed, the value of the euro quickly fell against the US dollar, there was some creative accounting to hide the difficulties that several countries had in meeting the criteria required for adoption of the euro, and three EU member states – Britain, Sweden and Denmark – stayed out altogether. Most euro zone countries had trouble meeting the terms of the stability and growth pact, signed in 1997 with a view to controlling government borrowing and budget deficits. Public debates typically qualified the potential benefits of the euro (including reduced exchange rate uncertainty, increased trade and investment, removal of exchange rate transaction costs, price transparency, low and stable inflation, and a challenge to the US dollar) with its potential costs (the loss of national sovereignty, of monetary policy as a tool of stabilization, and of flexibility to deal with the needs of wealthy and poor regions of the EU). And it was not long before wild talk even emerged that some countries might abandon the euro and switch back to their old currencies, regaining control over national fiscal policies. But this was little more than short-term buyer's remorse.

From this rather inauspicious start, the euro quickly became a challenger to the dominance of the dollar. Its initial precipitous decline against the US dollar had been wiped out by the end of 2003,[16] governments and corporations were increasingly borrowing in euros, nearly 40 per cent of foreign exchange transactions are today carried out in euros, central banks are holding more of their reserves in euros, and euros are increasingly used by consumers outside the euro zone, notably in Eastern Europe. Speculation has also grown that the dollar is threatened by fallout from US domestic economic policies and unpopular foreign policies.[17] Some wonder whether the dangers of the US current account deficit (the gap between what it earned abroad and what it spent abroad) have been given enough attention,[18] and others speculate that the 'size effect' alone makes the euro a competitor to the dollar.[19] Even Jeffrey Frankel has conceded that the euro could surpass the US dollar as the leading reserve currency if the euro zone economy becomes bigger than that of the US (which will happen if the UK and other countries adopt the euro), and if confidence in the dollar continues to be undermined by US economic policy.[20]

Why is the future of the euro so important to the global status of the EU? The answer, quite simply, is that its creation was overtly a political act, and that history has shown that a strong currency is an essential part of global political influence. The absence of a strong currency, for example, is one reason why claims that China has superpower qualities are so weak.

Geopolitical power depends on financial power, argues Kunz, and each supports the other: the end of the dollar order would 'drastically increase the price of the American dream while simultaneously shattering American global influence'.[21] Frankel notes the link between loss of key currency status, loss of international creditor status, and discussion of the historical decline of great powers.[22] Cohen argues that monetary supremacy provides insulation from external influence over policy, as well as reducing the constraints on foreign policy, and that the expansion of the 'authoritative domain' of a currency translates directly into effective political power.[23] Currency hegemony brings with it several opportunities: the comparative advantage for markets and institutions of the hegemon, the advantage for trade of having other countries peg their currencies to that of the hegemon (removing exchange rate uncertainty), and the ability to finance balance of payments deficits with liabilities denominated in the hegemon's currency.[24]

At least four conditions will need to be met if the euro is to depose (or take its place alongside) the dollar. First, it must show strong internal stability in the form of low inflation, which in turn means that the European Central Bank must establish credibility by achieving price stability, and avoid being frustrated by excessive government spending.[25] Inflation rates in the euro zone have to date been respectable, holding in the low single figures since the early 1990s,[26] but the record on government spending has been mixed: ten of the twelve euro zone countries have been unable to meet the goals of the stability and growth pact, and France and Germany have led the lobbying for an easing of restrictions. Whatever problems the euro zone countries have, however, they pale by comparison with the modern tradition of deficit spending in the United States. Thanks mainly to tax cuts and increased military spending, the US budget deficit in 2004 was running at 4.4 per cent of GDP (down from a surplus of 2.5 per cent of GDP in 2000), compared to 3.7 per cent in France and 3.9 per cent in Germany, and the OECD was projecting that while the figure would fall in France and Germany, it was clear that the Bush administration had no intention of cutting overall federal spending.

Second, the euro must be more widely adopted as a reserve currency by central banks. For currencies to be attractive for purchase as reserves, they must be fully convertible and widely accepted, their financial markets must be broad, open and liquid, inflation must be low, there must be confidence in their value, and they must be widely used in trade and financial business.[27] Throughout the cold war, the dollar was the reserve currency of choice: it accounted for about 50–70 per cent of global holdings, while just 20 per cent were held in European currencies (mainly deutschmarks, with a sprinkling in British pounds and French francs).[28] Holdings in most of the European currencies automatically switched to euros in 1999, giving the euro a 20 per cent share. But euro zone countries were loth to switch more of their hold-ings to euros too quickly for fear of creating instability, so the key has been how soon third countries – notably the Asian countries that dominate the world's holdings of foreign exchange reserves – switch or diversify to the euro. This has not yet happened in any great quantities, and less than a third of global reserve holdings were held in euros in 2005 (compared to two-thirds in US dollars). But the euro zone has most of the qualities required to build the reserve status of the euro, and central bankers and political leaders in several countries, including Japan, Russia and South Korea, have expressed concerns about weaknesses in the dollar and have hinted that they might reduce their holdings.

Third, more economic activity will need to be denominated in euros, and more people will need to use euros and think of costs in terms of euros. Even though the EU is a much bigger trading power than the US, about half of global exports are still denominated in dollars (compared to about one-third in euros), which gives the United States the ability to reduce the risk it faces from global currency movements because a large share of its imports are priced in its own currency. Euro zone countries denominate their exports in euros, but until non-European countries follow suit, until a greater share of international trade is denominated in euros, and until the euro becomes a vehicle currency (one used in transactions between countries outside the euro zone),[29] it will not be able to compete with the dollar.

Finally, more private investors must hold portfolios in euros, and govern-ments and corporations must denominate more of their issues in euros. The European capital market is still too fragmented, so its liquidity is reduced and investors are disinclined to buy investments denominated in euros. The result is that most private holdings of international financial assets – such as bank accounts, bonds, and stocks – are still held in dollars. The strength of the dollar since the end of World War II has built upon itself – the more people who have used it, the more people who have wanted to use it. But the euro has at least two advantages. First, it is used on a daily basis by nearly 310 million consumers in 12 countries, as well as in several other areas outside the EU, including Montenegro and Kosovo. True, the dollar is used officially by 290 million American consumers and by several million more outside the US,[30] as well as circulating informally far more widely than the euro, but the euro is used in 12 of the richest countries in the world. Second, the euro offers investors ready access to a greater number and variety of assets than the dollar, and a desire to diversify their portfolios might encour-age investors to keep their holdings in more than one currency. The strength of the euro will only grow as its use expands.

The euro also benefits from weaknesses in the global status of the dollar, which can be traced back to the 1960s, to the first signs of economic competition from Europe and to the effects of US budget deficits generated by fighting the war in Vietnam. The problems have only worsened of late, thanks mainly to the twin deficits, on the budget and trade, which have led to the unprecedented sight of the country with the world's prime reserve currency also being its biggest net debtor.[31] Not everyone sees this as a problem; Levy and Brown argue that the US is 'continually extending its lead in the innovation and application of new technology, ensuring its continued appeal for foreign central banks and private investors. The dollar's role as the global monetary standard is not threatened.'[32] The Bush administration has reasoned that the US federal budget deficit will encourage economic expansion, which will in turn eventually bring government spending under control. But former US Treasury Secretary Robert Rubin and former Federal Reserve chairman Alan Greenspan have responded that a large deficit limits the ability of the government to deal with future crises, which could lead to a run on the dollar and a rise in interest rates, thereby hurting the stock market, weakening American banks, and reducing private sector investment.[33] Under these circumstances, currency traders would be encouraged to sell dollars, investors would be less inclined to hold assets denominated in dollars, governments would be less inclined to hold reserves in dollars, and it would be less likely that economic and financial activity would be denominated in dollars.

Perversely, the strength of the dollar has been a source of economic problems for the US: its reserve currency status is one reason why the US has been able to run large trade deficits without suffering adverse economic consequences. But if its credibility falls and governments switch to the euro, the dollar – and the US economy – will suffer. Most worrying of all for the United States is speculation that OPEC may one day decide to redenominate its oil in euros. If this happened, the US would have to buy euros with dollars before it could buy oil, the value of the dollar might fall further while the value of the euro rose, and the US economy would have to absorb increases in the price of petrol. Put another way, the US is playing with fire, which could work to the advantage of the euro.

And we must not forget the close association between currency credibility and political credibility. The Chinese yuan is not a contender for global status – despite the size and the transformation of the Chinese economy – in part because of the lack of transparency in the Chinese financial system, and in part because China has little political influence in the world. Its foreign policy interests do not reach as far as those of the United States or the EU, and the opinions of its leaders are not listened to so carefully. By contrast, one of the reasons why the dollar carries the weight that it does is because the political actions of the United States matter to the rest of the world. The same is increasingly true of the EU; as its policies have a broader reach, carried on the increasingly muscular shoulders of common trade policies and common foreign policies, so the credibility of the euro expands.

Some analysts have puzzled over why the euro has not *yet* displaced the US dollar, despite its success in unifying European financial markets. Others argue that it is too early for that displacement to take place, noting that the British pound continued to be a major world currency long after the relative decline of the British economy[34] and the rise of US economic power. In terms of the convertibility of the euro, the breadth and depth of euro zone financial markets, the political stability of the EU, and the level of trust in European financial institutions, the foundations are in place for the euro to challenge the dollar. The euro is a new currency, most currencies are still quoted against the dollar, few people – whether political leaders, financial professionals, or consumers – yet fully understand the political significance of the EU, and news from the EU still has less impact on international financial markets than news from the United States. But at no time since it became the world's premier currency has the dollar faced the kind of challenges that it now faces from the euro.

The changing balance of trade

Former EU trade commissioner Pascal Lamy liked to describe the EU and the United States as the two elephants of the global trading system, but perhaps he should have been more specific: the EU is like an African bull elephant, and the US more like a young Asian elephant. In 2004, the EU accounted for nearly 42 per cent of world merchandise exports (4.5 times as much as the US), for 41 per cent of merchandise imports (nearly 2.5 times as much as the US), for 48 per cent of commercial services exports (three times as much as the US), and for 45 per cent of commercial services imports (nearly four times as much as the US).[35] In trade terms, the EU has been a single actor – rather than a cluster of separate national importers and exporters – since the 1958 Treaty of Rome and its Common Commercial Policy (CCP).

The CCP is a common external trade policy whose official goals have been to reach and manage trade agreements with the rest of the world, and to apply uniform trade policy instruments. Its unofficial goal has been to make sure that the trade deficit between the EU and other countries is kept under control.[36] Whatever the measure, the CCP has been a runaway success. The EU acts as one in trade negotiations, and since the creation of the World

Trade Organization (WTO) in 1995 it has aggressively monitored external trade policies. Along the way, it has been able to protect its balance of trade: in 2003 it had a deficit of just over 1 per cent on trade in merchandise, and a surplus of 7 per cent on trade in services. By contrast, the US had a deficit of nearly 45 per cent on merchandise trade and a surplus of just over 20 per cent on services.[37] The EU has also been able to build steadily on its share of global trade. Between 1948 and 2003, the value of world merchandise trade grew by more than 11,000 per cent. During that time, the North American share was almost halved (falling from just over 27 per cent to just under 14 per cent in 2003), while the Western European share grew from nearly 32 per cent to 43 per cent. Meanwhile, the North American share of merchandise imports hovered at about 16–20 per cent, while the Western European share was in the range of 40–47 per cent.

The EU has not always won friends and influenced trading partners along the way. A notable bone of contention has been the Common Agricultural Policy (CAP), a system of subsidies to European farmers that has helped turn the EU from a major food importer into a major food exporter, but that has also been widely criticized – particularly by the United States and by the Cairns Group of countries (including Australia, Brazil, Canada, New Zealand and the Philippines) – for maintaining high prices. CAP has also been criticized for causing food over-production, allowing the misuse of EU funds, promoting environmental damage, undermining agricultural production in developing countries, benefiting large farmers at the cost of small farmers, and absorbing too much of the EU budget.[38]

CAP has also been a recurring bone of contention in the transatlantic trading relationship, the world's biggest and most politically important. The EU and the US each account for about one-fifth of each other's bilateral trade, and they are each other's biggest sources of foreign direct investment: by the end of 2002, that investment had reached nearly $1.7 trillion, of which 57 per cent was EU investment in the US, and 43 per cent was US investment in the EU. Nearly 4.4 million Americans work for European companies, and almost as many Europeans work for American companies.[39] 'Our multinationals are so thoroughly intertwined', quipped a bemused Pascal Lamy in 2003, 'that some of them have forgotten whether their origins are European or American'. In his view, the size and significance of the relationship has become such that 'it defines the shape of the global economy as a whole'.[40]

In the early post-war years, Europe–US trade relations were relatively calm, the Americans enjoying brisk economic growth and seeing no real threat from a Europe that was too busy recovering from war to offer much competition. Furthermore, common concerns about security during the cold war discouraged the US and Europe from politicizing trade. But the growth of the Community combined with the end of Bretton Woods to create a different climate. Disputes broke out over trade in steel (with both sides accusing each other of unfair trading practices), over CAP-driven limits on the number of chickens that US farmers could sell to Western Europe (a squabble that had to be taken to GATT for settlement[41]), over the implications of CAP itself, and – in the 1980s – over attempts by the US to take action against European companies involved in the building of the Siberian natural gas pipeline. Relations deteriorated even further with the passage of the 1988 Omnibus Trade Act, which allowed the US to take unilateral action against countries identified as pursuing unfair trade practices. The balance of transatlantic trade had meanwhile shifted firmly in favour of the Europeans; while the US had small trade deficits with Western Europe in the late 1980s, these turned into surpluses in 1990–92, only to turn once again into a deficit in 1993, which has since grown steadily, reaching \$113 billion in 2004.[42]

With the end of the cold war, and the creation in 1995 of the WTO and its binding dispute settlement system, the frequency of transatlantic trade disputes grew. The problem should not be over-stated: the bulk of transatlantic trade takes place peacefully and routinely, and trade disputes affect only a small fraction of total trade. But that fraction shows just how much the stakes have changed. Herein lies an irony: while EU–US economic connections are so close, and both sides have the same general interests in promoting free trade and supporting a multilateral rules-based trading system, they also seem to be increasingly at odds with one another. So serious has the situation become that Richard Morningstar, US ambassador to the EU, was prompted to suggest in 2001 that the number and the severity of the disputes was 'beginning to overshadow the rest of the relationship' and had the potential to harm the multilateral trading system.[43]

WTO archives offer some revealing data. In the period 1995–2004, a total of 324 disputes came before the WTO. Of those, the US was the defendant in 27 per cent and the plaintiff in 23 per cent, while the EU was defendant in 15 per cent and plaintiff in 17 per cent. A total of 46 disputes (14 per cent) involved both the US and the EU. In 29 of those cases, the EU was the plaintiff and in 17 the US was the plaintiff.[44] At the same time, not a single dispute was initiated by an individual EU member state. The EU has even gone beyond issues dealing with trade in goods and moved into areas outside its legal competence, including intellectual property rights, trade in services, and the tax regimes of third countries.[45] The Europeans and the Americans bring more cases to the WTO than anyone else, many of these cases involve both sides, and the Europeans have been more aggressive in bringing cases against the Americans than vice versa. Consider the following examples.

The beef hormone dispute   Although this involves barely $100–$200 million in lost US exports, it has important symbolism. The problem arose in 1989 when the EU banned the import of meat treated with growth-promoting hormones, claiming concerns about the health and safety of European consumers. The WTO ruled that the ban was inconsistent with earlier international agreements, and that there was no scientific justification. But the EU refused to lift the ban, instead offering compensation by buying more hormone-free beef. The US turned down the offer, and imposed tariffs on imports of agricultural products from the EU (mainly France, Germany, Italy and Denmark). The EU reduced the number of hormones that came under the ban, following up by arguing that the ban should be lifted, but the problem remains unresolved.

The banana wars   In 1993, as part of the single market programme, the EU implemented a policy under which preference was given to imports of bananas from EU overseas territories or former colonies, and banned imports from other countries, including several where US corporations were active. Aggrieved, the US took the matter to GATT, which ruled against the EU but did not have the power to take action. Inheriting the case, the WTO ruled against the EU and gave it until January 1999 to take action. The US meanwhile increased the pressure by threatening to impose 100 per cent duties on selected EU imports unless it met the WTO deadline. In a landmark ruling in April 1999, the WTO authorized the US to impose sanctions on products as varied as Danish ham and Roquefort cheese. The dispute was finally settled in July 2001, in favour of the United States.[46]

The dispute over Cuba   In March 1996, the US adopted the Cuban Liberty and Democratic Solidarity Act, otherwise known as the Helms-Burton Act. Designed to increase the economic pressure for political change in Cuba by deterring foreign investment in land and property expropriated by the Castro regime, it included a provision allowing foreign companies investing in Cuba to be sued in US courts, and executives from those companies to be barred from entry into the United States. The Act was criticized by the major trading partners of the United States, and the EU threatened retaliatory sanctions. The dispute added fuel to the flames of an earlier disagreement over another US law (the D'Amato Act) which required that sanctions be imposed on foreign firms investing in the Iranian and Libyan oil industries. The dispute went to the WTO, and was resolved in July 1998 when the US agreed to lift sanctions on European companies and to waive the ban on European executives entering the United States.

Genetically modified food Differences of opinion across the Atlantic about food safety have spilled over into a dispute about genetically modified (GM) food.[47] EU regulations on GM food – notably a four-year ban on GM crops introduced in 1999 – were criticized by the United States for violating free trade agreements, to which the Europeans responded by arguing that trade could not be free without informed consent. This was a particular problem for American farmers, given the size of the EU as an export market and given recent reductions in the size of those exports; between 1998 and 2002, the value of US corn exports to the EU fell from $63 million to $12.5 million. Falling commodities prices, falling demand, and the increased cost of US corn were all part of the problem, but the EU ban was also blamed. In 2003, the US – along with Australia, Canada, Mexico and New Zealand – filed a complaint with the WTO, charging that the EU's ban on GM food violated international trade agreements.

The Byrd Amendment In October 2000, the US Congress enacted the Continued Dumping and Subsidy Offset Act, otherwise known as the Byrd Amendment. Aimed at controlling dumping, it rewards companies that bring successful cases against foreign corporations that sell their products at unfairly low prices in the United States. The EU complained that it hurt their corporations twice, by subjecting them to higher tariffs and by giving US competitors a windfall income from those tariffs, and – along with Canada, India, and several other countries – challenged the statute in the WTO. When the US failed to act, the EU asked the WTO for permission to retaliate. This was given, but the plaintiffs chose to wait and see what action the US Congress took on repealing the Byrd Amendment. When action was not forthcoming, sanctions went into effect in April 2005.

Steel tariffs Claiming to be concerned about ailing American steel producers, the Bush administration in early 2002 imposed tariffs on US imports of cheaper foreign steel, much of it coming from the EU. Just as Helms-Burton had been described by critics as a domestic political ploy designed to bolster support for Bill Clinton among Cuban-American voters in Florida, so the steel tariffs were seen as a ploy to bolster support for George Bush in states that promised to play a key role in the 2004 presidential election, such as Michigan. The EU responded by threatening to impose countertariffs on various US imports, including orange juice from Florida, another key state in the election. In the face of EU criticism, and following a ruling by the WTO that they were illegal, the tariffs were lifted in December 2003.

The tussle over Airbus   For several years now, the US and the EU have exchanged rebukes over subsidies to their major civilian aircraft manufacturers. The United States has accused EU governments of helping Airbus, most recently with start-up costs for the Airbus A380 superjumbo, which poses direct competition to the Boeing 747. It also worries about advantages for the mid-sized Airbus A350, developed in response to Boeing's 787 Dreamliner (but which has not been selling well). The EU reaction to American accusations has been to argue that Boeing – the last remaining major US manufacturer of civilian aircraft – receives help from the US government in the form of space and military contracts and tax breaks. The US responds by pointing to the advantages that Airbus will accrue from sales of its A400M military transport plane, competing with the existing and potentially cheaper Lockheed Martin C-130. In negotiations over the issue, each side has accused the other of intransigence. In January 2005 they gave themselves 90 days to resolve the dispute rather than suing through the WTO. When this failed, the issue went to the WTO, which was expected to rule in 2007.

Tax breaks for corporations   In 2004, the United States stood down in the face of a long-standing dispute over tax assistance to corporations. Under laws introduced in 1984, US businesses could create foreign sales corporations (FSCs) that would allow them to be exempt from paying tax on exports; the main beneficiaries were large corporations such as Boeing, Caterpillar, IBM, and Microsoft. This was ruled to be an illegal form of trade subsidy by the WTO in 2000. The US responded by passing a replacement law, the Extra-Territorial Income Inclusion Act. This was also ruled illegal by the WTO, which authorized the EU to impose up to 100 per cent tariffs on $4 billion-worth of US imports. When the US failed to change its policies, the EU imposed a 5 per cent increase in duty on a wide range of US imports, ranging from paper, toys and jewellery to nuclear reactors, and threatened to increase the duties by 1 per cent per month. This was the first time that the EU had imposed sanctions on US imports as part of a trade dispute.[48] In October 2004 a new law was passed by the US scrapping the FSC scheme, but at the same time giving many industries tax breaks of a different kind, including the opportunity to repatriate profits at a greatly reduced rate of tax. The EU lifted the threat of sanctions, but at the same time challenged in the WTO some of the provisions of the new US legislation.

Why have the disputes between the US and the EU become so numerous and so fierce? First, the WTO dispute settlement system favours big states, there are increased opportunities for retaliation and cross-retaliation (taking action in areas outside the one under immediate dispute),[49] and the EU has grown. All these factors have encouraged the European Commission to exert the power of Europe rather than to react to pressures from abroad. Second, since the European and American markets are now the same size in terms of GDP, it is more difficult for one side to force concessions from the other, so both are pushed more frequently to the brink whenever disagreements arise. Third, transatlantic disputes involve clashes in domestic values, priorities and regulatory systems that cannot be addressed by international rules.[50] But above all, these disputes show that the EU has arrived as a trading super-power. Not only do its trading partners care – and care a great deal – about EU trade policies, but the EU has been able to use its size and power to wrest changes in global trade, and to exert pressure on the United States.

The rise of corporate Europe

A predictable effect of the European single market has been increased opportunities for cross-border corporate mergers, acquisitions, and joint ventures, leading to a revival of the European corporate presence in the global marketplace.[51] European companies already had a long history of international operations growing out of the colonial era, and in terms of total assets held overseas in the post-war years were more global in scope than their American competitors. But American businesses had several advantages over their European competitors:

- The corporate environment favoured American business. While American companies were egalitarian, dynamic, and heavily engaged in research and development, European companies tended to be nationalistic, hierarchical, conservative, and driven less by quantity than by quality.[52]
- While European corporations had become complacent as a result of their relatively easy access to colonial markets, American corporations were more competitive, and were building organized, large-scale, diverse multibusinesses that exploited economies of scale, provided a stimulus to suppliers and customers, and invested heavily in research and development.[53]
- While American corporations had access to the large American market, and developed management and operations techniques suited to large geographical areas, European businesses faced a host of barriers in their attempts to move into neighbouring states; these included merger taxes which discriminated against cross-frontier mergers, capital gains taxes on assets transferred as a result of mergers, double taxation on company

profits, the absence of European company law and commercial contract law, differences in regulations and standards, and limits on the movement of goods and services.

- The sheer size of the biggest American corporations gave them access to resources that European corporations mostly lacked, including support for marketing and for research and development.

The growth of the European single market in the 1960s changed the rules by increasing the opportunities for region-wide corporate operations and larger-scale production, but most mergers and joint ventures in Western Europe were still either national (taking place among companies in the same country) or international (involving European and foreign corporations), and there was relatively little intra-Community activity (involving companies in different EEC states). Among the corporate mergers that took place in the Community in 1966–69, 59 per cent were national, 26 per cent were international (involving mainly American firms), and just 8 per cent were intra-Community.[54] In fact, US corporations were far ahead of their European counterparts in taking a Europe-wide approach to production and marketing: IBM, Ford, General Motors, IT&T, Esso, Procter & Gamble and others were developing European brand images, splitting production among plants in different countries, manufacturing products jointly in two or more countries, and exploiting the reduction of trade barriers. In the few cases where European companies did the same, it was often in reaction to the American lead.[55]

Changes in laws and regulations during the late 1960s and 1970s eased the path for European corporations, but only slowly. While American multinationals continued to grow, and Japanese multinationals were added to the mix, European industry became less competitive, handicapped by slow progress in the completion of the single market. As late as the 1980s, the majority of mergers in the Community were still national, but intra-Community activity grew from 19 per cent in 1983–84 to 40 per cent in 1988–89, while the number of cross-border joint ventures registered by the Commission grew from 46 in 1982–83 to 129 in 1988–89. Meanwhile, the total number of mergers (national, intra-Community and international) grew from just 117 in 1982–83 to 492 in 1988–89.[56] In 1989–90 the number of intra-Community mergers finally overtook the number of national mergers for the first time,[57] since when the European mergers and acquisitions market has in several years been bigger than that of the United States.[58]

A flurry of activity during the 1990s continued to alter the business environment. Barriers to cross-border mergers were removed by changes in company laws and regulations, and progress on the single market increased the pressures and the opportunities for the development of pan-European corporations, as well as greatly increasing the number of consumers that they could reach. Community programmes aimed at encouraging research in information technology, advanced communications, and industrial technologies also paid dividends. With the removal of borders, national corporations lost the protection once offered by national governments, so that they now had to sink or swim. Many of them sank – in the airline market, several 'national champions' such as Swissair and KLM either went bankrupt or were bought out by other airlines – but many others became bigger and more productive. With the adoption of the euro, the increased availability of cheap and easy credit, and changes in European law in 2004, intra-European mergers became even easier. And when privatization programmes in many countries and the broader effects of globalization were added to the mix, the number of opportunities for mergers, acquisitions, and joint ventures grew, both within the EU and between European and non-European corporations.

Companies will usually merge for one or more reasons: to grow bigger, to seek out larger partners with access to capital for investment, to marry complementary businesses, to diversify in order to spread risk, to acquire new management, to make savings by cutting payroll and services, to make a profit by stripping the assets of another company, or to defend themselves in the face of mergers among competitors. All of these factors have achieved a new magnitude in the single European market, with the result that European business news in the last decade has been rife with stories of one merger after another: the rise of GlaxoSmithKline out of a string of mergers among British, Canadian and American pharmaceuticals companies; the rise of the French insurance company AXA (by 2005 the 13th biggest corporation in the world); the rise of the Royal Bank of Scotland to become (by 2005) the sixth biggest bank in the world; the aggressive string of mergers and acquisitions (including the 2000 takeover of the much larger German company Mannesmann) that have made Britain's Vodafone one of the world's biggest mobile phone businesses; and the 2004 takeover of Britain's Abbey by Spain's Banco Santander in Europe's biggest ever cross-border banking merger. Helped by weaknesses in the dollar, European companies have also reached more actively outside the EU, as did BP in 1998 when it took over Amoco in the United States, as did Daimler of Germany in 1999 when it took over the US automobile manufacturer Chrysler, and as did Deutsche Telekom in 2000 when it took over Voicestream in the United States.

The rise of the European corporate world is reflected in the statistics. In 1969, the *Fortune* list of the world's biggest 400 corporations showed that 238 (nearly 60 per cent) were American while 108 (27 per cent) were

European.[59] By contrast, the *Fortune* Global 500 list of the world's 500 biggest corporations in 2005 showed that 176 (35 per cent) were American and 158 (32 per cent) were from the EU. Where the five biggest of those companies (by revenues) in the late 1990s were American, by mid-2002 two had been displaced by European corporations: BP of Britain (ranked second in mid-2005), and Royal Dutch/Shell (ranked fourth in mid-2005). The long list of American companies that have for so long been staples of the international corporate world – including Ford, IBM, Boeing, Exxon, and Time Warner – is now littered with European names, including Allianz, Volkswagen, ING, Siemens, Carrefour, Fortis, HSBC, Peugeot, BNP Paribas, Tesco, and BMW. So active has been the European mergers market that companies that were once distinctly British or German or French have taken on identities that are increasingly European or international.

No discussion of the transformation would be complete without mention of Airbus, which has whittled away at the dominant global positions once enjoyed by American aircraft manufacturers. Founded in 1970 as a cooperative venture between France, Germany and Britain, and inspired by the argument that economies of scale were giving American manufacturers an advantage over their European competitors, whose national markets were too small to sustain them, Airbus has not only displaced all the large national European aircraft manufacturers, but has impacted the United States by contributing to the pressures that led to Lockheed opting out of the civilian aircraft market in the 1980s, and to McDonnell-Douglas being taken over by Boeing in 1997. Today, instead of several large American firms and several smaller European firms, the global market for civilian aircraft is dominated by just two: Airbus and Boeing. Airbus is 80 per cent owned by the European Aeronautic Defence and Space company (EADS), created in 2000 by a merger of its French, German and Spanish owners, and 20 per cent owned by BAE Systems of Britain.[60] It produces a line of 12 different airliners, the newest being the controversial 555-seat double-decker A380.

The impact of Europe has also been felt in other parts of corporate America. Symbolic of the change was the record fine of €479 million ($332 million) imposed by the European Commission in March 2004 on Microsoft, which was charged with abusing its dominant market position by bundling in its media player with its Windows operating system, thereby handicapping other companies that made media players. The Commission ordered Microsoft to begin offering a version of Windows without the media player installed, and to reveal its Windows software codes so that rival companies could more easily design compatible products. In 2005, Microsoft agreed to offer a version of its Windows XP Home Edition without the media player installed.

Even mergers within the United States have been the target of

Commission action. When telecom companies MCI/WorldCom and Sprint proposed a merger in 2000, it was blocked by the Commission for fear that the two companies would dominate internet operations in the EU (the merger was eventually abandoned). And when General Electric and Honeywell proposed a $43 billion merger in 2001, it was blocked by the Commission out of concern for its implications for the market in aircraft jet engines. But the Commission approved the 2002 merger between computer makers Hewlett-Packard and Compaq, as well as the 2005 merger between Sony and Bertelsmann, which created the world's biggest music company.

Interpreting the numbers

There are many – including Europeans themselves – who still question the vitality and dynamism of the European economy, and will quote one data set after another that illustrate American advantages: a robust and dynamic economy, a strong dollar, inventive entrepreneurs, productive workers, and helpful demographic trends. But we all know Benjamin Disraeli's admonition about lies, damned lies and statistics. The picture we construct depends upon the data we use, and how we interpret those data. Take, for example, the question of labour productivity. One set of numbers suggests that the United States has recently outpaced the EU, increasing its output per hour between 1994 and 2005 by 2.5 per cent annually, compared to just 1.5 per cent annually in the EU-15.[61] But a recent study by Robert Gordon, an American economist, suggests that if changes in productivity are seen over a longer timeframe, Europe does well compared to the United States: since 1950, US productivity has grown at an average annual rate of 2 per cent, while that of Europe has grown at 3.3 per cent.[62]

Take, also, the figures on per capita GDP, which seem to show that the United States is far in the lead: it was producing $41,400 per person in 2004, compared to $26,000–$35,000 per person in most Western European member states, and $5,000–$15,000 in Greece, Portugal and most Eastern European member states.[63] Explanations for the gap run the gamut from different tax rates to differences in culture and the achievements of trade unions, particularly those in France which won concessions on working hours in the early 1980s that were adopted by the French government, and which in turn helped fuel EU-wide changes.[64] But much again depends on how the data are interpreted, and which factors are added to the mix. Robert Gordon believes that social and even geographical factors may play a role in the higher US figures: with higher crime rates, more has to be spent in the US on home and business security and on keeping people in prison; with fewer people using public transport, more has to be spent in the US on roads and energy; and with a more extreme climate, Americans must spend more on air conditioning and heating. If such factors are artificially inflating US GDP, then perhaps the gap in transatlantic productivity is not as great as it appears.

Gordon's conclusions are debatable, as is the way in which GDP figures are conventionally used. Per capita GDP is an important measure of well-being, but it does not provide a complete picture, and when we also consider qualitative factors, a rather different picture emerges. In a recent report, the OECD argued that while cross-country rankings based on other measures of the quality of life are generally the same as that for per capita GDP, the same is not true when it comes to changes over time or to surveys on happiness and life satisfaction.[65] If we also consider qualitative factors such as the state of the environment, access to technology, wealth and income differentials, social class, gender and racial inequalities, access to education and health-care, and the quality of infrastructure, the US (as a national economy) would probably retain its lead in most areas, but Europe would have the advantage in other areas, and overall the gap would likely close.[66]

In the debate over quantity vs quality, there is something to be learned from the working habits of Europeans and Americans. The US leads Europe on per capita GDP in part because Americans have longer working days, and are usually limited to two weeks of annual holiday. Between 1990 and 2004, the average number of hours clocked up annually by employed workers fell by more than 10 per cent in France, 6 per cent in Germany and Britain, 4 per cent in Italy, and just 2 per cent in the US. By 2004, American workers were putting in 26 per cent more hours than French workers.[67] Interestingly, while the differential in per capita GDP between the US and the EU-15 remained almost unchanged between 1970 and 2000 (the EU-15 was producing only 70 per cent as much as the US), the gap in GDP per hour closed dramatically (from 65 percent of the US rate in 1970 to 91 per cent of the US rate in 2000).[68] The message is clear: Europeans are working fewer hours, but they are doing more with those hours. And the additional time that they have free to spend at home or on holiday with their families gives them a higher quality of life, or – at the very least – more time to actually enjoy life. Workplace pressures have been implicated in the break-up of the American family, and they may even factor into the slightly shorter life expectancy of Americans, which currently stands at 77 years compared to 78–81 years in most Western EU member states.[69]

Another area in which European quality may be more important than American quantity relates to demography. Those who question Europe's economic lead will often point to Europe's falling birth rate, and argue that because Europeans are living longer and becoming older, this will reduce the number of workers, who will carry an ever greater burden to meet the health-care and welfare costs of the retired. Thus, runs the logic, lower productivity combined with greater public spending on the elderly might reduce Europe's competitive edge. To make matters worse, warns *The Economist*, growth rates vary significantly from one EU country to another, and the economic tensions that are likely to rise will cause pressures on interest rates and perhaps under-mine the euro, with consequences that could be 'grim' and 'alarming'.[70]

There is no question (if we believe the projections) that the EU's popula-tion will shrink in coming decades, as it will in most industrialized states, and even in newly industrializing countries such as China. From a peak of nearly 730 million in 2000, the population of Europe (EU and non-EU member states combined) is projected to fall by 2050 to just over 650 million, a decline of more than 10 per cent (see Figure 4.3). Poland has

Figure 4.3   *Comparative demographic trends, 1950–2050*

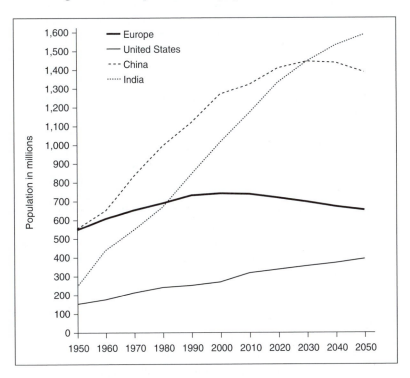

Source: United Nations Population Division, http://esa.un.org/unpp.

already begun a slow decline (as has Russia), the populations of Germany and Italy (and Japan) are expected to peak in 2010 and then to fall, Spain's will peak in 2020, and France's will peak in 2035. Alone among major European states, Britain is expected to see steady growth, its population rising by 14 per cent. In Europe today there are 35 people of pensionable age for every 100 of working age; by 2050, the ratio is forecast to have changed to 75:100.

By contrast, the population of the United States has been growing steadily for decades, and between 2000 and 2050 is expected to grow from 284 million to nearly 395 million, an increase of nearly 40 per cent. And compared to the already over-crowded cities and towns of Europe, which must expand into neighbouring rural areas, there is still considerable space to absorb the growth in the US; there are just 30 Americans to the square kilometre today, compared to 114 Europeans per square kilometre. The differential, claims Ferguson, 'condemns the EU to a decline in international influence', leaving Europeans with the choice of opening their borders to more immigration or transforming the EU into a 'fortified retirement community'.[71] For George Weigel, Europe's demographic decline has become 'a crisis of civilizational morale', and even poses a security threat to the United States because of the prospect of a Europe increasingly influenced by, and perhaps even dominated by, militant Islam imported by new immigrants.[72]

Such hyperbole does not always stand up to close scrutiny. If absolute wealth continues to be used as the core measure of comparative economic size, then clearly the US, China and India have an advantage over Europe. Their economies will become bigger, which will mean bigger markets, more consumers, more wealth and productivity, and greater economic influence in the world. Bigger economies will also help them sustain bigger militaries, which will mean greater political influence in the world, if such influence continues to be measured by firepower. Furthermore, China and India will have an advantage because their working-age populations will be much bigger as a proportion of the whole than the working-age population of Europe, where the taxpayer will have to meet the cost of maintaining growing numbers of retirees.

But if we look at the qualitative elements of population trends, a different picture emerges. Reductions in the labour force will continue to increase the pressure for technological change, which will in turn help make European workers more efficient. Workers will also be able to negotiate higher salaries, providing them with more disposable income. They will be able to spend more, helping boost the European marketplace. They will be able to save and invest more, helping strengthen European economies. They will pay more in taxes, helping governments raise the funds needed to take care of retirees, and the number of people living in poverty will likely decline. So while Europe's population growth may slow, the quality of life for Europeans will continue to improve. And we should not forget the impact of immigration on the European economy; more new immigrants will boost population growth and cancel out some of the numerical imbalances between workers and retirees. Finally, if demography *does* turn out to be a problem, then the US faces more competition from China and India than the EU faces from the US.

5

Europe's Political Leadership

Imagine a United States of Europe. In addition to being the world's biggest marketplace and trading power, it would have the centralized political institutions and common policies needed to speak with one voice on the global stage, and to convert its wealth into political influence. The euro would be used throughout its territory, and from that base would likely have displaced the US dollar as the world's leading currency. The European position on every critical problem – from terrorism to poverty, the Middle East, the environment, and trade – would dominate international debates. The directly elected European president would be one of the two or three most powerful and best known political leaders on the face of the earth. Foreign governments would listen carefully to European opinion, and would pay close attention to the state of their diplomatic and trade relations with Europe. The European flag would be one of the most recognizable of global icons. And few would question the superpower status of the EU.

But Europe is not a unified state. There is no independent government of Europe, and the presidents of the European Commission and the European Central Bank have only a fraction of the international visibility of their American counterparts. Europe lacks a clear identity, its personality changing from one issue to another and its image often confused by the hybrid nature of the EU itself. Its foreign policies are muddied by competing interests and hamstrung by the baggage of historical relationships among its member states. It lacks the kind of large, combined military traditionally associated with great powers. For most ordinary Europeans, the EU is not much more than a soulless bureaucracy turning out rather dull-sounding policies and regulations. It has been unable to produce the kind of visible and dramatic foreign policy results that we have come to expect from a superpower. While Americans are being told by their leaders and their media of the challenges posed by China, around which is thus being constructed the aura of a superpower, Europe is not seen as threatening, nor does it have a unified military, and so its global role is overlooked. Europeans themselves find little in the EU that excites or thrills, or that encourages a sense of belonging. In short, the EU has few of the visible trappings of great power that we associate with the United States or the former Soviet Union.

At least until recently, claims that Europe might be a significant presence on the world stage were usually met with responses ranging from disbelief to cynicism and outright rejection. This was certainly true during the 1990s, when the Balkan effect was at its height. Mark Almond dismissed the EU as a 'paper tiger',[1] Commission president Jacques Santer worried that it was 'simply not punching its weight',[2] and Charles Bremner wrote of the 'emptiness' of Europe's foreign policy ambitions.[3] Richard Rosecrance argued that there might never be a common European foreign or defence policy, and dismissed most European policy positions as 'lowest-common-denominator' agreements that had little influence on world politics.[4] Jan Zielonka summed it all up in the title of his 1998 book *Explaining Euro-Paralysis: Why Europe is Unable to Act in International Politics*. The idea that the EU could cope with a complex international environment, he concluded, was a 'grand delusion'.[5]

But that was the 1990s, when the bandwagon of doubt was filled to overflowing. A decade later, much has changed. Europe may not yet have a comprehensive common foreign policy, but it has learned from its mistakes, and its positions on international affairs have achieved more clarity and consistency. Those positions may not yet carry the weight of their American counterparts, but the European voice is increasingly heard at the high table of international debate, and the EU also enjoys two strategic advantages that are often overlooked, but that have helped redefine its role in the world. First, it has benefited from the declining credibility of the kind of unilateralism and hard power with which the United States has been associated. As noted in Chapter 2, Europeans were rarely in the position during the cold war to counter US policy, or the American view that it should strive to be strong in a weak Europe.[6] But Europe today has a new confidence, is no longer so willing always to defer to the Americans, offers a new set of interpretations of the international system, and brings a new style and a contrasting set of values and tools to bear on policy problems. Where American policymakers still emphasize realist self-interest, their Europeans counterparts tend towards a liberal worldview that is more universal, inclusive and multilateral.

Second, Europeans have a unique and powerful tool in their foreign policy kitbag: they can offer preferential access to the biggest capitalist marketplace in the world, and even – in select cases – full membership of the EU club, with all its attendant rights and benefits. American political leaders like to describe the United States as a beacon of democracy and capitalism, and rarely question the dictum that the United States provides vital global leadership on a wide range of issues. The Bush administration in particular has made much of its interest in promoting democracy. But since the end of the cold war, nothing has brought deeper and more lasting political and economic change to more people than access to Europe. Meeting the terms of entry has encouraged one Eastern European country after another to change its laws, practices and policies, and even North African and Middle Eastern countries have been swayed by the promise of non-member access to the European market. In the realm of international affairs, the Americans simply have nothing to compare with the irresistible attraction of Europe.

With advantages such as these in hand, it is easier today to find support for the idea that Europe matters. Roy Ginsberg quotes numerous issues on which the EU has made its mark, ranging from the Middle East peace process to events in Cuba, Cyprus, Iran and even (yes) the Balkans.[7] Karen Smith lists an impressive array of diplomatic and economic instruments that the EU has used in its international relations.[8] Even Rosecrance concedes that the EU is a 'magnetic force' in world politics, capable of pulling disparate countries into its web of economic and political associations and keeping them there.[9] And for Mark Leonard, all we have to do is recognize the 'invisible hand' of European power and we will conclude that Europe will 'run the 21st Century'.[10]

Europe's policy learning curve

Attempts to understand the role played by the EU in the world are complicated by a single troubling question: just what kind of beast is it? Academics have long wrestled with the problem, offering numerous possible answers but reaching a consensus on none.[11] It is less than a state but more than an international organization, say some. It is a federal superstate under construction, say others. It is *sui generis* (unique) say yet others, an explanation usually offered – it could be imagined – with a Gallic shrug of the shoulders, a downturn of the mouth and an upturn of the hands.

In 1970, Cosgrove and Twitchett offered three guidelines for measuring whether an international organization could be an actor on the international scene: the degree of autonomous decisionmaking power held by its central institutions, the extent to which its functions had an impact on interstate relations, and the depth of its impact on the formation of the foreign policies of states, particularly those of its members. On all three counts, they concluded, the EEC met the conditions for being a viable international actor.[12] The ungainly concept of 'actorness' soon entered the political lexicon, the idea being that the Community mattered because it was internally cohesive,

autonomous, had the ability to identify priorities and develop coherent policies, could negotiate with other actors in the international system, and
enjoyed legitimacy in the eyes of domestic audiences.[13] In 1977, Ralf
Dahrendorf argued that in spite of the 'now you see it, now you don't' quality of Europe, it undeniably existed, and made its presence felt by the actions
of its institutions.[14] Later, trying to downplay the comparison with states,
Allen and Smith suggested merely that the Community had a 'presence'
defined by its credentials, its legitimacy, its capacity to act, and the place it
occupied in 'the perceptions and expectations of policymakers'.[15]

But the lack of statehood continues to be quoted by those who deny that
the EU is a superpower. Only states have the necessary legitimacy, sovereignty, independence and common institutions – they argue – to be able to
develop common positions and negotiate with other states. Only states have
the degree of centralization and of internal structural coherence needed to
allow them to integrate policies and to both develop and implement a foreign
policy.[16] The EU may have become a major economic bloc that rivals the
United States in its overall volume of production and trade, argues Michael
Mann, but it is not a single state, and finds it 'much more laborious to devise
common policies'. The result is that while the US initiates policy, the EU
reacts.[17] But – as argued in Chapter 1 – insisting on a link between power
and statehood ignores the lessons of history, which is full of examples of
non-state actors with enormous power, from the Catholic Church and its
impact on the political and social development of medieval Europe, to al-
Qaeda today.

The debates aside, perhaps the most convincing recognition of Europe's
role as a global player is simply that it has come to matter. Its policies attract
more attention, its views are more widely discussed, and there is more analysis of its problems and its achievments. Why, otherwise, the harsh criticism
directed at the EU over the Balkans? Why, otherwise, the fury in
Washington when France and Germany refused to support the invasion of
Iraq? Why the growing number of books, articles and news stories that try to
tell us why the EU is *not* a major power? The sheer volume of denial brings
Hamlet to mind: the ladies are protesting too much. We may quibble over the
de jure personality of the EU, but right from the start it had a *de facto* international role that could not be ignored.[18] Expectations may have run ahead
of capabilities,[19] but the gap is closing, and out of the shadows has emerged
more substance.[20] How has all this happened?

With its limited original agenda, the European Economic Community
devoted little effort to developing common foreign policies. Given its handicaps and its marginal impact on US foreign policy during the cold war, the
EEC had only a modest international presence, and when it eventually began

to develop common external policies, this happened more by default than as the result of any proactive determination.[21] Not surprisingly, Zielonka concludes that 'disguise, ambiguity, and a general unwillingness to make bold choices' were features of European foreign policy from the outset.[22] Tellingly, the EU even today describes its activities as 'external relations' rather than as 'foreign policy'; it is a more ambiguous term, less suggestive of a developed and comprehensive set of processes and positions.

At their summit meeting in The Hague in 1969, Community leaders optimistically agreed that completion of the European single market meant paving the way for a Europe 'capable of assuming its responsibilities in the world of tomorrow'.[23] Duly inspired, they created European Political Cooperation (EPC), a process under which Community foreign ministers would meet regularly to coordinate their positions. But EPC was concerned more with *how* foreign policy should be agreed than with *what* that policy should be,[24] and there was no obligation on member states to act in concert. Its development, says Wallace, was a series of hesitant steps, followed by frustration at the meagre results, leading to a reinforcement of rules and procedures.[25] In 1973, British Prime Minister Edward Heath warned that Europeans would have to 'speak with a single voice' if they were to have real impact. As a result of the London Report in 1981[26] it was decided to move beyond consultation and towards joint action. The following year the Community for the first time agreed and took measures against third parties, imposing sanctions on the USSR after martial law was declared in Poland in the wake of the rise of the Solidarity trade union, and standing behind Britain over the war in the Falklands.[27]

Community foreign policy procedures remained informal until the adoption of the 1986 Single European Act, which gave EPC a legal basis and encouraged member states to 'endeavour jointly to formulate and implement a European foreign policy' under the overall leadership of the European Council. Community member states could still pursue independent national interests, but changes in the international environment had begun to demand new approaches, and the Community quickly took a leading position on Western relations with the soon-to-be-former Soviet bloc. Trade and negotiation agreements were signed with several Eastern European states, in 1989 the G7 summit agreed that the Community would coordinate Western aid to Poland and Hungary, and later that year the European Council agreed to create the European Bank for Reconstruction and Development to provide aid to Eastern Europe.

If Eastern Europe revealed the possibilities of the Community as a global actor, the 1990–91 Gulf crisis betrayed its limitations, just as it also confirmed the new dominance of the United States. A step forward was taken in 1992 when the Maastricht treaty included agreement on a Common Foreign and Security Policy (CFSP). The goals were loose and vague, with talk of the need to safeguard 'common values' and 'fundamental interests', 'to preserve peace and strengthen international security', and to 'promote international cooperation', and it was not a common policy in the same league as the Common Agricultural Policy. But its very creation was a sign of progress: the ambiguities suggested by the title 'European Political Cooperation' had been replaced by the more explicit tone of a Common Foreign and Security Policy,[28] which was part of the institutional structure of the EU[29] and – of course – included a new focus on security.

Developments in the Balkans provided the EU with a valuable set of lessons.[30] Europe looked instinctively to the US to provide leadership, while the US looked to the Europeans to take responsibility, and opinion was divided over the role of NATO. The EU lacked either the policies or the tools or the unity of purpose to provide leadership or to deal with large foreign policy challenges so soon after the end of the cold war, but the learning curve began to tighten. New organizational tools evolved, which were used with growing confidence: a series of 'joint actions' were taken under the terms of the CFSP (observing and providing logistical support for the 1993 Russian parliamentary elections, support for humanitarian aid convoys in Bosnia that same year, and preparation for the 1995 conference on non-proliferation of nuclear weapons), and in 1999–2000 the EU developed a series of 'common strategies' (on democracy in Russia, on the Ukraine, on the Mediterranean, and on Europe's plans for space). Finally, the EU agreed 'common positions' on relations with the Balkans, the Middle East, Burma and Zimbabwe, and on problems such as combating terrorism and how to deal with the International Criminal Court.

Along the way, European foreign policy also developed a distinctive style, which stood in contrast to that of the United States. If Americans still reserved the right to use coercion and the threat of force, Europeans emphasized diplomacy and negotiation. If Americans sometimes tended towards a unilateral approach to policy problems, Europeans preferred multilateral responses. If Americans defined problems according to the distinctive quasi-missionary worldview of the United States, Europeans took a more inclusive and less imperative view. If that hoary old chestnut of isolationism sometimes reared its head in discussions about US policy, there was never any doubt that the EU was engaged and connected. And if Americans saw a world divided by traditional state boundaries, the EU moved across those borders and looked at universal problems. For David Calleo, 'promiscuous Europe sees a world where everybody is a potential friend, [while] martial America lives in a world where every independent power is a potential enemy'.[31] For Leonard, the changes in Europe were easy to miss, because where US power was broadcast through 'bold declarations and blueprints', the European project had been both incremental and understated.[32] Discussions about the EU model have focused on the idea of 'effective multilateralism', or a belief that 'international relations should be organized through strong, negotiated, and enforceable multilateral regimes'.[33]

Europe's policy style can be explained in part by the very nature of its policymaking structure: because there is no common foreign policy and no single European government, because European Commission foreign delegations coexist with the diplomatic services of the individual members states, and because leadership of the EU rotates on a six-monthly basis among the member states, the EU has no choice but to accentuate consensus. This means that compromises are built in to EU policy positions from the start, which means in turn that these positions often lack the clear and sometimes uncompromising lines of their US counterparts. In addition, the political impact of the opportunities provided by the European marketplace creates many more opportunities for the kind of unintended effects of power discussed by Steven Lukes (see Chapter 1).

The softly-softly approach is most obvious in the EU's lack of a common military, but it is also reflected in the core foreign policy objectives of the EU: encouraging regional cooperation and integration, promoting human rights, advancing democracy and good governance, preventing violent conflict, and fighting international crime.[34] It is also reflected in the EU's preferred foreign policy tools, including declarations, high-level visits, diplomatic sanctions, diplomatic recognition, peace proposals, preventive diplomacy and peacekeeping, trade agreements, tariff and quota reductions and increases, embargoes, and boycotts.[35] These are all options available to traditional states as well, and in the hands of Europe might occasionally err on the side of waffle and fudge, but the big stick of Europe's economic clout ultimately backs up any soft talking. We may not be able (or want) to punish our enemies with the human and economic costs of a war, the EU seems to say, but we can withdraw the economic opportunities provided by access to our wealth and our marketplace.

For policy doves, the soft power approach is the best one for dealing with a potentially violent international environment, but for policy hawks – particularly in the United States – it smacks of weakness, a lack of resolution, and the A-word: appeasement. As long ago as 1996, James Woolsey, former director of the CIA, accused the EU of trying to appease Iran.[36] Dennis Hastert, Republican Speaker of the US House of Representatives, charged Spain with appeasing terrorists by changing its government in the wake of the March 2004 attacks in Madrid.[37] Conservative columnist Charles

Krauthammer has argued that if Europe retreats from Iraq it will repeat the appeasement of the 1930s.[38] Since Iraq, American bloggers and conservative websites have jumped on the EU with alacrity, accusing it of trying to coddle terrorists and dictators, and drawing comparisons with Chamberlain and Munich. Similar concerns have been voiced by a number of Europeans, including Václav Havel, who charged in 2005 that, over Cuba, the EU was 'dancing to Fidel Castro's tune', and that the common denominator of 'Europe's worst political traditions' was 'the idea that evil must be appeased'.[39]

Despite its mixed reception, European foreign policy cooperation has become habit-forming. Europe in the 1970s could do little more than either follow or rail against the American lead; today it has the means to agree common policies and to act upon them. The achievements were modest at first: the EU could never go very far by telling off Iran for its *fatwa* against Salman Rushdie or deploying election monitors in Cambodia and Zimbabwe. But the EU also coordinates its positions in the United Nations, and more often than not all the member states will vote the same way. It has also improved its institutional arrangements, replacing four foreign policy portfolios in the European Commission in 1999 with a single commissioner for external relations, and creating a new high representative for the CFSP. (The now defunct European constitution would have gone a step further by creating a European foreign minister.)

When asked what could most easily steer a government off course, British Prime Minister Harold Macmillan once famously replied, 'Events, dear boy. Events.' The unexpected can bring fundamental changes in policy, and give new insight into changes in capabilities and priorities. The September 2001 terrorist attacks in the United States were followed by the heady days of transatlantic policy agreement: the attacks themselves were universally deplored, international terrorism was defined by Americans and Europeans alike as a threat that could give them a new common cause, and there was general agreement on the need to quickly invade Afghanistan. But when the Bush administration made plans to invade Iraq and began talking about a 'war' on terrorism, the European foreign policy edifice seemed to crumple: the governments of Britain, Italy and Spain aligned themselves with US policy and those of France and Germany led the opposition. For some, European divisions were another sign of weakness, but for others they were an opportunity. All the transatlantic policy tensions that had been swept under the carpet during the cold war were now exposed to the clear light of day: never before had the differences in American and European values and priorities been more obvious.

The warning signs had long been clear in the results of European public opinion surveys. Since 1993, *Eurobarometer* polls have found about two-thirds of Europeans in favour of a common foreign policy (see Figure 5.1). By 2005, 83 per cent supported the EU having a common position in the event of an international crisis, 82 per cent supported the development of a European foreign policy independent of the United States, 69 per cent believed that the EU should have its own seat on the UN Security Council, and 67 per cent backed the idea of having a European foreign minister who could act as a voice for EU foreign policy. When asked to compare the global roles of the EU and the United States, there has been more support for the former than for the latter: on 'peace in the world' 63 per cent of Europeans favour the EU and 25 per cent the US, on protection of the environment the ratio is 62:18, on the fight against terrorism it is 60:43, and on the fight against poverty it is 49:20.[40]

In parallel, there has been growing support for the EU becoming a superpower in the mould of the United States. A 2002 survey taken in six countries found 65 per cent of respondents in favour of the EU becoming a superpower, while just 14 per cent felt that the United States should remain the sole superpower.[41] Majorities felt that becoming a superpower would help the EU 'cooperate more effectively with the United States in dealing with international problems', while only a minority saw it as a path to competing with the US. Although enthusiasm for the new role fell off when respondents were asked if they would still support the idea if it meant greater military expenditure by their governments, a majority was still in favour in most countries. Illustrating the different views of how to deal with international problems, large majorities in all the countries surveyed saw economic power as more important than military power in determining a country's overall level of influence in the world.

The public will, then, is clear: Europeans are suspicious and doubtful of American goals and values, want policy independence from the United States, and want the EU to exert itself. But two core obstacles remain to the achievement of a common and independent European foreign policy. First, there is the gulf between public and political opinion in the EU. Perhaps it comes down to the pragmatic leanings of European leaders and the idealism of European publics; the former think with their heads, and the latter with their hearts. Perhaps it comes down to a lack of confidence among leaders about surrendering the cold war tradition of deference to the United States, whose military they still believe they need for the most serious security problems. Perhaps Europeans do not really believe that Europe can go it alone, and have simply become addicted to America. Or perhaps it all comes down to a nostalgic belief that Europeans and Americans still have enough in common to allow them to continue to work together.

Figure 5.1 *Public support for a common European foreign policy, 2005*

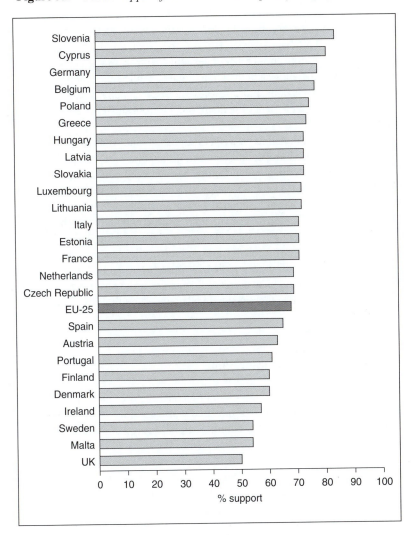

Note: Figures reflect public support for a common foreign policy among the member states of the EU.

Sources: European Commission, *Eurobarometer* 64, Autumn 2005.

Second, in contrast to the common trade policies pursued by the EU, where collective interests prevail, national interests limit the development of common EU foreign policies. Britain and France have their special interests in their former colonies, Austria, Finland, Ireland, and Sweden want to preserve their neutrality, and everyone is divided over their views on the United States and NATO: Atlanticists such as Britain, the Netherlands, Portugal, and several Eastern European member states still favour a strong NATO and a close security association with the United States, while Europeanists such as France and Germany look more toward European independence. There is more than a residual element of realism in the European approach to foreign policy.

But whatever the divisions between Europeanists and Atlanticists, between old Europe and new Europe, and between europhobes and europhiles, they have all missed one critical point: Europe has achieved political influence in spite of itself. Unlike the United States, which has sought and exercised power since 1945, the EU has accumulated power and influence without always trying. The rise of the European marketplace has combined with changes in the international system since the end of the cold war and the slowness of the United States to adapt to globalization to create a leadership vacuum into which the EU has steadily been pulled. While US foreign policy is increasingly out of step with the new needs and demands of the post-modern world, the EU is more attuned to those needs and demands, and finds itself filling the vacuum.

The decline of American leadership

The cold war is long over, but we still often hear the president of the United States described as the leader of the 'free world', a title – says Diamond – based on 'a shared vision of a common global project'.[42] But while there might have been a common project during the cold war (containing the Soviets), it is hard to find much sign of a common transatlantic project today. Yes, there is agreement on the promotion of democracy and capitalism, but there is not much agreement on the right methods to use. Yes, there is agreement that terrorism poses a critical threat, but there is not much agreement on the appropriate response, or even on the root causes. Yes, there is a common concern about nuclear proliferation, but European doves and American hawks cannot agree on how to proceed. For the Atlantic Alliance in particular, the end of the Soviet threat meant dissolution of its key *raison d'être*, and the fallout over Iraq served only to show that there is more that divides than binds the two old allies. Chomsky notes that the United States did not feel limited or bound by international law or treaty obligations during the cold war, and has since felt even less constrained.[43] Against the background of a more aggressively unilateralist US line on foreign policy, it has become easier to identify differences of opinion within the Alliance than points of agreement.

Those differences were always there. Western Europeans differed with Truman over Korea, with Eisenhower over Suez, with Kennedy over Cuba, with Johnson over Vietnam, with Nixon over Bretton Woods and the Middle East, with Carter over Afghanistan, with Reagan over almost everything, and with Clinton over the Balkans. They fretted about the qualifications of US presidents to be leaders of the Alliance; few came to office with much prior foreign policy experience, and most had to learn on the job. They also chafed against presidents governing without a long-term vision for US–European relations, and time and again making foreign policy without consulting the Europeans. Clinton was a case in point, with his decisions on Burma, Cuba, and Iran,[44] his refusal to sign the Kyoto protocol on climate change or the Ottawa Treaty on Anti-Personnel Mines, and his signature of the Helms-Burton Act on trade with Cuba. Finally, Europeans worry about an America that is parochial and introverted, and whose voters know so little about a world whose leadership has been assigned to their president.

Matters came to a head with George W. Bush, whose administration quickly fell out with the EU on most major matters of policy, and also on questions of policy style. On Iraq, argues Geoffrey Wiseman, a former diplomat, the United States transgressed five key norms of diplomatic culture: the use of force only as a last resort, transparency (obtaining information overtly and conveying views openly and frankly), continuous dialogue (engaging rather than isolating the enemy), multilateralism, and civility (an emphasis on tact).[45] And it is not only with the Europeans that the Americans now often disagree, but with much of the rest of the world. On one issue after another, it has become increasingly common to find the United States taking the minority position, and even occasionally the lone position.

Consider the example of the International Criminal Court (ICC), on which the United States has not only failed to show leadership but has also used questionable – even desperate – means to influence international political opinion. Created by a treaty signed in Rome in July 1998, the ICC is designed to prosecute those responsible for genocide, crimes against humanity, and war crimes. It found a champion in the EU: Germany was active in efforts to ensure its efficacy and independence, Britain, France and Germany became its biggest sources of funds, and every EU member state except the Czech Republic had ratified the Rome treaty by May 2005.

Following receipt of the required number of national ratifications, the Court was established in The Hague in July 2002, and issued its first arrest warrants in October 2005, aimed at Ugandan warlords.

American attitudes to the Court were quite different. Complaining that US soldiers might be subject to politically motivated or frivolous prosecutions, both Bill Clinton and George W. Bush criticized the Court, and the US has worked to undermine its provisions and its effects.[46] Along with China, it tried and failed to have the Court subordinated to the UN Security Council, where it has the power of veto. Clinton signed the treaty, but did not recommend that it be submitted to the US Senate for confirmation until American concerns were resolved. Bush rescinded the US signature, threatened to pull US personnel out of peacekeeping operations unless they were given immunity from prosecution, orchestrated a UN Security Council vote under which American troops were given a 12-month exemption to be renewed annually, and negotiated illegal 'impunity agreements' with individual governments under which they agreed not to surrender US nationals to the Court. Along the way, the US accused several EU member states of lobbying these governments not to sign the agreements with the US.[47] Finally, in August 2002, Bush signed into law the American Servicemembers Protection Act, which prohibited US cooperation with the ICC, allowed punishment of states that signed the treaty, and allowed the US to refuse to participate in peacekeeping operations unless US personnel were granted immunity from prosecution. As of early 2006, the United States still had not ratified the treaty, placing it in the company of China, Iraq, Iran, Israel, Russia, and Turkey.

With the ICC, the United States – so long a champion of human rights – has turned its back on an endeavour that has near universal support. But its political isolation does not stop there:

- While all 25 EU member states have signed and ratified the Comprehensive Nuclear Test Ban Treaty (opened for signature in September 1996), the United States is one of about 50 countries that has signed but not ratified. In the face of strong support for the treaty from the Clinton administration, the US Senate voted against ratification in 1999, meaning that the United States had – for the first time ever – rejected an arms control treaty. All five declared nuclear powers must ratify before the treaty can come into force, so the US vote was effectively a veto. The decision raised troubling questions about the example the US was setting to other countries with nuclear aspirations.

- In December 1997, the Ottawa Treaty on Anti-Personnel Mines was opened for signature, and quickly won so much support that it entered into force in March 1999. The Clinton administration refused to sign, arguing that landmines were a legitimate defensive weapon. The Bush administration followed suit, so that the United States in 2006 was one of about 40 countries – including Burma, China, Cuba, India, Iran, North Korea, Pakistan and Russia – that had still not ratified. All EU member states had signed and ratified except Finland and Poland.

- As of early 2006, Somalia and the United States were the only countries not yet to have ratified the Convention on the Rights of the Child, which was agreed by the UN General Assembly in 1989 and became the most rapidly and widely ratified human rights treaty in history. The US has signalled its intent to ratify, but claims that it needs time to examine the content of the treaty in more depth, and argues that it has a habit of considering only one human rights treaty at a time, so the convention must take its place in line. But this is a cover for conservative American criticism of the link between entitlements and economic, social and cultural rights.

'Only US leadership', claims Richard Haass, 'has the potential to be forceful and generous enough to persuade the other major powers to come together and build a more integrated world that can take on challenges to the common peace and prosperity'.[48] But a state cannot lead while it is acting unilaterally, or following a different path from those it claims to lead. Leadership demands inclusion, confidence building and a sense of common purpose, but the United States has become so isolated on so broad a range of issues that we now find it described as a 'rogue state',[49] and out of touch with world public opinion, which Patrick Tyler calls 'the second superpower'.[50] Pei notes the role of American nationalism in explaining both the way the United States acts and the way that it is perceived. He believes that America is a nationalistic society in spite of the fact that Americans swear off nationalism, and that the United States has a poor record of understanding the importance and effect of nationalism in other countries. This paradox helps explain why US foreign policy can sometimes appear hypocritical to others: this is especially true when the US appears to be trying to undermine global institutions or rejecting multilateral agreements in the interests of defending American sovereignty, and there is a tension between the universalistic appeals of American political ideals and its pursuit of parochial national interests.[51] (See Chapter 6 for more discussion.)

In September 2000, *The Economist* blithely argued that there was no need for Europe to try and provide a counterbalance to the US, because 'America shows no sign of abusing its power, and is unlikely to'.[52] But within less than three years, all had changed. The invasion of Iraq was widely seen as an abuse of power, and US leadership was in trouble. Henry Kissinger argues that 'American power is a fact of life, but the art of diplomacy is to translate power into consensus.'[53] The ability of the United States to promote a consensus has declined since the end of the cold war, and particularly since the invasion of Iraq and the launch of the 'war on terrorism'. Of course, there are countless examples of the US, the EU and other liberal democracies being in step on critical issues, but the rise of European power has drawn new attention to American exceptionalism. If the sense of inclusion, confidence, and common purpose in American global leadership is on a downward trajectory, the same cannot be said of Europe. In one area in particular, the power of Europe has become all but irresistible.

The lure of Europe

Promoting democracy has been the core organizing principle of US foreign policy since the end of the cold war. During the 1992 election campaign, Bill Clinton argued that the United States should 'lead a global alliance for democracy as united and steadfast as the global alliance that defeated communism'.[54] This view was reflected in his support for the Yeltsin administration, for Eastern European states prepared to pursue democratic political change, and for peace in Northern Ireland and the Balkans. At the heart of the rationale put forward by the Bush administration for the invasion of Iraq – at least, once weapons of mass destruction were not found – has been the need to set Iraq up as a democratic example for the rest of the Middle East. But the idea of bringing about democratic change by force is rife with contradictions, and not very effective to boot.

Generally, US foreign policy has followed Bertrand Russell's dictum that power is 'the production of intended effects', and has relied on its conscious and deliberate qualities. But – as noted in Chapter 1 – there is a difference between possessing power and exercising that power, or between latent and manifest power. Actor A may be able to purposefully encourage actor B to take action, but actor B may also be encouraged by virtue of the promise of potential rewards arising out of cooperation with actor A, or by the threat of exclusion from access to those rewards arising from non-cooperation.[55] Where the US model of power tends to focus on threats and observable power, the European model tends to focus on promise and possibility. And if we look at the lure of Europe – through enlargement, through the economic opportunities it offers, and through its magnetic attraction to immigrants and asylum seekers – we are quickly left with one irresistible conclusion: the European Union has become the most effective force in the world for the promotion of democracy and capitalism.

Peace, security, and economic cooperation were the original core goals of European integration, and the record on achieving these goals has been impressive. Cooperation in the 1940s and early 1950s helped allay fears that post-war Western Europe might be dragged into extremism by its political, economic and social difficulties, and the steps that led to the creation in 1958 of the European Economic Community paved the way for the triangular link between integration, democracy and capitalism to be set in stone: most of Europe today is peaceful, stable and wealthy. From that core, integration has proved an irresistible lure to countries right across the region, with membership of the EU being the icing on the cake for the select few. Ever since a sceptical Britain changed its mind about the potential of the EEC and made its first attempts to join, being left out has ceased to be an option for almost any country that meets the basic qualifications. For Rosecrance, the EU seems to have acquired a 'manifest destiny' to expand its membership,[56] just as the US felt the urge in the nineteenth century to move its boundaries westwards. But Europe's near neighbours also seem to have a clear desire to become part of the club. What is going on here?

First, membership of Europe is good for democracy, as was shown only too clearly in the cases of Greece (which joined in 1981), and of Spain and Portugal (which joined in 1986). They had all only recently shaken off authoritarian regimes, and membership of the Community not only helped them establish their new democratic credentials, but also gave them access to the meeting rooms of the big international organizations, strengthening their membership of the international community. They had already, it must be said, been brought into NATO (Portugal was a founder member, Greece joined in 1952, and Spain in 1982), but the practical changes that came out of Community membership were more immediate and telling: the terms of membership obliged them to open up their markets, reform their bureaucracies, and bring their laws and policies into line with those of other member states.

Second, the growth of Europe has helped redefine Europe's relations with the rest of the world. When Britain joined in 1973, the Community was handed an association with the Commonwealth, and found itself having to redefine its entire relationship with the Third World. When Greece, Spain and Portugal joined in the 1980s, ties to Latin America and the rest of the Mediterranean were strengthened, and then expansion to Austria, Sweden and Finland in 1995 helped shift the EU's geographic priorities eastward.[57] The most fundamental change of all came with the 2004 eastward enlargement, which obliged the Western European members of the club to broaden both their perspectives on the world and their definition of the idea of Europe. Academics have long quibbled about whether they should study

Europe or the European Union; today, we are rapidly approaching the point where there is no difference.

Then there are the economic benefits. The reconstruction of the six founding members was underpinned by the opportunities provided by access to a larger market, and even non-members felt the effects of being so close to that market. When Britain and Ireland joined in January 1973 and brought down the overall per capita GDP of the Community, new attention was drawn to the imbalance created by regional economic differences,[58] prompting the decision to create a European Regional Development Fund aimed at helping rebuild economically depressed parts of Europe. This was followed by a European Social Fund aimed at promoting employment and worker mobility, and – later – by a Cohesion Fund designed to help the poorest parts of the Community offset the costs of improved environmental regulation and investment in transport projects. These so-called structural funds have since become the second biggest item on the EU budget, channeling more than €30 billion ($36 billion) annually into closing the gap between the richer and the poorer parts of the EU. But their significance pales by comparison to the benefits offered by access to the European marketplace.

Portugal saw quick returns on its membership of the Community: its economy grew by 4.5 per cent annually in the period 1986–90, inflation fell from 22 per cent in 1985 to 12 per cent in 1991, and unemployment fell over the same period from 8.7 per cent to 4.6 per cent. It was helped by an upturn in the global economy and a fall in the price of oil, but Community membership was a critical part of the equation.[59] By contrast, the effects of failing to adapt to the single market were illustrated by the case of Greece, whose outdated economic structures could not cope with the new competition posed by Community membership. Its per capita GNP fell from 58 per cent of the Community average in 1980 to 52 per cent in 1992,[60] and even today it continues to suffer from a large government stake in major utilities, from red-tape that discourages the creation of new businesses, and from stiff job protection that handicaps women and younger workers.[61]

The most obvious example of the transformative possibilities of a combination of EU membership and sensible domestic policies can be found in Ireland. When it joined in 1973, Ireland was one of the poorest countries in Western Europe, with a per capita GDP that was only 53 per cent that of West Germany and only 58 per cent that of Britain. But by the 1990s it was enjoying double-digit annual economic growth, record low unemployment, booming exports, reduced rates of income, corporate and capital gains tax, and a flood of foreign investment, much of it headed for the high technology and financial sectors.[62] For decades (even as late as the 1980s), Irish workers had left home to seek jobs and opportunities in Britain and the United

States; by the 1990s, many were returning to Ireland, which was also attracting immigrants from other countries. Growth has lately tailed off, but by 2004 the Celtic Tiger had the ninth most productive economy in the world, with a per capita gross national income greater than that of any other EU member state except Luxembourg, Denmark, and Sweden.[63]

The EU cannot claim all the credit for Ireland's economic achievements, to be sure. Its growth did not begin until a good dozen years after it joined the Community, and some credit must be given to the general upturn that came to most capitalist economies during the 1990s. Doubts have also been cast on the part played in Ireland's renaissance by the EU's structural funds; if they were so important, why have other poorer EU states that have received even larger shares of the structural funds not had the same kind of success as Ireland?[64] What the case of Ireland shows is that the effect of sensible economic policies can be magnified by the opportunities offered by membership of the EU, a point that has important implications for its newest Eastern members.

The relaunch of the single market programme coincided with the end of the cold war, which meant that the gravitational pull of Europe was accelerating just as a cluster of prospective new members arrived on the scene. As Austria, Finland and Sweden prepared to join the EU in the mid-1990s, Europe Agreements were signed with several Eastern European countries in order to prepare them for eventual EU membership, and the EU's Agenda 2000 programme listed the measures that needed to be agreed in order to clear the way for eastward expansion. Negotiations opened in the period 1998–2000 with 12 countries, and ten of them joined in May 2004 (the exceptions being Bulgaria and Romania, which needed longer to prepare). Eastward enlargement expanded the EU economy by just 5 per cent, but the population of the EU grew by 20 per cent: with more than 450 million consumers, today's EU is by far the biggest capitalist marketplace in the world, with the potential for massive new economic growth in the East.

Opinion has been divided on the significance of eastward enlargement. While some have praised it for its speed and consistency, others have charged that it has been chaotic, that it has owed more to external pressures than to internal initiatives, that the triumph of democracy over dictatorship happened with almost no help from the Community, and that the changes helped the Community more than the Community helped Eastern Europe.[65] Even today, there are deep divisions over the implications of enlargement. While one school talks of enlargement fatigue, and warns of the economic costs of integrating poorer member states, the difficulty of reforming the EU decisionmaking system in order to keep up, and the impact of the redirection of structural fund investments from the West to the East, another school emphasizes the actual or potential benefits:[66]

- Because aspirant members must be stable democracies with a respect for human rights, the rule of law, and the protection of minorities,[67] enlargement supports democratic change by encouraging the democratization of institutions, processes, and political culture. By being bound more closely into the political structure of the West, security and stability are enhanced in the East.
- Because aspirant members must have a functioning free market, enlargement supports economic liberalization by opening markets in goods and services, stimulating economic growth and offering new trading opportunities. Market and regulatory pressures will also lead to an improvement in environmental standards. The combination of Western capital together with low labour costs and a largely untapped consumer market in the East is bound to be a winner.
- Because aspirant members must agree to adopt the common rules and policies of the EU, enlargement strengthens their institutions and their legal systems, and promotes cross-border cooperation on problems such as crime, drugs, and illegal immigration.

Whatever the debates about the wisdom of enlargement, it is happening regardless, and will continue to happen because the benefits outweigh the costs. The EU will become bigger, and its political and economic footprint will expand ever further beyond its borders. Leonard writes of a 'Eurosphere' that brings in 109 countries and two billion people. Including the EU, the former Soviet republics, the western Balkans, and virtually all of the Middle East and Africa, this is – he argues – a 'zone of influence which is gradually being transformed by the European project and adopting European ways of doing things'. For these countries, the EU is the largest trading partner, and the largest source of international bank credit, foreign direct investment, and overseas development assistance.[68] But while there is no denying the impact that the EU has had on political and economic developments further afield, its short- to medium-term impact is greatest closest to home. There are two bands of influence where the gravitational pull of Europe is particularly clear, and where the promise of access to Europe has brought the greatest pressures for democratic and free market change (see Map 5.1).

The first band covers neighbouring countries that qualify for membership of the EU: 18 in all, containing nearly 215 million people. Three of these (Iceland, Norway, and Switzerland) could join with few adjustments,

Map 5.1 *Bands of European influence*

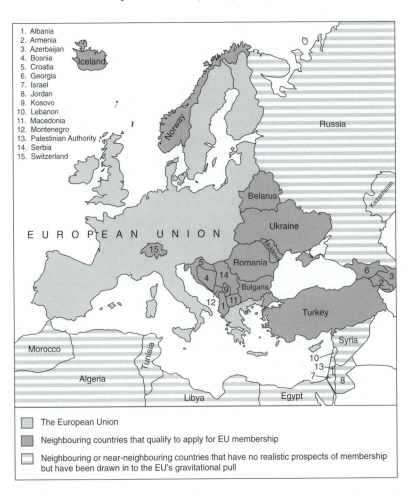

1. Albania
2. Armenia
3. Azerbaijan
4. Bosnia
5. Croatia
6. Georgia
7. Israel
8. Jordan
9. Kosovo
10. Lebanon
11. Macedonia
12. Montenegro
13. Palestinian Authority
14. Serbia
15. Switzerland

☐ The European Union

■ Neighbouring countries that qualify to apply for EU membership

☐ Neighbouring or near-neighbouring countries that have no realistic prospects of membership but have been drawn in to the EU's gravitational pull

because even as non-members they already find their laws and policies irresistibly impacted by the EU. Bulgaria and Romania will be the next to join, to be followed by Croatia and Macedonia, which are now officially candidate countries. Negotiations have also opened with Turkey, but it is not expected to join until 2015 or later. The other Balkan states – Albania, Bosnia and Herzegovina, Kosovo, Macedonia, Montenegro and Serbia – are considered no more than potential candidate countries for now, with too many outstanding problems and handicaps. Meanwhile, agreements have been signed with Armenia, Azerbaijan, Georgia, Moldova, and the Ukraine, encouraging trade liberalization and economic cooperation. Belarus may have eliminated itself from short-term consideration because of its authoritarianism, but the message that Europe sends is clear: mend your ways, and we will give you access to the same opportunities enjoyed by your more democratic neighbours.

The second band of influence consists of neighbours or near-neighbours of the EU that have no realistic prospects of membership but have been drawn in to the gravitational political and economic pull of their massive neighbour: there are 13 in all, containing about 350 million people. Since 1995, nine of these governments (Algeria, Egypt, Israel, Jordan, Lebanon, Morocco, the Palestinian Authority, Syria, and Tunisia) have – along with Turkey – been part of the Euro-Mediterranean Partnership aimed at promoting peace and cooperation in the Mediterranean basin. Under agreements signed with the EU, non-EU members agree to respect human rights and democracy and capitalism in return for preferential access to the European marketplace and the prospect of improved political, security, social, and cultural links. The EU does not have diplomatic relations with Libya, but the chances of improved ties have increased in recent years thanks to changes in the policies of the Gaddafi government. Partnership and cooperation agreements have also been arranged with Kazakhstan and Kyrgystan.

Meanwhile, the EU in 2003–04 launched a European Neighbourhood Policy designed to extend peace, stability and prosperity to neighbouring states, and to 'create a ring of friends' around the borders of the EU. More financial assistance is promised, along with more cross-border cooperation, increased trade, and better cooperation on a host of policies, including energy, the environment, transport, and research and development. Whatever critics may say about the balance between fluff and substance in EU initiatives, the effect of the Neighbourhood Policy will be to further deepen the political and economic influence of the EU on its neighbours. And the policy has not just regional implications, argues Aliboni, but also global geopolitical implications, impacting relations between the EU and the Arab world, Russia, and the United States.[69]

A third and more distant band of influence can be found in the EU's relationship with developing countries. Since the early 1970s, the EU has run an Africa Caribbean Pacific (ACP) programme under which preferential trade agreements, insurance funds, and investment tools are made available to 78 countries. Thanks in part to this programme the EU has become by far the biggest supplier of overseas development assistance (ODA) in the world: in 2003, the EU-15 supplied more than \$37 billion (€31 billion) in aid, or nearly 54 per cent of the world total. This far exceeded the figures for the

Figure 5.2 *Overseas development assistance, 2003*

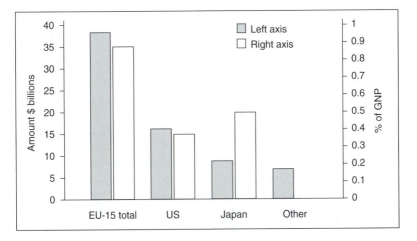

Source: UN Development Programme website (2005), www.undp.org.

United States ($16.3 billion) or Japan ($8.9 billion) (see Figure 5.2). And given that about one-third of US ODA over the last decade has gone to Israel, and about one-fifth to Egypt, the economic and political impact of the EU programme has been amplified. The EU is also generous in relative terms; it may not come close to the target of 0.7 per cent of GNP set by the UN General Assembly in 1970, but at 0.35 per cent of GNP it is still significantly above the figures for the United States (0.15 per cent) or Japan (0.20 per cent). And individual EU member states have surpassed the UN target: these include Denmark (0.84 per cent), Luxembourg (0.81 per cent), the Netherlands (0.80 per cent), and Sweden (0.79 per cent).

Attempts to explain the relatively low figures for the United States will sometimes point to the tradition of American philanthropy, suggesting that where the US falls short on official aid, it makes up through private giving. But the gap is not closed by much. The most recent figures (ranging from 1995 to 2003) suggest that there is just short of $16 billion in private giving annually from the 22 members of the OECD's Development Assistance Committee, compared to the more than $69 billion that was given in ODA in 2003.[70] The US is by far the biggest source, accounting for 68 per cent of that private giving, compared to the 19 per cent given by the EU-15. But an estimated 40 per cent of US giving goes to just one country – Israel – and even combining ODA and private philanthropy, the US (at nearly $27 billion) is still short of the EU (at more than $40 billion).

Of course, this may all be moot given questions about the quality of the EU's programme of ODA. For Babarinde, the EU's development programme is not only unsurpassed but has become 'the standard against which the rest of the world measures itself and is judged'.[71] The EU has also earned a more positive political image on development issues than the United States, where the Bush administration in particular has been criticized for its tough bargaining positions and its threats to blacklist WTO members with which it disagrees. But Arts and Dickson argue that EU development policy is more symbolic than exemplary: in the 1970s it was a model, making substantive and innovative attempts to contribute to North–South dialogue; today it is no more than a symbolic gesture policy that follows global trends.[72] Oxfam has accused the EU of double standards and of 'magisterial hypocrisy' by forcing developing countries to open up their markets on behalf of big business while maintaining barriers to their exports, by dumping highly subsidized agricultural surpluses with which small farmers are unable to compete, and by expanding the WTO agenda on trade liberalization in such a fashion as to benefit the EU and its corporations. But it makes similar charges against the United States, pointing to its farm subsidies and to the steel tariffs imposed by the Bush administration.[73]

Beyond all the agreements and the policies and the government aid, people are also reacting to the lure of Europe with their feet. Recent surveys have found that the United States has been losing its pre-eminent status as the land of opportunity, helped by the growing attraction of Britain (especially among Poles and Spaniards), Germany (among Turks and Russians) and France (among Lebanese).[74] The data on asylum seekers provide an important clue: in 2003, the EU-15 received just over 300,000 asylum applications, or about five times as many as the United States, and in 2005 the EU-25 received more than 70 per cent of all asylum applications to industrialized countries, compared to 22 per cent for North America.[75] The differences are a function of variations in policies (the relative ease with which asylum seekers can gain entry into different countries, and tightened restrictions in the US since 9/11) and of geographical proximity to the world's biggest sources of applications (the EU is closer to Serbia, Russia, Turkey, Iraq, and Iran than the United States), but they are also a reflection of the increased opportunities offered by Europe.

As the EU was busy expanding in 2003–04, strengthening economic ties with most of its neighbours, and bringing peaceful and gradual change to the lives of nearly 650 million people in 40 countries,[76] it was difficult not to notice the contrast with the coincidental attempts being made by the US-led coalition to bring democracy by force to 25 million Iraqis. It was also difficult to ignore the contrasting histories of the relationship between the EU and its 'near abroad' and of relations between the United States and its closest Southern neighbours. Latin America has never been able to evade the reality of American power in the Western hemisphere; hence the frustration reflected in the famous comment by nineteenth-century Mexican leader Porfirio Diaz: 'Poor Mexico; so far from God and so close to the United States.' Central America in particular has suffered, in the words of Arthur Schlesinger, 'a long and squalid history of US exploitation and intervention combined with neglect'.[77]

Under the Monroe Doctrine, the US during the nineteenth century defined Latin America as its exclusive sphere of influence. But it was more interested in its relations with other parts of the world, and a Latin American policy that was formally driven by concerns about security evolved into one of territorial expansion and of periodic military intervention. The Monroe Doctrine became intermingled with the concept of 'manifest destiny' (the belief that Americans should extend the 'boundaries of freedom' through continental expansion). Americans, argue Coerver and Hall, 'believed that they had developed a new and better society and that God had singled them out to spread the benefits of republicanism and economic opportunity to undeveloped or more backward areas', and thus US expansionism enjoyed a 'divine sanction'.[78] This theme can be found in the attitude of superiority that Schoultz feels the United States has shown toward its southern neighbours for more than two centuries. US policy in the region has been based on serving US interests, underlying which are 'a pervasive belief that Latin Americans constitute an inferior branch of the human species', motivated first by 'unreasonable radicalism', then by authoritarianism, and more recently by corruption. He likens the US attitude to Britain's idea of the White Man's Burden, or France's *mission civilisatrice*.[79]

One result of this lofty approach has been a tradition of resistance to American influence south of the Rio Grande, the level of defiance rising during the cold war when the US intervened regularly by outlawing suspect forces, supporting friendly governments, and overthrowing regimes it saw as dangerous.[80] The roll-call includes support for dictators (Trujillo in the Dominican Republic, Somoza in Nicaragua, and Batista in Cuba), attempts to topple unfriendly regimes (Allende in Chile, Castro in Cuba, or the Sandinistas in Nicaragua), and military interventions of sometimes dubious merit (in the Dominican Republic, Guatemala, Grenada, Haiti, and Panama).[81] The US has used a variety of methods to encourage democracy in Latin America, ranging from quiet diplomacy to intimidation, invasion, and occupation. But Lowenthal argues that none has ever succeeded in bringing enduring change except in those countries where local conditions were favourable, and the ebb and flow of American enthusiasm for the promotion of democracy has actually undermined the conditions for democracy.[82] Latin America's unequal relationship with its powerful neighbour encouraged it to pursue multiple strategies aimed at countering US influence, including cooperation among its governments, a search for external support, the use of international law, solidarity with other Third World nations, and a quest for social revolution.[83]

The key point here is that while Eastern Europe has been attracted by the promise it finds in European integration, and other neighbouring states have been attracted by the lure of access to the European marketplace, Latin America has long felt threatened by the United States, and so has been resistant to its influences. Reminders of Western hemisphere tensions were provided in November 2005 when George W. Bush visited several Latin American countries, and polls revealed that he was more unpopular there than anywhere outside the Arab world. Opposition to the war in Iraq had combined with criticism of American unilateralism, differences over economic policy, and a shift to the left in almost every country in the region to widen the gap, and large majorities of Argentineans, Brazilians, Chileans and Mexicans held negative views of the United States.[84] 'At a time when the Bush administration needs partners and allies across the globe', concludes Peter Hakim, 'the United States and its international agenda are discredited in Latin America'.[85]

The political influence of the European Union has been felt most obviously in the opportunities provided by economic development, and in the kind of democratic stability that typically accompanies the opening of the capitalist marketplace. But there is one further indication of its global political influence: the EU has become a model for regional economic integration all over the world.[86] If imitation is the sincerest form of flattery, it is also a telling consequence of latent power. When other Asian states in the 1960s began following the lead of Japan in restructuring their economies, it meant that Japan was exerting power by example. When other European states in the 1980s began following the lead of Margaret Thatcher in privatizing state-owned industries, it meant that Britain was also exerting power by example. Just as the success of the Canadian–American free trade area made the North American Free Trade Agreement (NAFTA) possible, so – argues Rosecrance – the success of the EU and NAFTA strengthen the prospects for a transatlantic free trade area.[87]

Directly or indirectly, the experience of the EU – warts and all – has driven the development of free trade arrangements on virtually every continent, the newcomers learning from its successes and its failures. At last count, there were 18 active regional integration organizations on all five continents (see Table 5.1). Among those is NAFTA, which includes the United States, Canada and Mexico. While the triggers for NAFTA were

Table 5.1   *Regional integration associations*

Name	Founded	Members
European Union	1952	25
Council of Arab Economic Unity	1957	13
Central American Common Market	1960	5
Association of Southeast Asian Nations (ASEAN)	1967	10
Andean Group	1969	5
Caribbean Community and Common Market	1973	14
Economic Community of West African States (ECOWAS)	1975	16
Latin American Integration Association	1980	11
Economic Community of Central African States	1983	10
South Asian Association for Regional Cooperation	1985	7
Arab Cooperation Council	1989	4
Arab Maghreb Union	1989	5
Asia Pacific Economic Cooperation (APEC)	1989	21
Southern Cone Common Market (Mercosur)	1991	4
Southern African Development Community	1992	14
North American Free Trade Agreement (NAFTA)	1994	3
East African Community (functioned 1967–78)	1999	3
African Union (AU)	2001	53

different from those for the EU, and its goals have been far less ambitious,[88] the EU was a motivating force in its development,[89] and the lessons for North Americans of the EU experience have not gone unnoticed. NAFTA was in turn to be a stimulant for other exercises in integration in the Americas; it may not have been the ignition switch, says Pastor, but it did 'put wind in their sails'.[90] Meanwhile, the African version – one of the newest – has gone so far as to name itself the African Union, to pursue the same general goals as the EU (including the promotion of peace, economic and political integration, and the coordination and harmonization of policies) and to set up an almost identical set of institutions: a Commission, a Court of Justice, a Pan-African Parliament, an Assembly (based on the European Council), and an Executive Council (based on the Council of Ministers). It may have enormous hurdles to cross, but the point is that it found in the EU a model worth emulating.[91]

6

Competing in the Market for Ideas

In the old cold war bipolar order, the conflict between the US and the Soviet Union revolved around two competing political and economic models: the American version emphasized democracy and capitalism, while the Soviet version emphasized state socialism and central planning. There was a related social rivalry as well, pitting American self-reliance and personal freedoms against the state-reliance and personal restrictions imposed by the Soviet model. But on the cultural front there was no contest: the Soviets had nothing that could match the global impact of Coca-Cola, blue jeans, Marlboro, Marilyn Monroe, or McDonald's. Buoyed by its cultural hegemony, the US was able to expand its economic and political influence even across the iron curtain.

In the new bipolar system, there are still two competing models, but the distinctions between them are of a different order: Europeans and Americans agree on the broad principles of democracy and capitalism, but differ on the best means of promoting the former, and have different ideas about the goals of the latter. And the new bipolarity is also distinctive for the heightened role played by competing social and cultural values, amplified by globalization and changes in technology. Never before in history, argues Rothkopf, has almost every individual at every level of society been able to sense the impact of international change. Globalization may have economic roots and political consequences, he argues, 'but it has also brought into focus the power of culture in this global environment – the power to bind and to divide in a time when the tensions between integration and separation tug at every issue that is relevant to international relations'.[1] And while he concludes that winning the battle of the world's information flows has become critical for the United States, it has become critical as well for the Europeans.

Social and cultural values have achieved a new prominence in the international debate because Europeans and Americans – loosened from the restrictive military ties of the cold war era, witnessing unprecedented levels of economic competition, and more openly and regularly reminded of how they differ on political priorities – have had more time and opportunity to explore those values, and along the way have become more conscious of their differences. While the EU pursues a liberal social agenda, the United States has a more conservative hue. While Europe leans towards the secular, religion sits at the heart of American public and political life. While Europeans build their welfarist social model, Americans argue the merits of individual responsibility and opportunity. While most Europeans believe that government is responsible for the provision of core public services, most Americans have a preference for the private sector. While post-material Europeans are conscious of the environmental impact of consumption, Americans are conspicuous and unapologetic consumers. While the EU pursues a post-modern agenda of globalization, science, peace, internationalism, social spending, and sustainable development, the American agenda is more nationalist, more insular, more independent, and more focused on what is best for America.

In the era of Huntington's clash of civilizations,[2] social and cultural factors stand as illustrations of the importance of soft power and of the unintended consequences of actions. The core goal of economic activity may be to sell products and services and to make profits, but it also leads to social influence. So while the main job of carbonated sweetened water is to quench thirst, when it is packaged in the distinctive aluminium cans of Coca-Cola or Pepsi-Cola it becomes an instantly recognizable icon of American capitalism, and indeed of the entire American way of life. So potent are Coke and Pepsi as global icons, indeed, that in response to concerns about American influence in the Middle East, several competing home-grown brands have been launched to offer consumers an alternative. First came Zam Zam Cola, introduced in Iran after the 1979 revolution; more recently have come Qibla Cola and Mecca Cola, targeted at Muslims concerned about (primarily) US policy in the Middle East.

Just as consumer brands have become central to the expression of influence, so the brand image of states has become central to notions of power. It is the 'X-factor' in international relations, or the unknown variable: we know much less about it than we think we know about military and economic power, but while we may not always be able to explain or measure its facets, we know it when we see it. And we can also be sure that where the United States continues to have a strong brand image, the European Union does not. Western culture may be synonymous with the great icons of European science, philosophy, art, music and letters, but they are still associated with individual states or with 'Europe' rather than with the European Union as a global actor. And while almost everyone who has access to the mass media is familiar with American cultural icons and even with the key events and personalities of American history and politics, the same cannot always be said about their European equivalents; George Washington is far better known than Jean Monnet. The promotion of a sense of a common European culture tends to be top down – witness EU programmes on cultural exchanges for example – rather than flowing naturally out of the habits and preferences of Europeans themselves. On the cultural front, at least, the United States is still a global hegemon.

But the balance is changing. Starbucks, Tommy Hilfiger, Disney, Xerox, Microsoft and Ford may figure prominently in the global popular consciousness, but so – for many years – have Philips, Siemens, BASF, Adidas, Mercedes, Renault and Fiat, and they have been joined more recently by trade names such as Allianz, Benetton, Ericsson, HSBC, Nokia, and Vodafone. Europeans are more willing to express their differences with the US on everything from abortion to capital punishment and gun control. As military power loses its validity in the eyes of many, so cold war bipolarity has been replaced with a post-modern bipolarity where Americans and Europeans compete in the international market not just for commodities and services but also for ideas. Military power still enters the equation as a tool by which political change might be wrought – or security threats headed off – in third countries. But today's international system is increasingly driven by values, which generate competing interpretations of the most pressing problems, and generate different recipes for dealing with those problems. It is a new variation on the old idea of the race to win hearts and minds. In the market for ideas, the two new superpowers are competing as much for philosophical and moral influence as they are for political advantage and economic profit.

Contrasting views of Europe and America

Great power inevitably generates strong opinions, if only because it cannot be ignored. Oscar Wilde once quipped that there is only one thing worse than being talked about, and that is not being talked about. The debate about those who wield great power is confirmation that they matter, that they are changing lives, and that they are forcing others to make choices. In their time, the Spanish, the Portuguese, the British, the Germans and the French all provoked strong feelings among those with whom they dealt, the balance between criticism and praise evolving with time and circumstances. Cold war superpowers generated a more voluble debate because they exerted much greater power and influence, and impacted the lives of so many more people. No surprise, then, that the debate about the global role of the United

States should have intensified since the end of the cold war: its power has been so much more visible and has a wider reach. No surprise, also, that anti-Americanism should have become more strident.

Exactly what is anti-Americanism? It has a long history, especially in Europe[3] and most particularly in France,[4] but despite its new prominence in popular debate, and despite the publishing boom it has generated (particularly since Iraq[5]), it remains difficult to define or to isolate, and it has more diverse origins than the label (and the suffix *-ism*) suggests. Generally speaking, anti-Americanism is hostility towards the foreign policy actions of the United States and towards some of the values and principles for which the United States appears to stand. What generates this hostility? The knee-jerk explanation preferred by many ordinary Americans, and even by some of their leaders, is that the criticism is driven by envy. Al-Qaeda hates us – George W. Bush often says – for our freedoms and democracy.[6] (But if true, then why does it not equally hate European states, or Canada, or Japan, for their freedoms and democracy?) Larry Diamond sees anti-Americanism partly as 'the inevitable resentment of US power' and partly as a result of 'envy at our wealth, success, and cultural dynamism'.[7] (But again, why no comparable dislike of Europe, Canada, or Japan?) For historian Paul Johnson, anti-Americanism is 'the prevailing disease of intellectuals today', and is a function of democracy-envy, and – in Europe – of 'cultural racism'.[8] Even a cursory review of American blog sites reveals repeated associations between the terms 'anti-Americanism' and 'envy'.

Others offer more nuanced explanations:

- Pei argues that it is in part a backlash against the nationalism that he feels is so much a part of US foreign policy. He describes the United States as 'one of the most nationalist countries in the world', and concludes that it is based not on notions of ethnic superiority but on a belief in the ideals of American democracy.[9]
- For Revel, anti-Americanism is often anti-capitalism in disguise.[10]
- For Chalmers Johnson it is a problem of blowback: the inevitable and predictable result of a US abandonment of a reliance on diplomacy, economic aid, and multilateralism in favour of military force and financial manipulation.[11]
- The Rubins identify two themes: the vision of the United States as a bad society that threatens to become a model for the world, and concerns about an America that seeks global conquest.[12]
- Sardar and Davies offer some 'obvious' explanations (such as US support for authoritarian regimes), and some less obvious reasons: the US has structured the global economy to enrich itself, the US is the

essential nation without which nothing can be resolved, the US is hypo-critical because it does not practice what it preaches, and the US gets to define right and wrong.[13]

- For Harold Pinter it is simply about American power: 'the crimes of the United States have been systematic, constant, vicious, [and] remorseless ... It has exercised a quite clinical manipulation of power worldwide, while masquerading as a force for universal good.'[14]
- For many Muslims, it is the seemingly uncritical support that the US provides to Israel, and the presence of US troops in Saudi Arabia.
- For many in non-Western societies, it is driven by fears of American cultural imperialism, and by the corrupting influence of American values, which threaten to undermine and displace traditional values.

The Economist sums it all up when it notes that while anti-Americanism 'spans the globe, the phenomenon is not everywhere the same. It mutates according to local conditions, and it is seldom straightforward.'[15] Whatever its sources, and whatever the dangers arising out of painting all Americans with the same brush, the extent of today's hostility towards the United States and/or US policy is without historical precedent. To be fair, the US has many advocates and supporters (particularly in Eastern Europe and India), but their numbers have slipped of late, and at no time has any one state been the target of such strongly critical opinions held by so many people. In a 2005 Pew Global Attitudes Survey, only 55 per cent of Britons had a favourable opinion of the US, along with 52 per cent of Russians, 43 per cent of the French, 42 per cent of Chinese, 41 per cent of Germans, 38 per cent of Indonesians, and 23 per cent of Turks and Pakistanis.[16] Anti-Americanism is found among sophisticated and educated elites as well as among the poor and illiterate. It is found on the political left as well as the political right. It is found in advanced industrialized societies as well as in states on the margins of viability. It is found among America's allies as well as among America's enemies. And it is fed and watered even by Americans themselves, who have been among the most ardent critics of US policy and are eagerly quoted by foreigners seeking more ammunition; Saul Bellow describes anti-Americanism as one of America's 'principal exports'.[17]

Because of the lack of survey data over an extended period, it is hard to know how attitudes towards the United States have changed over the long term, and how they compare with the Vietnam era when criticism of US policy was at an early peak. We know from Pew Global Attitudes data that positive opinion declined significantly in many countries between 1999 and 2005,[18] leading many to ask whether current levels of anti-Americanism are driven by the policies of the Bush administration, without question the most internationally disliked of all post-war US administrations, or if they will still be there when Bush leaves office. Pew Global Attitudes surveys suggest the latter. In assessing the results of recent polls, Andrew Kohut concludes that while Bush has been a lightning-rod for anti-American feelings, resentment is fuelled by American power and policies and by a widely held belief that the United States 'does too little to solve world problems and backs policies that increase the yawning global gap between rich and poor'.[19] But perhaps there is a simpler explanation: resentment stems from the growing social and philosophical differences between Americans and much of the rest of the world. In other words, it is the inevitable consequence of exceptionalism.

In contrast to what we know (or think we know) about anti-Americanism, critical perceptions of Europe are less common, less well understood, and have no equivalent history or equivalent body of analysis upon which to draw.[20] Where anti-Europeanism has arisen in recent years it has been mainly in the United States and as a reaction to French and German policy on Iraq.[21] There has also been criticism from the Muslim world, directed at those EU states that supported and participated in the invasion of Iraq, and there have been the occasional outbursts of short-term hostility, such as the outcry in February 2006 over the publication – first in Danish newspapers and then elsewhere – of cartoons depicting the prophet Muhammad, and considered offensive by many Muslims. Europe has also been generating its own domestic reaction from Muslims; Leiken argues that European states have appeared unable to regulate the entry of immigrants, and European society has seemed unwilling to integrate them.[22] The xenophobic and racist backlash has fed into the radicalization of Muslims, who are increasingly resentful of what Europe represents.

Otherwise, most anti-Europeanism is home-grown, and is directed not at EU foreign policy, nor at what the EU has come to represent as a global actor, but rather at what the EU means for Europe itself. Anti-Europeans (or eurosceptics or eurorealists as they are otherwise known) are alarmed by the threats they believe that integration poses to national sovereignty. They warn against the dangers of a centralized European superstate, the reduction in the powers of national legislatures, the threats posed to democracy by integration, and the implications of replacing national policies with common European policies. They argue that the EU does not advance free trade but has instead imposed a protectionist customs union on Europe, and that integration has meant increased state intervention and regulation over the free market, a move towards federal 'union by stealth', and the bureaucratization of Europe. Booker and North argue that the loss of democracy and power of states to govern themselves will leave behind a 'wasteland'.[23] Redwood believes that the creation of a United States of Europe will not likely make the world a safer or better place, but will more likely lead to a trial of strength between a 'democratic free trade' America and a 'bureaucratic and regulated' Europe.[24] The debate over Europe has no equivalent in the United States – there are few Americans who question the very existence of the United States, or feel that its presence has been bad for the 50 states.

There are several possible reasons for the relative lack of anti-Europeanism. Europe's global influence is less visible, and so there is less for potential critics to be concerned about. (In this respect, the importance of latent power is even more obvious.) Europe benefits from the reflected glow of the fires of anti-Americanism; with so much vitriol directed at US policy in recent years, Europe cannot help but come out looking better. Europe is not seen as threatening. While doubts have grown about American foreign policy motives, its reliance on military options, and the impact of American culture, Europe's motives are rarely questioned, it does not have a large military, and there is little evidence that Europe is a cultural powerhouse. Petiteville writes about the EU's advantages in the field of soft diplomacy (the use of 'economic, financial, legal and institutional means to export values, norms and rules and achieve long-term cultural influence'), notes that it has been used to good effect by Canada and the Scandinavian countries, but believes that it has added value in the EU because its weight in the world is now comparable to that of the United States.[25]

We must also appreciate that the EU in its present form has not been a significant mass on the international political or social radar for very long: perhaps no more than 10–15 years. There are still many who think of Europe as its individual states rather than as the European Union, and have not yet developed strong ideas about what Europe represents. They may have opinions about what Britain or France or Germany or Scandinavia represent, but the outlines of the EU are still fuzzy. In countless speeches, communiqués, government documents and critical analyses, US foreign policy is outlined and picked over in minute detail by governments, the media and public opinion. Foreigners are even polled during the US presidential election season on whom they would vote for if they could. By contrast, the EU's claims to a global role are widely doubted (where they are considered at all), and thus the values and positions for which it stands are less easily identified.

But perhaps the most fundamental explanation for the differences in the perceptions of Europe and America derives from the way the two superpowers see themselves. Let us begin with the United States. There is no question that Americans hold themselves and their country in high regard. Most Americans are probably not familiar with the term 'American exceptionalism', and yet they often think in exceptionalist terms, believing that the US is blessed, and is a beacon and an example for others. Most would also refuse to call themselves nationalists, and yet they live in a society that has projected a strong sense of national identity, bound together with symbols, values, heroes, and myths. Americans not only take pride in their national values but also see them as universally applicable. US Secretary of State Madeleine Albright suggested in 1998 that 'We are an indispensable nation. We stand tall. We see further into the future.'[26] Rothkopf speaks for many when he argues that 'Americans should not deny the fact that of all the nations in the history of the world, theirs is the most just, the most tolerant, the most willing to constantly reassess and improve itself, and the best model for the future.'[27] When a recent poll presented the statement 'Our people are not perfect, but our culture is superior to others,' 60 per cent of Americans agreed, but only 40 per cent of Germans, 37 per cent of Britons, and 33 per cent of the French.[28]

Americans may reject the label *nationalist* to describe themselves,[29] but most are only too ready to admit to being patriots.[30] A 2004 Harris poll found that about 84 per cent of Americans claimed to be 'very proud' to be American, while just 57 per cent of Spaniards expressed pride in their country, and 46 per cent of Italians, 43 per cent of Britons, and 33 per cent of the French. In Germany, only 23 per cent of the population can stir itself into feeling a sense of national pride.[31] The World Values Survey has found similar comparative results (see Figure 6.1). And if the polls are not proof

Figure 6.1   *Comparative national pride, 1999–2000*

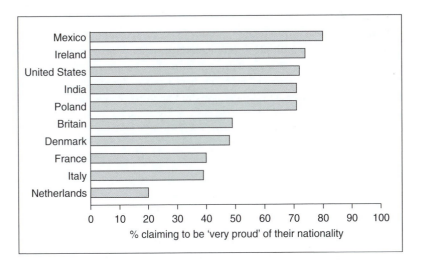

Source: World Values Survey, Institute for Social Research, University of Michigan.

enough, we need only look for confirmation at the visible symbols and routines of patriotism in the United States: the Pledge of Allegiance in schools, the performance of the national anthem at sporting events, the patriotic bumper stickers on American cars and trucks, the manner in which politicians pepper their speeches with phrases such as 'this is the greatest country in the world', and the chauvinistic behaviour of American fans and athletes at international sporting events. And in which other democratic society is flag-burning a hot-button public issue, or are leaflets published outlining the correct manner in which to handle and maintain the national flag?

If patriotism in Europe is more muted, then nationalism is widely rejected, mainly because of its negative associations with war and colonialism. This is not to suggest that it has disappeared altogether from the public scene – far from it. One of the great ironies of European integration is that while states build stronger economic and political ties among themselves, minorities within those states have taken the opportunity to agitate for a greater say over their own affairs. This led to the break-up of Czechoslovakia and Yugoslavia, the rise of Scottish and Welsh nationalism, and a strengthening of the separate identities of Basques, Catalans, Corsicans, and others. It also helps explain the quasi-nationalist backlash in Europe against non-white immigration, whose opponents often argue that white Christian culture is under threat from new arrivals from North Africa and the Middle East. But in spite of such developments, there is little broader sense among Europeans of the superior virtues of Europe, nor much of a sense of mission regarding the rest of the world.

Europeans also equivocate about the very concept of 'Europe'. Americans may have multiple different identities according to their heritage, and they may identify strongly with state or region, but the melting-pot has worked in the sense that most Americans have heeded Theodore Roosevelt's warning that 'a hyphenated American is not an American at all', and that they should identify strongly with America. By contrast, most Europeans still identify with their home countries first, and have mixed feelings about Europe:

- While 91 per cent of Europeans feel attached to their country, only 66 percent feel an attachment to the European Union.
- Support for membership of the European Union since 1995 has hovered between 46 and 56 per cent (although only 12–17 per cent feel that their country's membership of the EU has been altogether bad). Only 42–50 per cent feel that the image of the EU is positive, while 13–21 per cent feel that it is negative.

- Only 20 per cent of Europeans feel that the EU economy is doing better than the US economy, while 39 per cent feel that it is doing worse. At the same time, 46 per cent of Europeans feel that their quality of life is better than it is in the United States, while 32 per cent feel that it is worse.
- Strong majorities of Europeans feel that the EU is performing better than the United States on the protection of the environment, the provision of healthcare, and on fighting social disparities and discrimination, while small majorities feel it is performing better on education and unemployment. But strong majorities feel that the US is performing better on new technology, scientific and medical research, and the creation of companies.[32]

The results of polls like these often reflect perceptions rather than realities. A good example is offered by the EU's economic aspirations. In March 2000, EU leaders agreed the Lisbon Agenda, aimed at making the EU – within ten years – 'the most competitive and dynamic knowledge-based economy in the world, capable of sustainable economic growth with more and better jobs and greater social cohesion'. While the polls find most Europeans are optimistic that there will be improvements over the next few years on the economic, environmental, unemployment, and welfare fronts, and in the quality of their lives, only 35 per cent believe that the EU will become the world's leading economy by 2010, while 52 per cent believe it will not.[33] And yet while we can quibble about the meaning of 'competitive' and 'dynamic', the EU is already the world's biggest economy and its biggest trading power. This suggests that many Europeans do not yet fully understand the significance of the experiment of which they are a part. This is not surprising when polls find that only a minority of Europeans understand how the EU actually works (see Chapter 7). Nor when so much of the analysis of Europe is so focused on its problems rather than its achievements.

To summarize, then, we have a United States that has a strong sense of itself and a strong pride in what it represents, but we also have growing levels of anti-Americanism around the world. At the same time, we have a European Union that has a weaker sense of itself and more modesty regarding what it stands for, and we find less evidence of anti-Europeanism, except among Europeans themselves. Ironically, it is the very strength and certainty of American views about themselves that helps generate such strong critical feelings from others, and it is the equivocal views that Europeans have about themselves that makes them seem less threatening and less doctrinaire, and makes the values with which they are associated easier and more attractive for others to assimilate. Americans are more forthright and visible in promoting and defending their values, which is part of the reason why they will not reject the use of force in international relations (and perhaps also why gun control is so lax in the United States, and capital punishment still practised). Europeans have instead employed an 'invisible hand' of influence. Europe, says Leonard, 'has been able to extend itself into the lives of Europeans largely unchallenged by seeping into the existing structure of national life ... [Europeanization] has gone on largely behind the scenes'.[34] Much the same could be said about Europe's global reach – it is happening, but it is less obvious.

The culture wars

It is generally taken as axiomatic that American culture dominates the world, a view that is supported by multiple indicators: American films account for one-third of global box office takings, American brand names permeate the world of modern consumerism, in the world of popular music it is the American singers and bands that still steal most of the headlines, and perhaps – as Schlosser suggests – the golden arches of McDonald's have become 'more widely recognized than the Christian cross'.[35] Its cultural reach has been further extended by its technological leadership: 90 per cent of personal computers are driven by the Windows operating system, the Internet was developed in the United States, most Internet communication is run through American servers, the culture of the Internet is still predominantly American, the big names of the Internet world – from Amazon to Yahoo, Google and eBay – are all American (even if they often have local versions), and the United States symbolically refuses to give up control over ICANN (the Internet Corporation for Assigned Names and Numbers). The cultural power of the US is even seen by some in the spread of English, whether through popular media such as films, television, and books, or through consumer demand for American products, or through the role of the United States in promoting the rise of English as the language of business and technology.

America's international cultural footprint, it must be said, attracts some unfortunate hyperbole; thus Rothkopf's suggestion that 'American music, American movies, American television, and American software are so dominant, so sought after, and so visible that they are now available literally everywhere on Earth.'[36] The rural and urban poor of China, India, Latin America and sub-Saharan Africa might be puzzled by such an assertion, and there are some cultural sectors in which the American presence is almost invisible. Take, for example, the world of sport, which is central to culture.

The American brands have failed to infiltrate most markets, leaving baseball, basketball and American football as no more than minority sports in a world dominated by football, and where even the rugby and cricket world cups have picked up a widespread following; the former had a worldwide television audience in 2003 of 3.4 billion, while the International Cricket Council has 96 member states.

Most of those with access to American culture are willing consumers. But just as there has been increased resistance to American military power and political influence, so there has been increased resistance to American cultural influence, or to what the critics have dubbed 'cultural imperialism'. Microsoft may have been the driving force behind the spread of computer technology, but it has also been accused of bullying and uncompetitive behaviour, and of abusing its dominant market position. McDonald's may be present in almost every country in the world, but hamburgers are a long way from insinuating themselves into the national diets of those countries. And while CNN may have been the pioneering force behind the development of 24-hour television news, there have been multiple attempts to counter its international presence with home-grown local products, ranging from Britain's BBC World and Sky News to Europe's Euronews, Spain's TVE Canal 24 Horas, India's NDTV, Dubai's al-Arabiya, and Qatar-based al-Jazeera.

'Local content' has become the rallying cry of communities all over the world concerned about the inroads of American culture and technology, and particularly of American-dominated mass media. Whether the issue is one of giving rural populations in Asia and Africa more access to the Internet, and to websites in their own languages, or whether it is one of resisting the influx of American programming into local television, the signs are all there. On the broadcasting front, the EU has been particularly effective at responding, agreeing in 1989 its Television Without Frontiers directive, updated in 1997. This included a call for television stations – where practicable – to reserve at least half their broadcast time for films and programmes made within Europe. The target was quickly met and surpassed: about two-thirds of programming in the EU is today locally produced, and the days of *Dallas* and *Dynasty,* when popular American television dramas were required viewing in many European countries, are long gone. The Europeans also make more movies than the United States, and might be able to take on Hollywood in the competition for box office income were it not for two problems: the language barrier, and market fragmentation. US films do as well as they do thanks mainly to their massive home market – North America accounts for about 45 per cent of global box office takings.

And it should not be forgotten that culture moves in both directions along a two-way street. European (mainly British) television exports have done well in the United States, whether in the form of local translations (European shows being used as the model for American copies) or local versions (mainly of quiz shows and reality shows) or of redubbed versions (notably in the case of European children's shows that are popular in the US). Similarly, the Spanish-language TV channel Univision has recently developed a strong following among Americans in the 18–34 year-old age bracket; although based in the United States, the majority of its programming is made in Mexico. And although Hollywood dominates the global film industry, many of the biggest hits of recent years have come out of British culture: witness the success of the Harry Potter series and *The Lord of the Rings* trilogy, which, in 2006, accounted for six of the ten top-grossing films of all time.

For the European Union, the promotion of a European culture has been a priority. The steps taken have run the gamut from the potentially substantial to the superficially symbolic. There are programmes to select an annual European City of Culture, to promote knowledge of European history and to encourage artistic and literary creations, to improve the competitiveness of the audiovisual sector, to help with the production of European films and television shows, to encourage language training, to preserve minority languages, and to facilitate educational exchanges. All play their own modest role, but a common culture cannot be legislated or generated by grants and scholarships – it has to come out of a sense among people that they have a common background and a common set of interests and values. Nothing will more effectively generate a sense of European identity than the increased personal mobility of Europeans. As they travel in greater numbers across Europe's internal borders, and as they live and work in other EU member states, so the significance of their historical, linguistic and social differences will decline, and there will emerge a greater sense of a pan-European cultural unity.

That cultural identity does not yet even begin to match that of the United States, and it lacks the icons and traditions and commercial advantages that underpin American cultural hegemony. But then the EU has a history dating back barely two generations, and has only really entered the broader European consciousness since the late 1980s, and the broader global consciousness since the late 1990s. The European flag is widely visible and more widely recognized, and the euro is developing a presence as a symbol of Europe, but the Europeans still have a long road to travel. Inevitably though, as European power in the world becomes more visible, and as Europeans become more clear about what makes them distinctive from Americans, the brand image of Europe will become more clear and more influential.

Religion and politics

One of the most visible social distinctions between the EU and United States lies in the relationship between religion and politics. While Europe tends towards the secular, the United States is a more overtly religious society, and the effects of the differences are felt in social values, education, public discourse, and politics. These competing influences impact not just the way that Europeans and Americans think about themselves, but the manner in which the two actors project themselves globally. While Europe – except perhaps in its troubled relationship with Islam – pursues a secular relationship with the rest of the world, US foreign policy – particularly during the Reagan and Bush years – has been influenced by Christian values.

Most Europeans admit to basic beliefs in God and identification with organized religion, but church attendance has dropped (and is declining rapidly even in societies where religion is more important, such as Ireland, Italy and Spain), adherence to church teachings has declined, and the church rarely tries to exercise much political influence.[37] Europe has become, argues George Weigel, a 'post-Christian' society, and the differences between Europe and America over religion help explain their policy tensions.[38] What has happened, argues Crouch, is that modernization has brought secularization, consistent with nineteenth-century rationalist arguments about the incompatibility of religion and science.[39] There is some debate as to whether Europeans are better described – like the British – as 'believing without belonging'[40] (it is not belief in God that is challenged, but rather participation in organized religion), or – like the Swedes – as 'belonging without believing'[41] (many Europeans claim affiliation to religions and take part in religious ceremonies such as christenings, weddings, and funerals, but little more).

Religion influences the politics of particular issues in Europe, such as non-Christian immigration, education (witness the 2004 French law banning the wearing of religious symbols in schools) and globalization, and in selected cases remains a potential source of political mobilization, but otherwise Western Europe has the highest level of secularization in the world, with religious beliefs pushed into the private sphere and towards the margins of political and social life.[42] Symbolically, attempts were made in 2003–04 to include a statement in the draft EU constitution describing the European Union as a Christian union. Supporters argued that Christianity had been a dominant influence on European civilization, and that the Judeo-Christian heritage was a core value of the EU; this won support among Catholic Europeans, including those in aspirant member states such as Poland, but among few others. Opponents argued that Europe was not about religion, and that giving undue prominence to religion was potentially divisive, that it would offend non-Christians and those without faith, and that it might even prohibit the admission of non-Christian states such as Turkey.[43] In the event, the statement was deleted.

In the United States, conservative commentator Pat Buchanan claims that a 'European-style' de-Christianization is the goal of many American liberals, and that they are succeeding.[44] The indications are found in court decisions banning prayer in schools and removing displays of the Ten Commandments from public buildings, and in attempts to remove the words 'under God' from the Pledge of Allegiance. But the worries of Buchanan and others fly in the face of the evidence: church attendance in the United States is booming, many Americans allow their religious beliefs to influence both their personal behaviour and their political choices, and despite long-held claims of the importance of the separation of church and state, there are many who argue that the two are so intertwined that the United States has developed a 'civil religion', or a religion of democracy.

The clues can be found in the way many Americans interpret national history in religious terms, in the way God's will is evoked to justify public policy, in the way presidents assert the divine purpose of the United States and routinely end speeches with an appeal for God to bless America, and in the way that the United States is often described as a nation favoured by God.[45] 'Fundamentalism' and 'the religious right' are part of the routine daily discourse of politics, conservative Christians have played an important role in politics (most notably in the 2004 presidential election), prominent Christians such as Jerry Falwell, Pat Robertson and Ralph Reed have enjoyed strong political profiles, there is an unspoken requirement that candidates for high office should at least go through the motions of declaring their faith, presidents are expected to be moral leaders and to be seen to have links with religious groups and to participate in religious ceremonies, and there is a strong link between religion and policy on a wide variety of issues. Polls even find that more Americans would vote for an openly homosexual candidate for the presidency than would vote for an openly atheist candidate.

There is little transatlantic difference in the numbers of people who claim to belong to a religious denomination (91 per cent in North America, 88 per cent in Western Europe, and 84 per cent in Eastern Europe), but more North Americans attend religious services once per week or more (47 per cent, compared to 20 per cent of Western Europeans and 14 per cent of Eastern Europeans), God is considered important in the lives of many more North Americans (83 per cent, compared to 49 per cent of Western and Eastern Europeans), and many more North Americans believe there is a personal

God (62 per cent, compared to 42 per cent in Eastern Europe and 35 per cent in Western Europe).[46] While 70 per cent of Americans claim to believe in God, just 22–24 per cent of Germans, Britons, and the French make the same claim, and while nearly two-thirds of Americans hold that religion is important in their lives, less than one in five Germans, Britons, Spaniards or of the French feel the same way.[47] When asked if it is necessary to believe in God in order 'to be moral and have good values', 58 per cent of Americans agree, compared to 38 per cent of Poles, 33 per cent of Germans, 30 per cent of Canadians, 27 per cent of Italians, 25 per cent of Britons, and 13 per cent of the French.[48]

Only on the question of the relationship between church and state is there closer agreement between Europeans and Americans: when asked if religion is a matter of personal faith that should be kept separate from government policy, 90–94 per cent of Britons, Poles, the French, Germans, Italians and Canadians agree, compared to 80 per cent of Americans.[49] History tells us of the clear distinction drawn by the American founders between church and state, and Americans point with some pride to the tradition in their country of religious freedom, noting that many Europeans fled to the United States in order to be able to pursue their religion free of state interference and proscription. But while they may talk of freedom of religion, many still allow religion to spill over into social and educational choices, and to impinge upon the rights and choices of those who do not share their views.

Hutton notes that while Europeans understand that religion cannot obstruct science, Americans generally take a different view.[50] Nowhere has this been more clear than in the debate over evolution and creationism (the belief that humans, the Earth and the universe were created by a Supreme Being or deity, literally as described in the Bible). Americans live in the most technologically advanced society on earth, and yet many seem to be resolutely turning their back on modern science when it comes to explaining the origins of the Earth and mankind. In 1996 the Catholic Church itself acknowledged that evolution explained the origins and development of the human race, but a solid majority of Americans disagree. In a 2004 opinion survey, 82 per cent claimed to believe in some form of creationism (either God created humans in their present form, or God guided the process), and only 13 per cent believed that humans evolved from less advanced life without the guidance of God. There was little difference of opinion between Democrats and Republicans: 51 per cent and 66 per cent, respectively, supported the creationist view.[51]

In Europe by contrast, according to an albeit less reliable Internet poll conducted under the UN 'Planet Project' in 2000, only 18 per cent of respondents believed that God created humans, while 82 per cent believed that humans descended from other species. When plans were announced by the Vardy Foundation in Britain in 2003 to open six schools that would teach creationism alongside evolution, the philosophy was dismissed by Richard Dawkins of Oxford University as 'educational debauchery' and 'utter nonsense'.[52] In September 2004 the Serbian education minister caused outrage – and was forced to resign – when she announced that evolution would no longer be taught in schools, in a country where religion had only recently begun to be taught.

While there is little or no discussion about creationism either in public or in the education system in Europe, in the United States there has been a vigorous debate about the legal status of evolution and creationism in public education, with various attempts dating back nearly a century to prohibit the teaching of evolution (reaching a peak in the famous Scopes Monkey Trial of 1925), and more recent attempts to have evolution represented as a theory rather than a fact. The debate has spawned the 'intelligent design' movement, which argues that life is too intricate to have evolved without help from an 'intelligent designer', whose identity is left an open question. George W. Bush believes that evolution and creationism should be taught alongside each other, with American children allowed to make their own choices regarding which they believe. The majority of Americans agree with him: according to a July 2005 poll, nearly two-thirds of Americans felt creationism should be taught alongside evolution in public (state) schools, while 38 per cent favoured replacing evolution with creationism.[53]

The links between religion and politics spill over into international relations. While Europe pursues essentially secular foreign policies, and there is little evidence of religious values or principles impacting its policy choices, the foreign policies of the United States have been impacted by religion.[54] This is nothing new, and Judis points out that religious concepts and themes have coloured the pronouncements and policies of American leaders dating back to colonial times; he also notes that 'America's difficult moments have come when it has allowed religious conceptions to colour its understanding of the real world.'[55] In 1998, Congress passed the International Religious Freedom Act, making freedom of religion and conscience a 'core objective' of US foreign policy. Religion played into foreign policy when the Bush administration attacked international family planning initiatives, and in 2002 cut funding to the UN Population Fund on the grounds that it supported forced abortions and sterilization in China, and in March 2006 when Secretary of State Condoleezza Rice (in response to Afghan plans to execute a Muslim who had converted to Christianity) said, 'There is no more fundamental issue for the United States than freedom of religion and religious conscience. This country was founded on that basis, and it is at the heart of democracy.'[56] It is hard to imagine a European leader making the same kind of argument.

More famously, religion has been a factor in US foreign policy towards Israel; while support for Israel must be seen in the context of the impact of the large and highly effective pro-Israeli lobby in the United States,[57] the total restoration of Israel is considered by many American evangelicals to be a prerequisite for the Second Coming. A link has even been made between religion and American cultural imperialism, the argument being that American missionaries and religious groups have – often with the support of the US government – been agents for the spread of American political, economic, and social values.[58]

It is important not to make too many generalizations about the relative roles of religion in the two superpowers. There are many Americans who claim to have no religious affiliation, just as there are many Europeans who are committed members of one religious group or another. American religious leaders have been among the most vocal critics of the war in Iraq, while a number of European religious leaders have equivocated. And the precise impact of religion on politics in the United States is still widely debated,[59] particularly given America's famous support for the gap between church and state, and its lack of a state religion or established church. But while no discussion of American politics is ever really complete without reference to the role of religion, it rarely factors in to discussions about the political and social identity of Europe.

Most importantly, a secular Europe has distinct strategic advantages over a Christian America in the international arena. In a world where there are many religions, and where fundamentalism has become a critical factor in the politics of many societies, the association between religion and political power inevitably works against the United States, while its secularism works in favour of Europe. Where the United States is distrusted and widely perceived as a threat because of its military power, it is also distrusted and widely perceived as a threat because its political objectives are not seen to be free of religious sub-text. As for secular Europe, even when it sends doubtful messages regarding its attitude towards Muslims living within its borders, there is minimal association between its political power and its religious affiliation. If America is overtly Christian, Europe is – at most – neutral on religion.

Contrasting social models

Differences over religion are just one of the most visible of the distinctions between European and American society and culture. They help explain a host of additional differences – for example, over abortion, homosexuality, euthanasia and censorship – but they must take their place alongside a variety of additional qualities that distinguish the two superpowers and that illustrate the social boundaries of the new bipolar system. Pre-eminent among them are the contrasting views on the role of the state. Europe's emphasis on the provision of education, healthcare, and a host of other free or subsidized services stands in contrast to the American focus on the promotion of individual welfare. The logic of capitalism permeates society on both sides of Atlantic, but while Americans are more focused on the accumulation of wealth, Europeans are more ready to criticize capitalism as the primary source of many social ills, whether it is the gap between the rich and the poor, racial and sexual discrimination, environmental problems, or the decline of the family.

When asked in a 2003 poll to choose between the freedom to pursue one's goals without state interference and the power of the state to guarantee that nobody is in need, just over half of Americans opted for personal freedom, compared to about one-third of Germans, the French, Britons and Poles, and less than one-quarter of Italians and Russians. While two-thirds of Europeans felt that the state should play an active role in society so as to guarantee that no-one was in need, only one-third of Americans felt the same way.[60] When asked if it was the responsibility of the state to take care of very poor people who could not help themselves, only 73 per cent of Americans agreed, compared to 87–95 per cent of Britons, Russians, Poles, Germans, Italians, and the French.[61] And when it comes to succeeding in life, only one-third of Americans believe that it is determined by forces outside their control, compared to half of Britons and the French, and two-thirds of Italians and Germans.[62]

An example of the distinctiveness of the European and American social models is offered by attitudes towards capital punishment. The United States is far from being the only country that allows and uses capital punishment: more than 110 other countries allow for the death penalty for at least some offences, although many have scrapped it in practice. However, the US is unique among liberal democracies because the death penalty is outlawed in all 25 EU member states, as well as in Australia, Canada, New Zealand, Norway, and Switzerland, and it has been abolished in practice in Russia. European opposition was strong enough to merit the inclusion of a specific ban on capital punishment in the 2003 draft EU constitution, and the EU has made the abolition of the death penalty a condition of membership; thus Turkey in 2004 had to amend its constitution to abolish the death penalty. Belarus is now the only European country that still recognizes the death penalty.

The United States not only continues to allow the death penalty, which can be used for those who break federal law, and for capital crimes in 38 of the 50 states, but it is also one of the very few countries that allows the execution of juveniles. It is one of only two countries in the world (along with Somalia) that has failed to ratify the UN Convention on the Rights of the Child, which forbids capital punishment for juveniles, and is one of only seven countries in the world that is known to have executed juveniles since 1990 (the others are the Congo, Iran, Nigeria, Pakistan, Saudi Arabia, and Yemen). Although the number of American juveniles receiving the death penalty is falling, the US has still executed more juveniles than any other country in recent history – a total of 17 since 1990.[63] Polls suggest that while about two-thirds of Americans support the death penalty, less than one-third support it for juveniles. But this has not been enough to generate much domestic debate about juvenile capital punishment, except when the media make an issue out of the trial of juveniles in capital cases.

Another example of transatlantic social differences can be found in atti-tudes towards homosexuality, the greater tolerance of Europeans contrasting with the more conservative views of most Americans. When asked in a 2003 poll if homosexuality was a way of life that should be accepted by society, more than three-quarters of Germans, the French, Britons, and Italians agreed, but barely half of Americans.[64] In Europe, same-sex marriages have been allowed in the Netherlands since 2001, in Belgium since 2003, and in Spain since 2005, while Britain, Denmark, Finland, France, Germany, Portugal, and Sweden all authorize same-sex civil unions or partnerships. But in the United States the issue has been deeply controversial.[65] Although about half of Americans support the creation of a separate but equal legal status for same-sex couples[66] – typically in the form of a civil union or laws protecting domestic partnerships – only Massachusetts currently recognizes same-sex marriages, while six states have given same-sex partners some kind of legal protection. Meanwhile, 16 states have passed constitutional amendments against same-sex marriage, and 27 states have adopted statutes defining a marriage as a union between two people of the opposite sex.

The list of contrasting social values goes on:

- Abortion is legal on both sides of the Atlantic, but while it has blended into the social landscape in most European countries, it still generates controversy in the US, where the prospects of limiting access to abortion or even of making it illegal continue to bubble under the surface.
- Alcohol is freely available in shops, pubs and clubs across the EU with few restrictions on time, and yet there are still restrictions in the United States, including the widespread ban on alcohol sales on Sundays and a

minimum drinking age of 21 (compared to 18 in most European countries), and the United States remains one of the few Western industrialized countries ever to have agreed a national prohibition on its sale (from 1920 until 1933).

- Guns are more freely available in the United States, and indeed are seen by many as a core element of American culture. Access, claims the gun lobby, is even guaranteed by the Constitution.
- Television programming in the EU is subject to less stringent censorship than is the case in the United States, where strong language and sexual situations on most television channels (except on premium cable or satellite) are either dubbed over or cut.

Europeans and Americans agree on the pursuit and promotion of democracy and capitalism, but when they disagree so much on social values it becomes more difficult to see how they can agree on political objectives. The way in which they relate to other states and societies, the issues that they regard as most challenging, the manner in which they are perceived by themselves and by others, and the solutions they propose to the most pressing international problems – all will be impacted by their contrasting perceptions of norms and priorities. Europe has a strategic advantage in that its values are those that we are more likely to find in the kind of post-modern societies that liberal democracies become. For its part, American exceptionalism may be preventing the United States from becoming the model that many hope it could be; its unique set of social values is acting as an encumbrance to its attempts to lead, and it is surrendering the moral advantage to the Europeans.

Taking the lead on the environment

The EU has recently developed a reputation as a leader on the environmental front, but herein lies an irony. Europe was the birthplace of the industrial revolution and was generally slow to pick up on early pressures to clean up the environment and better manage natural resources. It was the Americans who introduced the idea of national parks, and many of the philosophical concepts and practical solutions behind environmentalism were introduced by Americans such as George Perkins Marsh, John Muir, and Gifford Pinchot.[67] The United States was later at the forefront of legal and institutional responses to environmental problems: it began passing national clean air and clean water legislation in the 1950s and 1960s, created the federal Environmental Protection Agency in 1970, and was years ahead of the Europeans in introducing lead-free fuel. But the Reagan administration did its best to gut national environmental initiatives, the Bush administration has been famously unsupportive of attempts to deal with climate change and America's looming energy problems, and whatever their advances on the regulatory front, and in spite of how much they have championed green lifestyles, Americans as a whole have ultimately failed to change their habits in such a way as to make much positive difference.

It is not that Americans are less sympathetic than Europeans to the need for effective environmental management. When asked in 2003 if people should be willing to pay higher prices in order to protect the environment, more Americans (70 per cent) agreed than Europeans (53–60 per cent in the Big Four countries), and the statement 'Protecting the environment should be given priority even if it causes slower economic growth and some loss of jobs' had 69 per cent support in the US, slightly more than in France (66 per cent), and not much less than in Italy, Britain and Germany (78–82 per cent).[68] But when Europeans talk about paying more or about managing economic growth in order to protect the environment, they are doing so from the perspective of people living in small, crowded and expensive countries where public transport is a way of life for many, and resource consumption is already relatively low. For Americans, whose resource demands are substantial, who are more aggressive consumers, and where public transport is the choice of the minority, making sacrifices is of an altogether different order.

At the heart of transatlantic differences is the concept of sustainable development. Usually defined as development that 'meets the needs of the present without compromising the ability of future generations to meet their own needs',[69] sustainable development has been one of the core principles of EU environmental policy since the 1986 Single European Act.[70] Debates continue about just how much difference it has made in practice – there is much talk in Brussels, but less evidence of real change in policy. But with or without policy change, Western Europeans in particular have altered their consumption habits to fit with the goals of sustainable development. They are conscious of the limitations on natural resources, and of the links between cause and effect, and they are less demanding consumers. Some of the results are reflected in the data: Europeans produce about half as many emissions of greenhouse gases as Americans, they generate about two-thirds as much waste, and they consume less than one-third as much water and about half as much energy (see Figure 6.2).

On the issue of climate change in particular, the Europeans have been leaders and the Americans have been laggards. In 1992, the Framework Convention on Climate Change was agreed with the goal of reducing the

Figure 6.2   *Comparative environmental records*

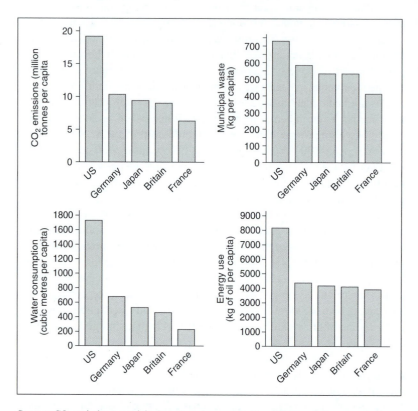

Sources: CO_2 emissions, municipal waste, water consumption: OECD website, www.oecd.org; figures are for 2003 or latest year available. Energy use figures: World Bank website, www.worldbank.org; figures are for 2000.

carbon dioxide emissions implicated in climate change (otherwise known as global warming or the greenhouse effect).[71] It was signed by 175 countries, but the United States (source of about 25 per cent of global CO_2 emissions), and the EU (source of about 13 per cent of emissions) played a key role in designing the convention and in running the negotiations that followed. The convention involved a commitment only to voluntary reductions in emissions, and it was clear by the 1990s that emissions were rising. In 1997, in an attempt to agree a protocol containing specific reductions in emissions of CO_2 and other greenhouse gases by 2008–12, signatories to the convention met in Kyoto, Japan. The EU favoured a 15 per cent reduction by 2010 (on

1990 levels), but the Clinton administration was prepared to accept only a return to 1990 levels by 2010, and objected to the fact that China and India were to be exempted. The final agreement compromised by allowing different reductions for different countries, including 8 per cent for the EU and 7 per cent for the US.[72] This limited political agreement was significant, but the reductions agreed were too small to stabilize atmospheric concentrations of greenhouse gases.

Climate change is symbolic of a broader set of approaches that have made European environmental initiatives distinctive. The United States has lost its position as a leader and an initiator. Where once it was commonly joked that California made the first move, the rest of the US followed later, and the Europeans tagged along last, the roles have been reversed. Thanks in part to the pressures of the single market, Europe has become a leader on the development of new understandings of the mechanics of cross-border environmental problems, and on the development of creative new responses to those problems.[73] Europe has taken on a new leadership role in promoting global environmental sustainability, and has been increasingly at odds with the United States along the way.[74] In this particular segment of the market for ideas, it is clear that the balance of power has changed.

The Europeans and the Americans disagreed again at a meeting of parties to the convention in The Hague in 2000, this time over implementation. The US wanted more credit for agricultural land and forests that act as a 'sink' for CO_2, but the EU felt that this was an opt-out that would divert the US away from developing emission reduction technology and changing its energy consumption habits. Then in 2001 the Bush administration dropped a bomb by announcing its opposition to the Kyoto protocol, citing concerns about potential damage to the US economy, and the lack of obligations on China and India. The EU was furious at this development, as much for the decision as for the abrupt and unilateral manner in which it was announced. Several EU states felt that the EU should go ahead and apply Kyoto without the United States, and that if abandoned it would waste years of careful negotiation and consensus building. The Bush administration held rigidly to its position, even in the face of polls showing that a majority of Americans believe that climate change is a problem, and that the US should have ratified and abided by Kyoto.

7

The Meaning of Europe

It is never easy to place a precise date on the end of one era and the beginning of another, unless it is conveniently indicated by some landmark event: a war, a decisive battle, or the death of a powerful leader. There is no agreement, for example, on when the cold war began. The end of World War II is taken as the usual point of reference, but was it the end of the war in Europe in May 1945, the end of the war in the Far East in August 1945, the breaking of the Berlin Crisis in March 1948, or some point in between? Equally, it is not easy to mark the precise end of the cold war. For convenience, it is usually dated from the dissolution of the Soviet Union at midnight on 31 December 1991, but it probably ended earlier, perhaps when the Berlin Wall came down in 1989, or perhaps when Gorbachev had begun to lose control of the USSR and the ideological conflict with the West petered out.

It is just as difficult to agree when the new post-cold war unipolar system was born, finally and clearly establishing the United States as the world's last remaining superpower. Was it as the Soviet Union began to implode, was it when the Soviet Union was formally dissolved, or was it later? The 1990–91 Gulf war might be seen as confirmation that the global role of the USSR had fundamentally changed, because it was neither willing nor able to exert its old-style opposition to Western military action. But perhaps the confirmation of American hegemony was nothing to do with the Soviets; perhaps it was more a function of American leadership in the Gulf, or perhaps it came when the European Community failed to assert itself in the Balkans. All we can say with any certainty is that somewhere between the late 1980s and the early 1990s there was an elemental shift in the global balance of power, such that by the mid-1990s only the United States had that all-important combination of military, economic, political and cultural power that elevated it in the minds of most to being a global actor without parallel.

We have seen how some analysts have argued that the unipolar 'moment' segued quickly and painlessly into a unipolar 'era'. They have seen little sign of any other power rising to challenge the dominating global role of the United States, and they continue to see American power streaming on beyond the distant horizon. China and India may one day be able to challenge that power, they conclude, and we may one day have a multipolar system, but not any time soon. We have seen how conventional definitions of power support this view. But we have also seen how a new understanding of the qualities of power can paint a different picture, in which globalization and interdependence change the nature of the game, heightening the importance of multilateralism and the use of soft power. Some time in the last decade, according to this line of argument, there has been a diminution of America's unipolar authority, encouraged by the rise of Europe, and allowing the European superpower to step into the breach, thereby creating a new bipolar international order.

The implications of American power are generally well understood, if only because we have lived with it for so long. We might not always be able to itemize or agree upon the details, but most of us would feel instinctively that we know what the US represents, if for no other reason than that American power *matters*. For its supporters, the United States stands for democracy, capitalism, and security in a troubled world; for its detractors, it stands for militarism and cultural imperialism. For its supporters, the United States is the most dynamic, creative and open of all contemporary societies; for its detractors, it is worryingly exceptionalist, is socially and politically divided, and does not always live up to its possibilities as the world's largest national economy. For its supporters, the United States has been a champion of the universal ideals for which all those who yearn for liberty continue to strive; for its detractors, it is a rogue state that insists – with declining success – upon interpreting the world according to its own values and agenda, and upon pursuing policies that all too often leave it isolated.

By contrast, the European model of power is not only more difficult to pin down, but its significance is widely doubted. The majority view is that Europe is a cluster of sovereign states with separate national identities. Few Europeans understand how the European Union works, or have thought through its implications, or could say how European interests differ from national interests, or could identify many of the distinctive features and values of the European project. Nationalism may have been on the decline since World War II, encouraged by the removal of cross-border limits on the movement of people, money, goods and services, and by Europe's attempts to build a sense of a shared history, a common culture, and a European 'citizenship'.[1] But Europe is still typically seen as no more than the sum of its parts, and is compromised by widespread and often badly informed euroscepticism. For its supporters, it stands for democracy, capitalism and peace; for its detractors it is elitist, bureaucratic, and undemocratic. For its supporters, the European single market has reinvigorated European capitalism and made Europe the economic equal of the United States; for its detractors, it has failed to free the marketplace, is still heavily protectionist, and has done too little to address long-term economic problems such as unemployment and low productivity. For its supporters, the EU offers a softer and more inclusive model of international cooperation; for its detractors, its global role will remain marginal – or certainly incomplete – so long as it does not become a military power.

But this book has argued that the nature of power has changed, that Europe's economic presence cannot be ignored, that it has exploited its civilian qualities and American unilateralism to expand its political influence, and that it represents a distinctive set of social values. The world during the cold war may have lived with a model of power driven by American preferences and precepts, but this is no longer true; it must pay heed to the European power alternative. What difference does that alternative make to the functioning of the international system? How is the post-modern concept of power (particularly the European model) different from the cold war realist concept (particularly the American model)? The values for which the United States stands, even if they are more often observed in theory than in practice, are well known; what, by contrast, does Europe stand for, and what are the implications? And given their competing perspectives on the world, what are the prospects for Europe and the United States continuing to work together?

What does Europe represent?

Since 1973, the European Commission has monitored public opinion in the member states of the EU, relying in part on a regular series of surveys undertaken under the auspices of its Eurobarometer polling service. These surveys include attempts to gauge how much Europeans know about the EU, both in general terms and in regard to specific elements of European integration. What they have revealed is that the average European knows remarkably little about the EU, and has some startling misconceptions regarding the details of how it works. When asked to give themselves a score out of 10 on their general level of knowledge, with 10 meaning they know a great deal and 1 meaning they know little, about two-thirds of respondents give themselves failing scores of 5 or less, and nearly one in ten admit to knowing nothing at all. On the specifics, the results are not encouraging: most Europeans know little about the EU's history, and there is widespread confusion about how it functions. On attitudes towards the EU, opinion is mixed, with Europeans equivocating about how much they identify with Europe, about how much benefit they feel their country has derived from Europe, and about how much they trust the EU and its institutions.[2]

This knowledge deficit is not unique to Europe, and neither is the climate of equivocation. Similar surveys in the United States have found equally significant gaps in public knowledge, and anyone who teaches politics at an American university will be able to verify the remarkably low level of knowledge among undergraduates about even the basics of the American system of government. And polls will repeatedly find that Americans – while patriotic, and proud of what their country represents – are never shy about criticizing their system of government or worrying about the direction in which the country is moving. Polls in the first half of 2006, for example, found that only 35–40 per cent of Americans approved of the job performance of George W. Bush, that 55–65 per cent believed that the US was headed in the wrong direction, and that 65–70 per cent disapproved of the job being done by the US Congress.

Where the two societies part company is over their respective levels of confidence regarding the underlying values and principles for which they each stand. The United States has a clear advantage arising out of its longer history; the American experiment has been under way for more than 230 years, and Americans are repeatedly reminded during public discourse of the features of their national identity, and of the value they place on democracy, freedom, and equality. Europeans, too, are reminded through the same channels of their identity and of the value they place on the same three commodities, but their views are founded mainly on their citizenship of individual member states of the EU, and much less is known or understood about what Europe represents, and about the extent to which it overlaps with – or contradicts – national values.

Assessments of the philosophical character of the EU are likely to be heavily influenced by reminders of the difficulties of building Europe, and by reference to the arguments and strains that have often marked interstate relations within the EU, whether driven by differences over policy priorities, over the nature and goals of European integration itself, over political and social values, or even over history and culture. But while no-one questions that the European project has been beset by crises – from the 1965 'empty-chair crisis' to concerns in the 1980s about eurosclerosis, to worries in the 1990s about the Danish rejection of Maastricht, to early failures to build a single currency, to the 2003 split over the US-led invasion of Iraq, to concerns about the effects of the 2004 expansion into Eastern Europe, to the 2005 French and Dutch rejections of the draft constitutional treaty – the EU has survived regardless, and continues to stand as one of the most remarkable political and economic achievements of the modern era.

Europe has worked because more than two dozen countries, with long histories of internecine warfare and conflict, have voluntarily come together to pool their resources and to build shared systems of decisionmaking and to agree common policies. They have brought down most of the barriers to the free movement of people, money, goods and services, they have agreed an extensive body of common laws, and along the way they have established Europe as a new and irresistible player in the international system. And in spite of the equivocation revealed by some polls, other polls have shown an emerging European consensus on a wide range of foreign policy questions, on the distribution of power and influence in the world, and on the need for Europe to assert itself. This consensus has emerged in part as a result of the constant process of negotiation that has been under way among Europeans since 1945 as they have built the EU and its common policies, but it has also been a by-product of changes in the international system, none of them more telling or more important than the reaction among Europeans to American global leadership.

What, then, does Europe represent, and how might we define 'European-ism'? Václav Havel has suggested that most Europeans never actually think about the idea of being European, and are taken by surprise when asked by opinion pollsters to declare their European affiliation. The lack of a tradition of conscious Europeanism in Europe can, he believes, be explained by a sense of superiority and a long-held belief among Europeans that they did not need to define themselves in relation to others.[3] Clearly that view took a hard knock with World War II and the cold war transition to American leadership, which combined with the internal polit-ical, economic and social problems of the continent to raise doubts about what Europe represented. Instead of encapsulating European values or a European view of the world, 'Europeanism' came to be associated with a more narrow support for the process of integration. For Scruton, it is the 'attitude which sees the well-being, destiny and institutions of the major European states as so closely linked by geographical and historical circum-stances that no cogent political action can be successfully pursued in one state without some reference to, and attempt to achieve integration with, the others'.[4] He notes the strong undercurrent of Europeanism within dissi-dent movements in Eastern Europe, and the significance for these movements of membership of the EU, which went beyond the question of economic prosperity.

It has only been more recently that hints have emerged that the term 'Europeanism' might be more aptly applied to the collective identity of Europeans, and the values and principles for which they stand. It was not surprising during the cold war that there were few signs of such an iden-tity, because Europeans found themselves carried along on the currents of tension created by political and military competition between the US and the USSR, and were too focused on thinking creatively about how they could avoid allowing nationalism ever again to lead to generalized war to worry about their external identity. Now that Europe is at peace, has built policies and goals to which it is collectively committed, is freed from its military and economic dependence upon the United States, and has been so often reminded of its differences with the US, Europeans have had more time and encouragement to think about what makes them distinctive.

In January 2003, eight European governments – led by Britain and Spain – published the 'Letter of Eight' in which they explained their support for the US stance on Iraq. On 15 February, massive anti-war demonstrations were held in London, Berlin, Paris, Rome, Madrid and Barcelona, and were hailed by former French finance minister Dominique Strauss-Kahn as marking the birth of a new 'European nation'.[5] Encouraged by these events, the German philosopher Jürgen Habermas – with the support of French philosopher Jacques Derrida – attempted to impose more clarity on the idea of Europe. In an article published in *Frankfurter Allgemeine Zeitung* on 31 May, they hailed 15 February as the signal for the birth of a 'European public sphere'. They argued that a 'core Europe' (excluding Britain and Eastern Europe) should be a counterweight to the influence of the United States, and believed that in reaction to nationalism, values and habits had evolved which had given contemporary Europe 'its own face'. They noted several features of 'a common political mentality' that had helped others recognize Europeans as such, rather than as Germans or Italians or Spaniards. Six such features were described in their article:

- Secularization, and suspicion of 'transgressions of the border between politics and religion'.
- Trust in the 'organizational and steering capacities' of the state, and scepticism about the achievements of markets. Thanks to the spread of the ideals of the French Revolution, they said, politics had been welcomed in Europe, but capitalism was less well regarded because of its association with class conflict.
- An absence of 'naively optimistic expectations about technological progress'.
- A preference for the welfare state's guarantees of social security.
- A low threshold of tolerance for the use of force, prompted by memories of twentieth-century totalitarianism and the Holocaust.
- Support for multilateralism, 'the mutual limitation of sovereignty', and a regulated international order within the framework of a reformed United Nations.[6]

In a similar vein, Hutton has compared and contrasted the economic and social characteristics of the EU and the United States. He argues that while the American liberal definition of rights does not extend beyond the political to the economic and social, the European conception of rights is broader, encapsulating free healthcare, free education, the right to employment insurance, and so on. He suggests that while Americans are provided with opportunities, it is also understood that they must accept the related risks and expect no social intervention to cushion the blow of failure. For Europeans, the conception of a fair society sees a larger role for the state, ensuring a fair distribution of risk and reward.[7] Elsewhere, Timothy Garton Ash – reflecting the suggestion by Hannah Arendt that Europeanism is to some extent a reaction to Americanization[8] – has written of 'Europe as Not America', suggesting that Habermas and Strauss-Kahn are arguing that Europe is both different from and better than America, and that a European identity can and should be built upon the differences.[9]

The idea of Europe as Not America, while tempting as a short and easy route to independence of thought and action, might be read as meaning that Europe can only be seen as distinctive in reference to the United States. In truth, however, Europe has – like all societies – free-standing features and values that have grown out of its own unique experience. Thus we need to look at Europe on its own terms, using the United States only as a point of comparison and differentiation. In particular, attention needs to be paid to what the rise of the EU means – or is likely to mean – for the international system. There is an emerging consensus that the EU has transformed the place of Europe in the world, but there is much less certainty about its global significance.

Like all societies, Europe is a product of its history, its culture, its society, and of its external relationships. While the United States has a long history as a sovereign state, however, Europe is still a community of sovereign states, making it difficult always to tease out the common themes in what it represents. There is also a danger in trying to make generalizations, mainly because there are always exceptions to the rule, but also because generalizations overlook contradictions within the cases being compared. For example, the US is often associated with unilateralism, and yet polls found before the Iraq war that nearly two-thirds of Americans were uncomfortable with US policy, believing that the US should invade only with UN approval and with the support of its allies. Equally, Europe is often associated with a resistance to using military options to pursue foreign policy goals, but Britain and France have both engaged in multiple modern conflicts, either unilaterally or in alliance with the United States or each other, and both countries were readier to use force in Kosovo – including the commitment of ground troops

– than was the United States. Finally, while the present Bush administration became well known for its opposition to the Kyoto protocol on climate change, polls have found majority support in the United States for adopting the protocol and for taking action to stop climate change.[10] But even in the face of such contradictions and inconsistencies, there are many values and features – or perhaps they are better described as tendencies and inclinations – that make Europeanism distinctive from Americanism (see Table 7.1), and that serve to bind the concept of a distinctive model of European power in the world. What, then, might be (provisionally) included under the rubric of Europeanism?

In international relations, Europeanism emphasizes the post-modern values of peace, multilateralism, internationalism, soft power, and civilian means for dealing with conflict. Where Europeans tend to identify with the liberal view of the international system, American policy is more impacted by realist interpretations. Nye writes of the cultural influence of the EU in

Table 7.1   *Comparing Europeanism and Americanism*

Europeanism	*Americanism*
Peace	War
Multilateral	Unilateral
Internationalism	Nationalism
Soft power	Hard power
Civilian	Military
Liberal worldview	Realist worldview
Sustainable development	Consumerism
Universal	Provincial
Post-modern	Modern
Welfarism	Materialism
Community	Individual
State-reliance	Self-reliance
Social liberalism	Social conservativism
Progressive	Orthodox
Secular	Religious
Modest	Ambitious
Pragmatic	Utopian
Settled	Restless
Risk aversion	Risk tolerance
Past	Future

the world, of the symbolic value contained within the concept of European unity itself, and argues that external actors see it as 'a positive force for solving global problems'. He contrasts this with the carrot and stick emphasis of the United States on economic and military might as a critical element in foreign policy.[11] Where Europeans tend towards a post-modern view of the international system, Americans tend towards the modern view, with its emphasis on national interests, security, and consumerism. Van Staden argues that while European states have become used to pooling their sovereignty and working out interdependent common policies, the United States has become reluctant to water down its sovereignty by becoming immersed in systems of global governance.[12] Fukuyama argues that 'Europeans believe that they are transcending sovereignty, whereas Americans believe that legitimacy comes from democratic, sovereign states'.[13] Where many Europeans long ago acknowledged that they were citizens of an international system, in which diplomacy and multilateralism played a vital role, and in which engagement was the only realistic option, there are still many Americans for whom there are only two acceptable alternatives: American leadership, or isolationism.

On the economic front, Europeans are as entrepreneurial as Americans, but there is more concern in Europe with creating a level playing field and with redistributing opportunity and wealth. As Prestowitz puts it, one of the most fundamental of transatlantic differences is that 'Americans emphasize equality of opportunity, [while] Europeans focus more on equality of results.'[14] Europeans have a preference for the welfare state over the interests of materialism, and incline towards state-reliance over self-reliance. Rifkin contrasts the American emphasis on economic growth, personal wealth, and individual self-interest with the European emphasis on sustainable development, quality of life, and community, and concludes that the EU is developing a new social and political model better suited to the needs of the globalizing world of the new century; in short, that the European dream is eclipsing the American dream.[15]

On social issues, Europeans hold attitudes that tend towards the liberal and the secular. While championing the role of government in the marketplace, Europeans are keen to minimize the role of government in making moral decisions or defining personal choices. As noted in Chapter 6, the positions of Europeans on such issues as abortion, capital punishment, gun control, censorship, doctor-assisted suicide, evolution, and same-sex marriage make them quite distinctive from mainstream opinion in the United States. While Europeanism tends towards the progressive and the temporal, Americanism tends towards the orthodox and the spiritual. While Europeanism tends towards freedom of personal choice, Americanism is more ready to allow government to limit that choice and to regulate the behaviour of individuals.

Finally, in terms of their aspirations, Europeans tend towards the modest and the pragmatic, and are less mobile – in personal and labour terms – than Americans. While Americans tend to be future-oriented, and to use code-words such as 'dreams' and 'visions', Europeans are more aware of the past, and less ambitious about the possibilities for change. Europeans also tend to be more risk-averse than Americans. Looking at recent election results in Europe and at welfare and labour policies, *The Economist* concludes that risk aversion has become 'the defining feature' in continental Europe's largest countries, and that while the American system rewards risk taking, 'Europeans think it is better to be safe than to be sorry'.[16]

These are no more than preliminary assessments of the features of Europeanism. The emergence of a distinctive European identity has not yet been studied in great depth, in part because 'Europe' is still more focused on regulating the marketplace and developing common policies than it is on defining what Europe represents. But once more Europeans wake up to the possibilities of Europe as an assertive and powerful global actor, they will be more inclined to think about what Europe represents. And the longer that the United States continues to pursue policies that place it so clearly at odds with public and political opinion in much of the rest of the world, the greater will be the pressure on Europeans to more carefully define and champion the goals to which they aspire.

The doubtful future of the Atlantic Alliance

No discussion of Europe as a superpower would be complete without an assessment of the future of the Atlantic Alliance, or of Atlanticism, or even more generally of 'the West'. Question marks have hung over that future almost since the end of the cold war. In 1993, Owen Harries – then editor of *The National Interest* – warned against assuming that the West was a 'natural presence' that was here to stay, argued that it had taken the presence of a threatening 'East' to bring it into existence and to maintain its unity, and concluded that it was unlikely that it would survive the disappearance of that threat. He argued that while the countries of the West were tied by a common civilization, this was not the same as achieving political unity. Division and conflict had been all too common within the West, and Europeans had only been attracted to a political West when faced with great and imminent danger.[17] More recently, Kupchan has warned that the cultural distance between Europe and the US may be widening, putting the two sides on diverging social paths.[18] Moïsi wonders if the West still even exists. The response to Islamic fundamentalism, international terrorism and weapons of mass destruction has not had the same unifying effect as the Soviet threat, he concludes, because the EU and the US differ over how to respond. But they do not need to think the same way; they need to better understand each other's way of doing things.[19]

Optimists (or idealists) continue to argue that Europeans and Americans can – and, indeed, must – continue to work together, because they have core common values, such as a belief in democracy and free markets, and because they can achieve more in partnership than in opposition. Writing in 1997, well before the crisis over Iraq, Mastundano suggested that 'rather than edging away from the United States, much less balance against it, Europe [has] been determined to maintain the patterns of engagement that characterized the Cold War'.[20] For Lambert, writing just before the Iraq invasion, the Atlantic Alliance had been enormously successful, and 'most of the good things that have happened in the world … have come as a result of the two continents working together to a greater or lesser degree of harmony'. But he also conceded that the Bush administration no longer felt a sense of urgency in its relationship with Europe, and concluded that it was time for Europeans 'to make determined and consistent efforts to present their ideas to the United States' and to 'demonstrate that they are partners to be valued and respected'.[21]

Writing after Iraq, Ikenberry saw no sign of 'other major states … making systematic choices to pull away from and balance against the United States', and felt that US relations with Western Europe had remained 'relatively stable' and that deep shifts had not surfaced.[22] For Gordon and Shapiro, also writing after Iraq, the Alliance was in better shape than was often portrayed. The crisis over Iraq was not inevitable, it was an experience that neither side wanted to repeat, and the Alliance had to be saved because it continued to play a vital and irreplaceable role in maintaining international peace and prosperity.[23]

Contrasting with these assessments, there is the more pessimistic (or cynical) view that asks whether Europe and America any longer have enough in common to be able to understand each other, let alone work out points of agreement. As noted in Chapter 1, transatlantic relations during the cold war were rarely as happy as they seemed on the surface, and the Alliance was often no more than a marriage of convenience. This arrangement suited both sides for what could be gained, but regular disputes reminded them that the Alliance was a delicate relationship that had not developed deep roots. The end of the cold war and the increasing intensity of the disputes between the two partners – whether over trade, over foreign and security policy, or over social values – simply served to draw new attention to the problems, and long before Iraq there was a body of opinion that maintained that Europe and the US were growing apart politically, culturally, socially and even morally.

Lundestad reminds us that studies of the Alliance have long been sprinkled with words such as *crisis, clash, divorce, troubled*, and *unhappy*.[24] Particularly since Iraq, it has become more difficult to find analyses that do not highlight the problems and raise questions about the prospects for the maintenance of a common view of global problems and priorities. Pond wrote in 2004 of the 'near-death' of the Alliance, noting that while transatlantic differences in the past had focused on perhaps two or three questions at a time, by 2003 there was a long list of differences over policy and policy style, which exacerbated one another and created problems that were reinforced 'by long-standing mutual disapproval of domestic social choices made on the other side of the Atlantic'.[25] Mowle concludes that while both sides share similar goals with respect to global issues, they are increasingly unable to agree on how to proceed. He notes the role of realism in the US approach, and the US desire to maintain its freedom of action and sovereignty, but also notes that the same can be said regarding much of what the EU does, and that this explains much of their disagreement. He argues that the transatlantic alliance is not in a state of crisis, because the EU 'cannot directly oppose or replace the United States' and because the interests of the EU remain closer to those of the US than to other centres of world power; instead, they remain 'allies at odds'.[26]

Dorfman argues that the United States needs a cooperative relationship with Europe in order to solve the dilemma of Iraq as well as a host of other Middle Eastern problems: European political support would add to the credibility of US efforts, and would have played an invaluable role in Iraq with debt forgiveness, financial support for rebuilding infrastructure, the training of police and the military, and advice on how to deal with the historical, economic, cultural and political realities that Europeans better understood because of their long association with the region.[27] Bereuter and Lis argue that common interests – including free trade, democracy, and the struggle against terrorism and weapons proliferation – suggest that transatlantic cooperation is as imperative today as it was at the height of the cold war.[28] They also need each other as they face the challenge of China.

But whatever happens as a result of the short- and medium-term fallout from Iraq, whatever policies are pursued by George W. Bush's successors, and whatever progress is made (or not made) on mending fences, it is clear that the Alliance will never be the same again. Iraq was just the highest and most visible peak in a mountain range of transatlantic disputes that stretch back to 1945 and beyond, and it was symbolic of a host of broader and deeper problems that interfere with the health of the Alliance. In the eyes of most Europeans, Iraq exemplified the most unfortunate kind of American unilateralism, highlighted the contrasting perceptions that Europeans and Americans now have of global problems and their best solutions, revealed a Europe that is more willing than at any time before to publicly and openly oppose American policy, exposed a seam of public opinion in the United States that is unwilling to tolerate criticism or opposition from Europe, and made many Europeans more aware of their subconscious desire for greater foreign and security policy independence. It also exemplified the problems that can be created when the United States claims to be speaking on behalf of the global community and claims to identify itself with global interests, when in fact there may not always be much correlation between US and non-US interests.

Most tellingly, the debates that took place before, during, and after Iraq drew attention to the altered state of the international system, and to the limits of the cold war-style realist interpretations championed by many American policymakers: the idea that the state is the most important actor in international relations, that security is the most important item on the agenda, that states must rely on themselves in order to ensure their security, and that force is an effective tool of statecraft. In contrast, Iraq drew new attention to the liberal worldview of Europeans: the international agenda is more varied than realists suggest, international organizations and institutions are also important actors in the international system, and a greater premium should be placed on cooperation and multilateralism. These debates have coincided with a new discussion about the global role played by the European Union. Increasingly, the term *superpower* appears in discussions about Europe, and not just in conjunction with its economic personality, but also in conjunction with its political influence in the world, with its position as a distinctive social actor, and with the new light it sheds on discussions about security issues and about the nature of civilian power.

Meaningful future cooperation is unlikely without a change in attitude and approach from both sides of the Atlantic. The United States must realize that the world has changed since 1990 and that the policies and interpretations that came out of the cold war do not always any longer apply. In particular, it must understand that power is not irredeemably associated with the military and with nation-states, and that civilian international organizations – or clusters of states working together – can also wield power, and can do so peacefully. It must also understand that exceptionalism does no-one any favours; it isolates American thinking, prompts reactionary thinking from abroad, and places American interests above those of the international community that the United States claims to lead. Huntington has argued that the United States is blind to the fact that it no longer enjoys the pre-eminent position that it occupied at the end of the cold war, and that it must relearn the game of international politics, make compromises, and make rational recalculations of power rather than pursuing 'a wish list of arrogant, unilateralist demands'.[29] Relearning does not mean that the United States must cease struggling for what it believes is right, but rather that it must renounce the hubris that often accompanies great power, that it must acknowledge the limitations on that power, and that it must take a more universal and inclusive view of global problems.

In his 2003 State of the Union address, George W. Bush argued that 'The course of this nation does not depend on the decisions of others.' This is nonsense. In the interdependent post-modern global community, the course of all nations depends on the decisions of others, which makes it all the more important to understand and work with others. There was a time when the United States could ignore most protests from states that disagreed with American policy. It was the world's biggest economy and had the world's biggest military, and most of those states needed the US more than the US needed them. And at the end of the day it could always fall back on threats and coercion to get its way; none but the Soviets could really oppose it, and even the Soviets were limited in how much they could achieve. But this is no longer true. The United States is no longer a lone superpower, and it no longer faces opposition from a discredited 'evil empire'. Instead, it faces opposition not just from its enemies but from a cluster of wealthy, democratic, capitalist European states that often act and function as one. In this new bipolar international environment, the United States must learn to reach accommodations. And it cannot refuse and fall back on isolationism – it is too late for that. The autarkical streak that can often be found running through popular debates in the United States is unrealistic and unsustainable in the era of globalization, and anyone who believes that the US can go it alone and build a metaphorical wall around itself is fooling only themselves.

As for the Europeans, they must begin to better appreciate and understand the possibilities of Europe. European integration has achieved much of what it set out to achieve, including generalized peace in Europe, economic and social solidarity, the development of a single European market, common policies on shared problems, the promotion of the European model of society, and a reassertion of the European role in the world. These achievements have not been easily won, and much remains to be done, but Europeans are still too doubtful about those achievements, still too ready to be diverted by the crises rather than celebrate the achievements, and still too reluctant to realize and appreciate the benefits and responsibilities of Europe. It is too late to fall back on narrow nationalism; Europeans still recognize and celebrate their separate national identities, and rightly so, but the ties that bind the member states are too numerous and too tightly knotted to allow a reversion to the era of the sovereign nation-state. The slogan 'strength through unity' may have been over-used, but it remains apposite: Europeans have had to make sacrifices on the road to integration, but the compensation has been dramatic. Europe is a superpower; not one that threatens and coerces, but one that offers a new set of interpretations and possibilities to a world that has too long been dragged along behind the increasingly bankrupt philosophy of hard power and militarism.

The European superpower has an important role to play in redefining our understanding of the international system, and in helping its American counterpart adjust its perceptions and values. At no time since it became a superpower has the United States been faced with so compelling a set of alternatives as it does today from Europe. The Soviets offered only military and ideological competition; the Europeans offer economic, political, ideological, social, cultural and moral alternatives. Europe not only offers another interpretation of how international affairs might be managed, and of how threats to the international community might be defined and resolved, but it also poses limits to the ability of the United States to mould that community according to its priorities and principles. The European Union is a superpower, and the new pole in a post-modern bipolar international order. It is time to acknowledge this, and to better understand the implications.

Notes and References

Introduction

1. Quoted by Samuel Huntington, 'The Lonely Superpower', in *Foreign Affairs* 78:2, March/April 1999, pp. 35–9.
2. Paul Kennedy, 'The Greatest Superpower Ever', in *New Perspectives Quarterly* 19:2, Spring 2002.
3. Andrew Moravcsik, 'Striking a New Transatlantic Bargain', in *Foreign Affairs* 82:4, July/August 2003, pp. 74–89.
4. The BRIC thesis was developed in 2003 by a team at the investment bank Goldman Sachs. See Dominic Wilson and Roopa Purushothaman, 'Dreaming With BRICs: The Path to 2050', Global Economics Paper No. 99, Goldman Sachs, 1 October 2003.
5. Walter LaFeber, 'The United States and Europe in an Age of American Unilateralism', in R. Laurence Moore and Maurizio Vaudagna (eds), *The American Century in Europe* (Ithaca, NY: Cornell University Press, 2003).
6. For a review of the literature, see Geir Lundestad, *The United States and Western Europe Since 1945* (Oxford: Oxford University Press, 2003), pp. 4–5. For a discussion of crises within NATO, see Elizabeth D. Sherwood, *Allies in Crisis: Meeting Global Challenges to Western Security* (New Haven, CT: Yale University Press, 1990).
7. Robert Kagan, *Of Paradise and Power: America and Europe in the New World Order* (New York: Knopf, 2003).

Chapter 1

1. Bertrand Russell, *Power: A New Social Analysis* (London: Allen and Unwin, 1975), p. 25.
2. The two major approaches to understanding power in the international system are 'defensive realism' (see Kenneth N. Waltz, *Theory of International Politics* (Boston, MA: McGraw-Hill, 1979) for example) and 'offensive realism' (see John J. Mearsheimer, *The Tragedy of Great Power Politics* (New York: Norton, 2001) for example). Both are based on deliberate actions by great powers against other great powers.
3. Anthony Sampson, *The New Europeans: A Guide to the Workings, Institutions, and Character of Contemporary Western Europe* (London: Hodder and Stoughton, 1968), p. 207.
4. François Duchêne, 'The European Community and the Uncertainties of Interdependence', in Max Kohnstamm and Wolfgang Hager (eds), *A Nation*

Writ Large? Foreign Policy Problems Before the European Community (London: Macmillan (now Palgrave Macmillan), 1973).

5. See discussion in Franck Petiteville, 'Exporting "Values"? EU External Co-operation as a "Soft Diplomacy"', in Michèle Knodt and Sebastiaan Princen (eds), *Understanding the European Union's External Relations* (London: Routledge, 2003).

6. See Robert A. Dahl, 'The Concept of Power', in *Behavioral Science* 2, 1957, pp. 201–5.

7. Kenneth J. Waltz, *Theory of International Politics* (Boston, MA: McGraw-Hill, 1979), pp. 191–2.

8. For discussion, see Kenneth E. Boulding, *Evolutionary Economics* (Beverly Hills, CA: Sage, 1981) and Philip Mirowski, *More Heat Than Light: Economics as Social Physics, Physics as Nature's Economics* (Cambridge: Cambridge University Press, 1989).

9. Joseph Schumpeter, *Essays: On Entrepreneurs, Innovations, Business Cycles and the Evolution of Capitalism* (New Brunswick, NJ: Transaction, 1989), p. 166.

10. Joseph Schumpeter, *Capitalism, Socialism and Democracy* (New York: Harper Perennial, 1962).

11. See, for example, A. J. P. Taylor, *The Struggle for Mastery in Europe, 1847–1918* (Oxford: Oxford University Press, 1971), p. xxiv, and George Modelski, *Principles of World Politics* (New York: Free Press, 1972), p. 149.

12. Michael Mandelbaum, 'Is Major War Obsolete?', in *Survival* 40:4, Winter 1988–89, pp. 20–38.

13. John Mueller, *Retreat From Doomsday: The Obsolescence of Modern War* (New York: Basic Books, 1989), pp. 4–5; John Mueller, *The Remnants of War* (Ithaca, NY: Cornell University Press, 2004).

14. For discussion, see Mary Kaldor, 'American Power: From "Compellance" to Cosmopolitanism', in David Held and Mathias Koenig-Archibugi (eds), *American Power in the 21st Century* (Cambridge: Polity, 2004), pp. 187–91.

15. Richard Rosecrance, *The Rise of the Trading State: Commerce and Conquest in the Modern World* (New York: Basic Books, 1986).

16. Klaus Knorr, *Power and Wealth: The Political Economy of International Power* (New York: Basic Books, 1973), pp. 3–4.

17. Joseph S. Nye, *Bound to Lead: The Changing Nature of American Power* (New York: Basic Books, 1991) and *Soft Power: The Means to Success in World Politics* (New York: Public Affairs, 2004), pp. 5–7.

18. Robert Cooper, 'The Goals of Diplomacy, Hard Power, and Soft Power', in Held and Mathias Koenig-Archibugi, *American Power*, p. 169.

19. Joseph S. Nye, *The Paradox of American Power* (Oxford: Oxford University Press, 2002), p. 39.

20. See discussion in Steven Lukes, *Power: A Radical View* (Basingstoke: Macmillan (now Palgrave Macmillan), 1974), pp. 11–12. See also Dennis H. Wrong, 'Problems in Defining Power', in Marvin E. Olsen and Martin N.

Marger (eds), *Power in Modern Societies* (Boulder, CO: Westview, 1993), pp. 11–13.

21. Lukes, *Power*, pp. 21–5.

22. For discussion, see J. M. Roberts, *The Penguin History of the World* (London: Penguin, 1990), pp. 255–67, 459–71.

23. Robert O. Keohane and Joseph S. Nye, *Power and Interdependence: World Politics in Transition* (Boston, MA: Little, Brown, 1977), pp. 24–5.

24. Nathan Gardels, 'The Rise and Fall of America's Soft Power', in *New Perspectives Quarterly* 22:1, Winter 2005, pp. 6–19.

25. See Oran R. Young, *Governance in World Affairs* (Ithaca, NY: Cornell University Press, 1999).

26. Richard G. Whitman, *From Civilian Power to Superpower? The International Identity of the European Union* (Basingstoke: Palgrave (now Palgrave Macmillan), 1998).

27. Anne-Marie Slaughter, *A New World Order* (Princeton, NJ: Princeton University Press, 2005).

28. Jack S. Levy, *War in the Modern Great Power System, 1495–1975* (Lexington, KY: University Press of Kentucky, 1983), pp. 16–18.

29. W. T. R. Fox, *The Super-Powers: The United States, Britain and the Soviet Union – Their Responsibility for Peace* (New York: Harcourt Brace, 1944), pp. 20–1. The term had earlier been used by the author John Dos Passos, who in turn had attributed it to a businessman describing a large business empire. See John Dos Passos, *USA* (London: Penguin, 1981), pp. 1155–61.

30. Steven L. Spiegel, *Dominance and Diversity: The International Hierarchy* (Boston, MA: Little, Brown, 1972), pp. 70, 98.

31. Jan Nijman, *The Geopolitics of Power and Conflict: Superpowers in the International System 1945–1992* (London: Belhaven, 1993), p. 2.

32. Eugene J. McCarthy, *The Limits of Power: America's Role in the World* (New York: Holt, Rinehart and Winston, 1967), pp. 6–7.

33. Nijman, *Geopolitics of Power and Conflict*, p. 31.

34. Christer Jönsson, *Superpower: Comparing American and Soviet Foreign Policy* (London: Pinter, 1984), Chapter 1.

35. Ken Aldred and Martin A Smith, *Superpowers in the Post-Cold War Era* (Basingstoke: Macmillan (now Palgrave Macmillan), 1999), p. 31.

36. Paul Dibbs, *The Soviet Union: The Incomplete Superpower*, 2nd ed. (London: Macmillan (now Palgrave Macmillan), 1988).

37. Mann argues that 'effective power' requires a combination of ideological, economic, military and political power. See Michael Mann, 'The First Failed Empire of the Twenty-First Century', in Held and Koenig-Archibugi, *American Power*, p. 52.

38. John Lewis Gaddis, *The United States and the End of the Cold War* (Oxford: Oxford University Press, 1992), p. 5.

39. See, for example, William H. Overholt, *The Rise of China: How Economic Reform is Creating a New Superpower* (New York: Norton, 1993); David L.

Shambaugh (ed.), *Greater China: The Next Superpower?* (Oxford: Oxford University Press, 1995); Laurence J. Brahm, *China's Century: The Awakening of the Next Economic Powerhouse* (New York: Wiley, 2001); Ted Fishman, *China, Inc.: How the Rise of the Next Superpower Challenges America and the World* (New York: Scribner, 2005); Francis A. Lees, *China Superpower: Requisites for High Growth* (New York: St Martin's Press, 1997), and Geoffrey Murray, *China: The Next Superpower: Dilemmas in Change and Continuity* (New York: St Martin's Press, 1998).

40. H. Lyman Miller, 'A Superpower? No Time Soon', in *Hoover Digest* 2, Spring 2005.

41. Robert Sutter, 'Why Does China Matter?', in *Washington Quarterly* 27:1, Winter 2003–04, pp. 75–89.

42. Hubert Védrine, with Dominique Moïsi, *France in an Age of Globalization* (Washington, DC: Brookings Institution Press, 2001), p. 2.

43. Immanual Wallerstein, *The Politics of the World Economy: The States, the Movements, and the Civilizations* (Cambridge: Cambridge University Press, 1984), p. 38.

44. Josef Joffe, 'Defying History and Theory: The United States as the "Last Remaining Superpower"', in G. John Ikenberry (ed.), *America Unrivaled: The Future of the Balance of Power* (Ithaca, NY: Cornell University Press, 2002).

45. See, for example, the discussion in Benjamin R. Barber, *Fear's Empire: War, Terrorism, and Democracy* (New York: Norton, 2003); Emmanuel Todd, *After the Empire: The Breakdown of the American Order* (New York: Columbia University Press, 2003); Lloyd Gardner and Marilyn Young (eds), *The New American Empire* (New York: The New Press, 2005), and V.G. Kiernan, *America: The New Imperialism* (London: Verso, 2005).

46. See, for example, Charles Krauthammer and Robert Kaplan, quoted by Michael Mann, 'The First Failed Empire of the Twenty-First Century', in Held and Koenig-Archibugi, *American Power*; and Joseph S. Nye, 'Hard Power, Soft Power, and the "War on Terrorism"', in Held and Koenig-Archibugi.

47. Geir Lundestad, *The American 'Empire'* (Oxford: Oxford University Press, 1990), p. 37.

48. Chalmers Johnson, *The Sorrows of Empire: Militarism, Secrecy, and the End of the Republic* (New York: Metropolitan, 2004).

49. Noam Chomsky, *Hegemony or Survival: America's Quest for Global Dominance* (New York: Metropolitan, 2003).

50. Michael Mann, *Incoherent Empire* (New York: Verso, 2003).

51. Niall Ferguson, *Colossus: The Price of America's Empire* (New York: Penguin, 2004), p. 2.

52. Charles Krauthammer, 'The Unipolar Moment', in Graham Allison and Gregory F. Treverton (eds), *Rethinking America's Security: Beyond Cold War to New World Order* (New York: Norton, 1992).

53. Charles Krauthammer, 'The Unipolar Moment Revisited', in *The National Interest* 70 (Winter 2002–03), pp. 5–17.

54. G. John Ikenberry, 'Introduction', in Ikenberry, *America Unrivaled*, p. 1.

55. G. John Ikenberry, 'Liberal Hegemony or Empire? American Power in the Age of Unipolarity', in Held and Koenig-Archibugi, *American Power*.

56. William C. Wohlforth, 'The Stability of a Unipolar World', in *International Security* 24:1 (Summer 1999), p. 8.

57. William C. Wohlforth, 'US Strategy in a Unipolar World', in Ikenberry, *America Unrivaled*.

58. Josef Joffe, 'How America Does It', in *Foreign Affairs* 76:5, September/ October 1997, pp. 13–27.

59. Samuel Huntington, 'The Lonely Superpower', in *Foreign Affairs* 78:2, March/ April 1999, pp. 35–49.

60. Robert Kagan, 'America's Crisis of Legitimacy', in *Foreign Affairs* 83:2, March/ April 2004, pp. 65–87.

61. Robert J. Lieber, *The American Era: Power and Strategy for the 21st Century* (New York: Cambridge University Press, 2005), p. 17.

62. Robert E. Hunter, 'Europe's Leverage', in *Washington Quarterly* 27:1, Winter 2003–04, pp. 91–110.

63. Richard Haass, *The Opportunity: America's Moment to Alter History's Course* (New York: Public Affairs, 2005), p. 8.

64. The suggestion for the term 'American exceptionalism' is usually credited to Alexis de Tocqueville and his assertion in 1835 that 'The position of the Americans is ... quite exceptional, and it may be believed that no democratic people will ever be placed in a similar one.' See Alexis de Tocqueville, *Democracy in America* (various editions and years), Vol. II, First Book, Chapter IX.

65. Byron E. Shafer (ed.), *Is America Different? A New Look at American Exceptionalism* (Oxford: Clarendon Press, 1991), p. v.

66. Trevor B. McCrisken, *American Exceptionalism and the Legacy of Vietnam: US Foreign Policy Since 1974* (Basingstoke: Palgrave Macmillan, 2003), Chapter 5.

67. William J. Clinton, speech at George Washington University, 5 August 1996.

68. Kenneth N. Waltz, 'America as a Model for the World? A Foreign Policy Perspective', in *PS*, December 1991, p. 669.

69. Walter Lippmann, *US Foreign Policy* (London: Hamish Hamilton, 1943), pp. 5–6.

70. See, for example, Waltz, *Theory of International Politics*; Robert Gilpin, *War and Change in World Politics* (Cambridge: Cambridge University Press, 1981); Stephen M. Walt, *The Origins of Alliances* (Ithaca, NY: Cornell University Press, 1987), and Mearsheimer, *The Tragedy of Great Power Politics*.

71. Paul Kennedy, *The Rise and Fall of Great Powers: Economic Change and Military Conflict from 1500 to 2000* (New York: Random House, 1987).

72. Ibid., p. 515.
73. Samuel P. Huntington, 'The US – Decline or Renewal?', in *Foreign Affairs* 67:2, Winter 1988/89, pp. 76– 97.
74. Paul Kennedy, 'The Eagle Has Landed', in *Financial Times*, 1 February 2002.
75. Christopher Layne, 'The Unipolar Illusion: Why New Great Powers Will Arise', in *International Security* 17:4 (Spring 1993), pp. 5–51.
76. Richard Haass, *The Reluctant Sheriff: The United States After the Cold War* (New York: Council on Foreign Relations, 1997), p. 2.
77. Charles A. Kupchan, 'After Pax Americana: Benign Power, Regional Integration, and the Sources of a Stable Multipolarity', in *International Security* 23:2, Fall 1998, pp. 40–79.
78. Richard Haass, 'What To Do with American Primacy', in *Foreign Affairs* 78:5, September/October 1999, pp. 37–49.
79. Haass, *The Opportunity*.
80. Garry Wills, 'Bully of the Free World', in *Foreign Affairs* 78:2, March/April 1999, pp. 50–9.
81. G. John Ikenberry, 'America's Imperial Ambition', in *Foreign Affairs* 81:5, September/October 2002.
82. Earl H. Fry, Stan A. Taylor and Robert S. Wood, *America the Vincible: US Foreign Policy for the Twenty-First Century* (Englewood Cliffs, NJ: Prentice-Hall, 1994).
83. Huntington, 'The Lonely Superpower'.
84. John W. Kingdon, *America the Unusual* (New York: Worth, 1999).
85. Clyde Prestowitz, *Rogue Nation: American Unilateralism and the Failure of Good Intentions* (New York: Basic Books, 2003).
86. *Bulletin of the European Communities* 3 (110 1970), p. 10.
87. See François Duchêne, 'Europe's Role in World Peace', in Richard Mayne (ed.), *Europe Tomorrow: Sixteen Europeans Look Ahead* (London: Fontana, 1972), pp. 43, 47.
88. Johan Galtung, *The European Community: A Superpower in the Making* (London: George Allen & Unwin, 1973), p. 17.
89. David Buchan, *Europe: The Strange Superpower* (Aldershot: Dartmouth, 1993).
90. See Richard Rosecrance, 'Mergers and Acquisitions', in *The National Interest* 80, Summer 2005, pp. 65–73.
91. See, for example, John Newhouse, *Europe Adrift* (New York: Pantheon, 1997).
92. Galtung, *The European Community*, p. 17.
93. Jan Zielonka, *Explaining Euro-Paralysis: Why Europe is Unable to Act in International Politics* (Basingstoke: Macmillan (now Palgrave Macmillan), 1998), pp. 13–15. See also Carolyn Rhodes (ed.), *The European Union in the World Community* (Boulder, CO: Lynne Rienner, 1998), and Brian White, *Understanding European Foreign Policy* (Basingstoke: Palgrave Macmillan, 2001).

94. Stanley Hoffman, 'Goodbye to a United Europe?', in *New York Review of Books*, 27 May 1993, reprinted in Hoffman, *The European Sisyphus: Essays on Europe 1964–1994* (Boulder, CO: Westview, 1995).

95. Martin Feldstein, 'EMU and International Conflict', in *Foreign Affairs* 76:6, November/December 1997, pp. 60–75.

96. Irving Kristol, 'The Emerging American Imperium', in American Enterprise Institute Online, 1 January 2000, www.aei.org.

97. Paul Johnson, 'America's New Empire for Liberty', in *Hoover Digest* 4, Fall 2003.

98. Charles Aldinger, 'US, Europe Must Heal Rifts Over Iraq – NATO Chief', Reuters, 29 January 2004, http://today.reuters.com/news.

99. John C. Hulsman and William L. T. Schirano, 'The European Union is Dead', in *The National Interest,* Fall 2005.

100. Trevor C. Salmon and Alistair J. K. Shepherd, *Toward a European Army: A Military Power in the Making?* (Boulder, CO: Lynne Rienner, 2003).

101. See, for example, Noel Malcolm, 'The Case Against '"Europe"', in *Foreign Affairs* 74:2, March/April 1995, pp. 52–68, and John Redwood, *Superpower Struggles: Mighty America, Faltering Europe, Rising Asia* (Basingstoke: Palgrave Macmillan, 2005).

102. See, for example, Ken Aldred and Martin A. Smith, *Superpowers in the Post-Cold War Era* (Basingstoke: Macmillan (now Palgrave Macmillan), 1999), p. 164.

103. Reinhard Rummel, *The Evolution of an International Actor: Western Europe's New Assertiveness* (Boulder, CO: Westview, 1990).

104. Tomasso Padoa-Schioppa, *Europa, Forza Gentile* (Bologna: Il Mulino, 2001). See review by Cesare Merlini in *International Spectator* 36:3, July–September 2001.

105. Andrew Moravcsik, 'The Quiet Superpower', in *Newsweek*, 17 June 2002, p. 27.

106. Party of European Socialists, 'Common Security in a Changing Global Context', PES Group Paper, March 2004.

107. William Wallace and Jan Zielonka, 'Misunderstanding Europe', in *Foreign Affairs* 77:6, November/December 1998, pp. 65–80.

108. Huntington, 'The US – Decline or Renewal?'.

109. Ronald Steel, 'The Rise of the European Superpower', in *The New Republic*, 2 July 1990, pp. 23–5.

110. Charles A. Kupchan, *The End of the American Era: US Foreign Policy and the Geopolitics of the Twenty-First Century* (New York: Vintage, 2002), Chapter 4.

111. Jeremy Rifkin, *The European Dream: How Europe's Vision of the Future is Quietly Eclipsing the American Dream* (New York: Jeremy Tarcher/Penguin, 2004).

112. T. R. Reid, *The United States of Europe: The New Superpower and the End of American Supremacy* (New York: Penguin, 2004).

113. Rockwell A. Schnabel, *The Next Superpower? The Rise of Europe and its Challenge to the United States* (Lanham, MD: Rowman and Littlefield, 2005).

114. Stephen Haseler, *Super-State: The New Europe and its Challenge to America* (London: I B Taurus, 2004).

115. Mark Leonard, *Why Europe Will Run the 21st Century* (London: Fourth Estate, 2005).

116. Don Cook, *Charles de Gaulle: A Biography* (New York: Putnam, 1983), p. 334.

117. Romano Prodi, 'Shaping the New Europe', speech to the European Parliament, Strasbourg, 15 February 2000.

118. Reid, *United States of Europe*, p. 4.

119. Interview with *Der Spiegel*, 8 November 2004. See Spiegel Online, www. spiegel.de.

120. D. G. Griffin, *Parapsychology, Philosophy and Spirituality: A Postmodern Exploration* (New York: State University of New York Press, 1997), pp. xiii–xiv.

121. Robert Cooper, *The Breaking of Nations: Order and Chaos in the Twenty-First Century* (London: Atlantic, 2003).

122. Kaldor, 'American Power: From "Compellance" to Cosmopolitanism', pp. 205–7.

Chapter 2

1. See Christopher Layne, 'America as European Hegemon', in *The National Interest* 72, Summer 2003, pp. 17–29.

2. See Jim Hoagland, 'Europe's Destiny', in *Foreign Affairs* 69:1, 1989/90, pp. 33–50.

3. Christopher Thorne, *The Far Eastern War: States and Societies, 1941–45* (London: Unwin, 1986), pp. 211–12.

4. Tom Brokaw, *The Greatest Generation* (New York: Random House, 1998).

5. William I. Hitchcock, *The Struggle for Europe: The Turbulent History of a Divided Continent, 1945–Present* (New York: Anchor, 2004), p. 159.

6. Beatrice Heuser, *Transatlantic Relations: Sharing Ideals and Costs* (London: Royal Institute of International Affairs, 1996), p. 16.

7. Geir Lundestad, 'The United States and Western Europe Under Ronald Reagan', in David E. Kyvig (ed.), *Reagan and the World* (Westport, CT: Greenwood Press, 1990).

8. For a discussion of the deliberations, see Robert Skidelsky, *John Maynard Keynes 1883–1946: Economist, Philosopher, Statesman* (London: Palgrave Macmillan, 2003), pp. 762–7.

9. Armand Van Dormael, *Bretton Woods: Birth of a Monetary System* (New York: Holmes and Meier, 1978).

10. President Harry S. Truman, address to Congress, 12 March 1947.
11. Michael J. Hogan, *The Marshall Plan: America, Britain, and the Reconstruction of Western Europe, 1947–52* (New York: Cambridge University Press, 1987), pp. 26–7.
12. Alan S. Milward, *The Reconstruction of Western Europe 1945–51* (Berkeley, CA: University of California Press, 1984), pp. 46–8.
13. Ibid., p. 94.
14. Heuser, *Transatlantic Relations*, p. 16.
15. Pascaline Winand, *Eisenhower, Kennedy and the United States of Europe* (Basingstoke: Macmillan (now Palgrave Macmillan), 1993), p. 1.
16. D. C. Watt, *Survey of International Affairs 1962* (London: Oxford University Press, 1970), p. 137.
17. Roger Morgan, 'The Transatlantic Relationship', in Kenneth J. Twitchett (ed.), *Europe and the World: The External Relations of the Common Market* (London: Europa, 1976).
18. Hitchcock, *The Struggle for Europe*, pp. 156–8.
19. See Derek Urwin, *Western Europe Since 1945: A Political History*, 4th ed. (London: Longman, 1989), pp. 106ff.
20. Michael Mandelbaum, *The Nuclear Revolution: International Politics Before and After Hiroshima* (Cambridge: Cambridge University Press, 1981), pp. 153–4.
21. Maurice Vaisse, 'Post-Suez France', in William Roger Louis and Roger Owens (eds), *Suez 1956: The Crisis and Its Consequences* (Oxford: Clarendon Press, 1989).
22. Hitchcock, *The Struggle for Europe*, pp. 177–83.
23. Tony Judt, *Postwar: A History of Europe Since 1945* (New York: Penguin, 2005), p. 299.
24. Elizabeth D. Sherwood, *Allies in Crisis: Meeting Global Challenges to Western Security* (New Haven, CT: Yale University Press, 1990), p. 36.
25. Geir Lundestad, *The United States and Western Europe Since 1945* (Oxford: Oxford University Press, 2003), p. 115.
26. Ibid., p. 153.
27. See Anthony Gorst and Lewis Johnman, *The Suez Crisis* (London: Routledge, 1997), pp. 151, 160.
28. Morgan, 'The Transatlantic Relationship'.
29. See Marvin R. Zahniser, *Uncertain Friendship: American–French Diplomatic Relations Through the Cold War* (New York: Wiley, 1975), Chapter 8, and Robert O. Paxton and Nicholas Wahl (eds), *De Gaulle and The United States: A Centennial Reappraisal* (Oxford: Berg, 1994).
30. Dan Hiester, 'The United States as a Power in Europe', in Robert S. Jordan (ed.), *Europe and the Superpowers: Essays on European International Politics* (London: Pinter, 1991), p. 31.
31. Charles de Gaulle, quoted in Barton J. Bernstein, 'The Cuban Missile Crisis: Trading the Jupiters in Turkey?', in *Political Science Quarterly* 95:1, Spring 1980, pp. 97–125.

32. Sherwood, *Allies in Crisis*, p. 111.
33. Stanley Hoffmann, 'Europe's Identity Crisis: Between the Past and America', in *Daedelus* 93:4, Fall 1964.
34. David P. Calleo, 'Western Transformation After the Cold War', in Geir Lundestad (ed.), *No End to Alliance: The United States and Western Europe: Past, Present and Future* (Basingstoke: Macmillan (now Palgrave Macmillan), 1998).
35. Richard J. Barnet, *The Alliance: America, Europe, Japan; Makers of the Post-war World* (New York: Simon and Schuster, 1983), p. 238.
36. Quoted by ibid., p. 264.
37. Urwin, *Western Europe Since 1945*, p. 198.
38. Douglas A. Borer, *Superpowers Defeated: Vietnam and Afghanistan Compared* (London: Frank Cass, 1999), pp. 207–8.
39. For details see Urwin, *Western Europe Since 1945*, pp. 257–60.
40. Judt, *Postwar*, p. 454.
41. Morgan, 'The Transatlantic Relationship'.
42. Hiester, 'The United States as a Power in Europe', p. 33.
43. Ibid., p. 33.
44. *Bulletin of the European Communities* 3(1) 1970, p. 12.
45. Ken Aldred and Martin A. Smith, *Superpowers in the Post-Cold War Era* (Basingstoke: Macmillan (now Palgrave Macmillan), 1999), p. 153.
46. Mike Bowker and Phil Williams, *Superpower Détente: A Reappraisal* (London: Sage, 1988), pp. 261–2.
47. Z, 'The Year of Europe?', in *Foreign Affairs* 52:2, January 1974, pp. 237–48.
48. For background, see Roy H. Ginsberg, *The European Union in International Politics: Baptism by Fire* (Lanham, MD: Rowman and Littlefield, 2001), pp. 110–12.
49. See *Sunday Times* Insight Team, *The Yom Kippur War* (London: Andre Deutsch, 1975), pp. 421–7.
50. 'New Strains on US-Europe Alliance', in *US News and World Report*, 12 November 1973, p. 32.
51. Sherwood, *Allies in Crisis*, pp. 138–42.
52. Aldred and Smith, *Superpowers*, p. 154.
53. Ginsberg, *The European Union in International Politics*, pp. 114–15.
54. Bowker and Williams, *Superpower Détente*, pp. 244–53.
55. President Ronald Reagan, State of the Union address, 26 January 1982.
56. Lundestad, 'The United States and Western Europe Under Ronald Reagan'.
57. Chalmers Johnson, *Blowback: The Costs and Consequences of American Empire* (New York: Holt, 2001).
58. Quoted in *Boston Globe*, 5 December 1984.
59. See Hiester, 'The United States as a Power in Europe'.
60. Michael Howard, 'A European Perspective on the Reagan Years', in *Foreign Affairs* 66:3, 1987/88, pp. 478–93.

61. Ibid.
62. *Report of the Congressional Committtees Investigating the Iran-Contra Affair* (Washington, DC: GPO, 1987).
63. Howard, 'A European Perspective on the Reagan Years'.
64. By November 2005 it stood at just over $8 trillion.
65. Margaret Thatcher, *The Downing Street Years* (London: HarperCollins, 1993), pp. 327–31.
66. Bowker and Williams, *Superpower Détente*, p. 253.
67. Howard, 'A European Perspective on the Reagan Years'.
68. Margaret Thatcher, eulogy broadcast at funeral of Ronald Reagan, 11 June 2004.
69. Willem van Eekelen, 'WEU and the Gulf Crisis', in *Survival* 32:6, 1990, pp. 519–32; Scott Anderson, 'Western European and the Gulf War', in Reinhardt Rummel (ed.), *Toward Political Union: Planning a Common Foreign and Security Policy in the European Community* (Boulder, CO: Westview, 1992).
70. *New York Times,* 25 January 1991.
71. Jacques Delors, 'European Integration and Security', in *Survival* 33:2, Spring 1991, pp. 99–109.
72. Margaret Thatcher, in *Wall Street Journal*, 3 September 1990.
73. J. Bryan Collester, 'How Defense "Spilled Over" Into the CFSP: Western European Union (WEU) and the European Security and Defense Identity (ESDI)', in Maria Green Cowles and Michael Smith (eds), *The State of the European Union: Risks, Reform, Resistance, and Revival* (Oxford: Oxford University Press, 2000).
74. John J. Mearsheimer, 'Back to the Future: Instability in Europe After the Cold War', in *International Security* 15:1, 1990, pp. 5–56.
75. See Jarrod Wiener, 'Transatlantic Trade: Economic Security, Agriculture, and the Politics of Technology', in Wiener (ed.), *The Transatlantic Relationship* (Basingstoke: Macmillan (now Palgrave Macmillan), 1996).
76. *Rebuilding America's Defenses: Strategy, Forces and Resources for a New Century* (Washington, DC: Project for the New American Century, September 2000).
77. See Irving Kristol, *Neo-Conservatism: The Autobiography of an Idea* (Chicago: Ivan Dee, 1999), and Stefan Halper and Jonathan Clarke, *America Alone: The Neo-Conservatives and the Global Order* (Cambridge: Cambridge University Press, 2004).
78. Sherle R. Schwenninger, 'Revamping American Grand Strategy', in *World Policy Journal* 20:3, Summer 2003, pp. 25–44.
79. President George W. Bush, State of the Union address, 29 January 2002.
80. Nicole Gnesotto, 'Reacting to America', in *Survival* 44:4, December 2002, pp. 99–106.
81. Survey co-sponsored by the German Marshall Fund, results reported in BBC News Online, 4 September 2003, http://news.bbc.co.uk.

82. European Commission, *Eurobarometer*, October 2003.
83. 'Chirac Firm on Iraq War Opposition', in BBC News Online, 21 February 2003; 'Chirac Reopens Iraq Wounds', in BBC News Online, 3 June 2003.
84. 'Analysis: Schroeder Challenges the US', in BBC News Online,13 February 2003.
85. There is a long tradition of anti-French sentiment in the United States. See, for example, John J. Miller and Mark Molesky, *Our Oldest Enemy: A History of America's Disastrous Relationship with France* (New York: Doubleday, 2004); Kenneth R. Timmerman, *The French Betrayal of America* (New York: Crown Forum, 2004), and Richard Z. Chesnoff, *The Arrogance of the French: Why They Can't Stand Us – and Why the Feeling Is Mutual* (New York: Sentinel, 2005).

Chapter 3

1. Thomas Risse, 'US Power in a Liberal Security Community', in G. John Ikenberry (ed.), *America Unrivaled: The Future of the Balance of Power* (Ithaca, NY: Cornell University Press, 2002).
2. Stanley Hoffmann, 'Towards a Common Foreign and Security Policy?', in *Journal of Common Market Studies* 38:2, June 2000, pp. 189–98.
3. Alfred van Staden, 'The Case for Complementarity', speech to conference organized by the German Council on Foreign Relations, Berlin, June 2003, reproduced on Tech Central Station website, www.techcentralstation.be.
4. In order, they are Russia, China, Japan, Britain, France, Germany, Saudi Arabia, Italy, India, and South Korea. Calculated from figures in International Institute for Strategic Studies, *The Military Balance 2004–2005* (Oxford: Oxford University Press, 2004).
5. Ibid.
6. See discussion in Robert J. Art, 'To What Ends Military Power?', in *International Security* 4:4, Spring 1980, pp. 3–33.
7. See discussion in Andrew J. Bacevich, *The New American Militarism: How Americans Are Seduced by War* (New York: Oxford University Press, 2005).
8. See discussion in Frances G. Burwell, 'Introduction', in Frances G. Burwell and Ivo H. Dalder (eds), *The United States and Europe in the Global Arena* (Basingstoke: Macmillan (now Palgrave Macmillan), 1999).
9. Robert Kagan, *Of Paradise and Power: America and Europe in the New World Order* (New York: Knopf, 2003).
10. The campaign to discredit Senator John Kerry's Vietnam record during the 2004 US presidential race was a case in point.
11. See discussion in Anand Menon, Kalypso Nikolaidis and Jennifer Walsh, 'In Defence of Europe – A Response to Kagan', in *Journal of European Affairs* 2:3, August 2004, pp. 5–14.

12. Ronald Steel, *Temptations of a Superpower* (Cambridge, MA: Harvard University Press, 1995), p. 6.
13. Larry Diamond, 'Patching Things Up', in *Hoover Digest* 3, Summer 2003.
14. Andrew Moravcsik, 'Striking a New Transatlantic Bargain', in *Foreign Affairs* 82:4, July/August 2003, pp. 74–89.
15. Niall Ferguson, 'What is Power?', in *Hoover Digest* 2, Spring 2003.
16. 'A Famous Victory and a Tough Sequel', in *Financial Times*, 10 April 2003, p. 10.
17. Minxin Pei, 'Lessons From the Past: The American Record on Nation-Building', Carnegie Endowment Policy Brief No. 24, April 2003.
18. Bruce Bueno de Mesquita and George W. Downs, 'Why Gun-Barrel Democracy Doesn't Work', in *Hoover Digest* 2, Spring 2004.
19. Joseph S. Nye, *The Paradox of American Power: Why the World's Only Superpower Can't Go It Alone* (New York: Oxford University Press, 2002).
20. Charles Aldinger, 'US, Europe Must Heal Rifts Over Iraq – NATO Chief', Reuters, 29 January 2004, http://today.reuters.com/news.
21. Ferguson, 'What is Power?'.
22. In the White House budget plan sent to Congress in February 2006, the administration asked for $439.3 billion for defence.
23. On the sustainability of US economic policy and hegemony, see David H. Levey and Stuart S. Brown, 'The Overstretch Myth', in *Foreign Affairs* 84:2, March/April 2005, pp. 2–7.
24. See Daniel Keohane, 'The European Defence Plans: Filling the Transatlantic Gaps', in *International Spectator* 38:3, July–September 2003.
25. See the comments of correspondent Andy Rooney on the ABC television programme *60 Minutes*, 24 October 2004, www.cbsnews.com.
26. See discussion in Max Boot, 'The Struggle to Transform the Military', in *Foreign Affairs* 84:2, March/April 2005, pp. 103–18.
27. See discussion in Earl Tilford, 'Operation Allied Force and the Role of Air Power', in *Parameters: US Army War College Quarterly* 29:4, Winter 1999–2000, pp. 24–38, and Timothy L. Thomas, 'Kosovo and the Current Myth of Information Superiority', in *Parameters: US Army War College Quarterly* 30:1, Spring 2000, pp. 13–29.
28. Arnold Beichman, 'The Politics of Vengeance', in *Hoover Digest* 3, Summer 2004.
29. Samuel Huntington, *The Clash of Civilizations and the Remaking of World Order* (New York: Simon and Schuster, 1996).
30. Chester A. Crocker, 'A Dubious Template for US Foreign Policy', in *Survival* 47:1, Spring 2005, pp. 51–70.
31. Jeffrey Record, 'The Limits and Temptations of America's Conventional Military Primacy', in *Survival* 47:1, Spring 2005, pp. 33–50.
32. Senator Jesse Helms, floor debate in the US Senate, 27 April 1998.
33. Alexander Haig, 'The Promise and Peril of Our Times', Foreign Policy Research Institute, 25 November 2003, at www.fpri.org.

34. Robert E. Hunter, 'Europe's Leverage', in *Washington Quarterly* 27:1, Winter 2003–04, pp. 91–110.
35. See discussion in Reinhardt Rummel and Peter Schmidt, 'The Changing Security Framework', in William Wallace (ed.), *The Dynamics of European Integration* (London: Pinter, 1992).
36. Stephanie Anderson, 'The EU: From Civilian Power to Military Power?', in *International Studies Review* 6:3, September 2004, pp. 505–7.
37. Andrew Shonfield, *Europe: Journey to an Unknown Destination* (Harmondsworth: Penguin, 1973).
38. See Richard Whitman, 'The Fall, and Rise, of Civilian Power Europe?', National Europe Centre Paper 16, Australian National University, July 2002.
39. Thus, for example, the suggestion by former Commission president Romano Prodi in 2000 that Europe should become a 'global civil power' (see Chapter 1).
40. See François Duchêne, 'Europe's Role in World Peace', in Richard Mayne (ed.), *Europe Tomorrow: Sixteen Europeans Look Ahead* (London: Fontana, 1972), and François Duchêne, 'The European Community and the Uncertainties of Interdependence', in Max Kohnstamm and Wolfgang Hager (eds), *A Nation Writ Large? Foreign Policy Problems Before the European Community* (London: Macmillan (now Palgrave Macmillan), 1973). Duchêne's ideas are nicely summarized by Jan Zielonka, *Explaining Euro-Paralysis: Why Europe is Unable to Act in International Politics* (Basingstoke: Macmillan (now Palgrave Macmillan), 1998), pp. 226–7.
41. Kenneth J. Twitchett, 'External Relations or Foreign Policy?', in Twitchett (ed.), *Europe and the World: The External Relations of the Common Market* (London: Europa, 1976).
42. Hedley Bull, 'Civilian Power Europe: A Contradiction in Terms?', in Loukas Tsoukalis (ed.), *The European Community: Past, Present and Future* (Oxford: Basil Blackwell, 1983).
43. Hanns W. Maull, 'Germany and Japan: The New Civilian Powers', in *Foreign Affairs* 69:5, Winter 1990/91, pp. 91–106.
44. Karen E. Smith, 'Still "Civilian Power EU"?', European Foreign Policy Unit Working Paper 2005/1.
45. International Institute for Strategic Studies, *The Military Balance 2004–2005* (Oxford: Oxford University Press, 2004).
46. Robert Kagan, *Of Paradise and Power: America and Europe in the New World Order* (New York: Knopf, 2003), p. 53.
47. See discussion in Trevor C. Salmon and Alistair J. K. Shepherd, *Toward a European Army: A Military Power in the Making?* (Boulder, CO: Lynne Rienner, 2003), pp. 22–6.
48. Anne Deighton, 'Conclusion', in Deighton (ed.), *Western European Union 1954–97: Defence, Security and Integration* (Oxford: European Interdependence Research Unit, 1997), p. 170.
49. It began life as the Western Union, and was renamed the Western European Union in 1954.

50. Geir Lundestad, *The United States and Western Europe Since 1945* (Oxford: Oxford University Press, 2003), p. 82.

51. William Wallace, 'Foreign and Security Policy', in Helen Wallace, William Wallace and Mark A. Pollack (eds), *Policy-Making in the European Union*, 5th ed. (Oxford: Oxford University Press, 2005).

52. Christopher Hill, 'The Capability–Expectations Gap, or Conceptualizing Europe's International Role', in *Journal of Common Market Studies* 31:3, September 1993, pp. 305–28.

53. Wallace, 'Foreign and Security Policy'.

54. *The Economist*, 'War in Europe', 6 July 1991.

55. Quoted by Noel Malcolm, 'The Case Against "Europe"', in *Foreign Affairs* 74:2, March/April 1995, pp. 52–68.

56. Adrian Treacher, 'From Civilian Power to Military Actor: The EU's Resistable Transformation', in *European Foreign Affairs Review* 9:1, Spring 2004, pp. 49–66.

57. Ibid.

58. For more details, see J. Bryan Collester, 'How Defense "Spilled Over" Into the CFSP: Western European Union (WEU) and the European Security and Defense Identity (ESDI)', in Maria Green Cowles and Michael Smith (eds), *The State of the European Union: Risks, Reform, Resistance, and Revival* (Oxford: Oxford University Press, 2000)

59. Bastian Giegerich and William Wallace, 'Not Such a Soft Power: The External Deployment of European Forces', in *Survival* 46:2, June 2004, pp. 163–82.

60. Sven Biscop, 'Ready and Able? Assessing the EU's Capacity for Military Action', in *European Foreign Affairs Review* 9:4, Winter 2004, pp. 509–27.

61. Anand Menon, 'Why ESDP is Misguided and Dangerous to the Alliance', in Jolyon Howorth and John T. S. Keeler (eds), *Defending Europe: The EU, NATO and the Quest for European Autonomy* (Basingstoke: Palgrave Macmillan, 2003).

62. Quoted in 'EU's Defence Plans Baffle NATO', in BBC Online, 3 December 2003, http://news.bbc.co.uk.

63. Dominique Moïsi, 'Reinventing the West', in *Foreign Affairs* 82:5, November/December 2003, pp. 67–73.

64. For discussion, see Karen E. Smith, 'The End of Civilian Power EU: A Welcome Demise or a Cause for Concern?', in *International Spectator* 35:2, April–June 2002, pp. 11–28; Trevor C. Salmon and Alistair J. K. Shepherd, *Toward a European Army: A Military Power in the Making?* (Boulder, CO: Lynne Rienner, 2003); Treacher, 'From Civilian Power to Military Actor'.

65. Giegerich and Wallace, 'Not Such a Soft Power'.

66. Hanns Maull, 'Germany and the Use of Force: Still a "Civilian Power"?', in *Survival* 42:2, 2000, pp. 71–3.

67. Knud Erik Jørgensen, 'Western Europe and the Petersberg Tasks', in Jørgensen (ed.), *European Approaches to Crisis Management* (The Hague: Kluwer Law International, 1997), pp. 131–52.

68.   Stelios Stavridis, 'Militarising the EU: The Concept of Civilian Power Europe Revisited', in *International Spectator* 36:4, October–December 2001.

69.   There were 25 active armed conflicts under way in August 2002, of which all but seven were internal armed conflicts. This number was down on previous years: 36 in 1997, 35 in 1998 and 1999, 37 in 2000, and 31 in 2001. Source: International Institute for Strategic Studies, *The Chart of Armed Conflict 2002* (London: IISS, 2002).

70.   Andrew Moravcsik, 'How Europe Can Win Without an Army', in *Financial Times*, 2 April 2003; Andrew Moravcsik and Kalypso Nicolaidis, 'Urgent: How to Fix Europe's Image Problem', in *Foreign Policy* 148, May/June 2005, pp. 72–7.

71.   NATO, Text of the Report of the Committee of Three on Non-Military Cooperation in NATO, approved 13 December 1956. www.nato.int/docu/basictxt/bt-a3.htm.

72.   Simon Duke, *The New European Security Disorder* (Basingstoke: Macmillan (now Palgrave Macmillan), 1994), p. 228.

73.   Alyson J. K. Bailes, 'US and EU Strategy Concepts: A Mirror for Partnership and Difference?', in *International Spectator* 39:1, January–March 2004.

74.   Robert E. Hunter, 'The US and the European Union: Bridging the Strategic Gap?', in *International Spectator* 39:1, January–March 2004.

75.   Quoted by E. J. Dionne, 'West Europe Generally Critical of US', in *New York Times*, 16 April 1986.

76.   Dominique de Villepin, '2004 – Just Another year of Fighting Terrorism?', in *Globalist*, 2 January 2004.

77.   Simon Duke, 'The European Security Strategy in a Comparative Framework: Does it Make for Secure Alliances in a Better World?', in *European Foreign Affairs Review* 9:4, Winter 2004, pp. 459–81.

78.   Party of European Socialists, 'Common Security in a Changing Global Context', PES Group Paper, March 2004, p. 6.

79.   Richard Whitman, 'The Strange Superpower: Europe's Global Role', keynote address at opening of EU Center of Excellence, Indiana University, April 2006.

80.   Duke, *The New European Security Disorder*.

81.   Fraser Cameron, in debate with Andrew Moravcsik: 'Should the European Union Be Able to Do Everything that NATO Can?', in *NATO Review* 3, Autumn 2003.

Chapter 4

1.   In the period 1994–2003, more than $3 trillion was invested in the EU-15, or twice the amount invested in the United States. In that same period, the EU invested three times as much overseas as the United States and 15 times as much as Japan.

2. The European market has extended even to non-EU member states: Iceland and Norway are members of the control-free Schengen agreement, and participate in the single market through the European Economic Area.
3. This is particularly true of controls on the movements of Eastern Europeans to the West.
4. Adam Posen of the Institute for International Economics, quoted by David H. Levey and Stuart S. Brown, 'The Overstretch Myth: Can the Indispensable Nation be a Debtor Nation?', in *Foreign Affairs* 84:2, March/April 2005, pp. 2–7.
5. Arnold Beichman, 'The Politics of Vengeance', in *Hoover Digest* 3, Summer 2004.
6. Levey and Brown, 'The Overstretch Myth'.
7. Robert C. Pozen, 'Mind the Gap: Can the New Europe Overtake the US Economy?', in *Foreign Affairs* 84:2, March/April 2005, pp. 8–12.
8. 'What Ails Japan? A Survey of Japan', in *The Economist*, 20 April 2002.
9. These and other historical economic data come from OECD, *The World Economy: Historical Statistics* (Paris: OECD Development Centre, 2003).
10. Commission of the European Communities, *Completing the Internal Market: The White Paper* (Luxembourg: Office of Official Publications of the European Communities, 1985).
11. European Commission, *Report of the Committee for the Study of Economic and Monetary Union* (Luxembourg: Office of Official Publications of the European Communities, 1989).
12. Charles Lockhart, *The Roots of American Exceptionalism: Institutions, Culture and Policies* (New York: Palgrave Macmillan, 2003).
13. Data from World Trade Organization website (2006), www.wto.org.
14. Jeffrey A. Frankel, 'Still the Lingua Franca: The Exaggerated Death of the Dollar', in *Foreign Affairs* 74:4, July/August 1995, pp. 9–16.
15. Lawrence Summers, speech to Euromoney Conference, New York, 30 April 1997.
16. At the time of its launch in 1999, the euro was worth $1.17. By July 2001, it was down to 84 cents. In January 2004 it was back up to $1.28.
17. In 2001–04 the dollar fell by 33 per cent against the euro, and would have fallen more had not Japan and China bought dollars to hold down the value of their own currencies. See 'Let the Dollar Drop', in *The Economist*, 7 February 2004.
18. Brad Setser and Nouriel Roubini, 'How Scary is the Deficit?', in *Foreign Affairs* 84:4, July/August 2005, pp. 194–200.
19. Richard Portes and Hélène Rey, 'The Emergence of the Euro as an International Currency', in David Begg et al. (eds), *EMU: Prospects and Challenges For the Euro* (Oxford: Blackwell, 1998).
20. Menzie Chinn and Jeffery Frankel, 'Will the Euro Eventually Surpass the Dollar as the Leading International Reserve Currency?', National Bureau of Economic Research Working Paper 11510, July 2005.

21. Diane B. Kunz, 'The Fall of the Dollar Order: The World the United States is Losing', in *Foreign Affairs* 74:4, July/August 1995, pp. 22–6.

22. Frankel, 'Still the Lingua Franca'.

23. Benjamin J. Cohen, 'The Political Economy of Currency Regions', in Edward D. Mansfield and Helen V. Milner (eds), *The Political Economy of Regionalism* (New York: Columbia University Press, 1997).

24. Portes and Rey, 'The Emergence of the Euro'.

25. Malcolm Levitt and Christopher Lord, *The Political Economy of Monetary Union* (Basingstoke: Macmillan (now Palgrave Macmillan), 2000), p. 163.

26. These figures stand in contrast to average rates of nearly 11 per cent during the 1970s and of 6.5 per cent during the 1990s. See Frank McDonald and Stephen Dearden, *European Economic Integration*, 3rd ed. (Harlow: Prentice-Hall, 1999), Table 3.3, p. 99.

27. See Roger Bootle, 'Should the Euro be the Reserve Currency?', in *Telegraph*, 27 February 2005; 'The Passing of the Buck?', in *The Economist*, 2 December 2004.

28. Figures from International Monetary Fund website (2005), www.imf.org.

29. For discussion, see Levitt and Lord, *The Political Economy of Monetary Union*, p. 164.

30. The US dollar is the official currency of Ecuador, El Salvador, and East Timor. It is also used alongside local currencies in several countries, including the Bahamas, Barbados, Bermuda, the Cayman Islands, Lebanon, and Panama.

31. 'The Passing of the Buck?', in *The Economist*.

32. Levy and Brown, 'The Overstretch Myth'.

33. See Steve Schifferes, 'Does the US Budget Deficit Matter?', in BBC News Online, 2 February 2004, http://news.bbc.co.uk, and 'Greenspan Concerned With Weak Dollar', in *CNN Money*, 19 November 2004.

34. Frankel, 'Still the Lingua Franca'.

35. World Trade Organization website (2006), www.wto.org. Figures are for trade in 2004, by dollar value.

36. McDonald and Dearden, *European Economic Integration*, p. 303.

37. Calculated from data on World Trade Organization website (2006), www. wto.org.

38. Actually, the proportion of EU agricultural spending has come down from more than 60 per cent of the budget in 1991 to about 46 per cent today.

39. Figures quoted by Raymond J. Ahearn, *US–European Union Trade Relations: Issues and Policy Challenges* (Washington, DC: Congressional Research Service, April 2005).

40. Pascal Lamy, speech before Congressional Economic Leadership Institute, Washington DC, 4 March 2003.

41. George M. Taber, *John F. Kennedy and a Uniting Europe* (Bruges: College of Europe, 1969), pp. 141–5.

42. Figures from US Census Bureau (2005), www.census.gov/foreign-trade.

43. Richard Morningstar, speech before the EU Committee of the American Chamber of Commerce, 23 January 2001.

44. WTO website (2005), www.wto.org.

45. Stijn Billiet, 'The EC and WTO Dispute Settlement: The Initiation of Trade Disputes by the EC', in *European Foreign Affairs Review* 10:2, Summer 2005, pp. 197–214.

46. See Robert Read, 'The "Banana Split": The EU–US Banana Trade Dispute and the Effects of EU Market Liberalisation', in Nicholas Perdikis and Robert Read (eds), *The WTO and the Regulation of International Trade: Recent Trade Disputes Between the European Union and the United States* (Cheltenham: Edward Elgar, 2005).

47. Nicholas Perdikis, 'EU–US Trade in Genetically Modified Goods: A Trade Dispute in the Making', in Perdikis and Read, *The WTO and the Regulation of International Trade*.

48. See 'EU Opens New Front in Trade War', in BBC News Online, 1 March 2004, and 'Bush Shakes up US Corporate Taxes', in BBC News Online, 22 October 2004, http://news.bbc.co.uk.

49. Billiet, 'The EC and WTO Dispute Settlement'.

50. Ahearn, 'US–European Union Trade Relations'.

51. For data on mergers and acquisitions, see Dealogic at www.dealogic.com.

52. For an interesting example of the view from the 1970s, see Michael Z. Brooke and H. Lee Remmers (eds), *The Multinational Company in Europe: Some Key Problems* (London: Longman, 1972), Chapter 6.

53. Alfred D. Chandler, *Strategy and Structure: Chapters in the History of the Industrial Enterprise* (Cambridge, MA: MIT Press, 1962), and 'The United States: Engines of Economic Growth in Capital-Intensive and Knowledge-Intensive Industries', in Chandler et al. (eds), *Big Business and the Wealth of Nations* (Cambridge: Cambridge University Press, 1997).

54. European Commission figures quoted by Christopher Layton, *Cross-Frontier Mergers in Europe* (Bath: Bath University Press, 1971), p. 3.

55. Ibid., pp. 4–5.

56. Ash Amin, D. R. Charles and Jeremy Howells, 'Corporate Restructuring and Cohesion in the New Europe', in *Regional Studies* 26:4, January 1992, pp. 319–31; Commission of the European Communities, 'Competition and Integration: Community Merger Control Policy', in *European Economy* 57 (1994).

57. Richard Owen and Michael Dynes, *The Times Guide to 1992: Britain in a Europe Without Frontiers* (London: Times Publications, 1989), p. 222.

58. Several proposed new mergers and acquisitions in late 2005 and early 2006 had – as this book went to press – revived ideas of economic protectionism in the EU, politely hidden behind the phrase 'economic patriotism'.

59. *Fortune Directory*, May 1970.

60. In April 2006 BAE systems announced that it was in discussions to sell its stake in Airbus to EADS.

61. The difference, according to *The Economist*, lies in advances in information technology, which the United States has used with great effect to boost efficiency. See *The Economist*, 21 May 2005.

62. Robert Gordon, 'Two Centuries of Economic Growth: Europe Chasing the American Frontier', 17 October 2002, http://faculty-web.at.northwestern.edu/economics/gordon/355.pdf.

63. World Bank figures, from www.worldbank.org/data. Among EU member states, only Luxembourg ($56,230) and Denmark ($40,650) had per capita levels of productivity comparable to those of the US.

64. Alberto Alesina, Edward L. Glaeser and Bruce Sacerdote, 'Work and Leisure in the US and Europe: Why so Different?', Working Paper 11278, National Bureau of Economic Research, April 2005, http://papers.nber.org/papers/w11278.pdf.

65. OECD, *Going for Growth 2006* (Paris: OECD, 2006).

66. See discussion in 'Grossly Distorted Picture', *The Economist*, 11 February 2006.

67. OECD, *OECD Employment Outlook, Statistical Annex* (Paris: OECD, 2005), p. 255. Americans were working 1,824 hours on average, and the French were working 1,441 hours.

68. Oliver Blanchard, 'The Economic Future of Europe', Working Paper, National Bureau of Economic Research, March 2004, http://papers.nber.org/papers/w10310.

69. OECD Health Data 2005, at OECD website (2006), www.oecd.org. Figures are for 2003.

70. 'Europe's Population Implosion', in *The Economist*, 19 July 2003.

71. Niall Ferguson, 'A World Without Power', in *Foreign Policy* 143, July/August 2004, pp. 32–9.

72. George Weigel, 'Is Europe Dying? Notes on a Crisis of Civilizational Morale', in *Newsletter of the Foreign Policy Research Institute* 6:2, June 2005.

Chapter 5

1. Mark Almond, *Europe's Backyard War: The War in the Balkans* (London: Heinemann, 1994), p. 339.

2. Speech by Jacques Santer to Davos World Economic Forum, 28 January 1995, on Europa website (2005), http://europa.eu.int/en/comm/js/davos.html.

3. Charles Bremner, 'EU Foreign Policy Left in Disarray by Balkan and Aegean Bungling', in *The Times*, 12 February 1996.

4. Richard Rosecrance, 'The European Union: A New Type of International Actor', in Jan Zielonka (ed.), *Paradoxes of European Foreign Policy* (The Hague: Kluwer Law International, 1998).

5. Jan Zielonka, *Explaining Euro-Paralysis: Why Europe is Unable to Act in International Politics* (Basingstoke: Macmillan (now Palgrave Macmillan), 1998).

6. Jacques Attali, 'A View from Europe (II)', in *Foreign Policy* 109, Winter 1997/98, pp. 54–8.

7. Roy H. Ginsberg, *The European Union in International Politics: Baptism by Fire* (Lanham, MD: Rowman and Littlefield, 2001).

8. Karen E. Smith, 'The Instruments of European Union Foreign Policy', in Zielonka, *Paradoxes of European Foreign Policy*.

9. Rosecrance, 'The European Union: A New Type of International Actor'.

10. Mark Leonard, *Why Europe Will Run the 21st Century* (London: Fourth Estate, 2005), Chapter 1.

11. For a review of the debate, see Ben Tonra, 'Conceptualizing the European Union's Global Role', in Michelle Cini and Angela K. Bourne (eds), *European Union Studies* (Basingstoke: Palgrave Macmillan, 2006).

12. Carol Ann Cosgrove and Kenneth J. Twitchett (eds), *The New International Actors: The United Nations and the European Economic Community* (London: Macmillan (now Palgrave Macmillan), 1970), pp. 12, 38–51.

13. See G. Sjöstedt, *The External Role of the European Community* (Farnborough: Gower, 1977). See also discussion in Ben Rosamond, *Theories of European Integration* (Basingstoke: Palgrave Macmillan, 2000).

14. Ralf Dahrendorf, 'International Power: A European Perspective', in *Foreign Affairs* 56:1, 1977, pp. 72–88.

15. David Allen and Michael Smith, 'Western Europe's Presence in the Contemporary International Arena', in *Review of International Studies* 16, 1990, pp. 19–37; David Allen and Michael Smith, 'The European Union 's Security Presence: Barrier, Facilitator, or Manager?', in Carolyn Rhodes (ed.), *The European Union in the World Community* (Boulder, CO: Lynne Rienner, 1998).

16. Sebastiaan Princen and Michèle Knodt, 'Understanding the EU's External Relations', in Knodt and Princen (eds), *Understanding the European Union's External Relations* (London: Routledge, 2003), p. 203.

17. Michael Mann, 'The First Failed Empire of the Twenty-First Century', in David Held and Mathias Koenig-Archibugi (eds), *American Power in the 21st Century* (Cambridge: Polity, 2004).

18. Jan Zielonka, 'Constraints, Opportunities and Choices in European Foreign Policy', in Zielonka, *Paradoxes of European Foreign Policy*.

19. See Christopher Hill, 'The Capability–Expectations Gap, or Conceptualizing Europe's International Role', in *Journal of Common Market Studies* 31:2, September 1993, pp. 305–28.

20. William Wallace, 'Foreign and Security Policy: The Painful Path from Shadow to Substance', in Helen Wallace, William Wallace, and Mark A. Pollack (eds), *Policy-Making in the European Union*, 5th ed. (Oxford: Oxford University Press, 2005).

21. Christopher Piening, *Global Europe: The European Union in World Affairs* (Boulder, CO: Lynne Rienner, 1997), p. 31; Adrian Treacher, 'From Civilian Power to Military Actor: The EU's Resistible Transformation', in *European Foreign Affairs Review* 9:1, Spring 2004, pp. 49–66.

22. Jan Zielonka, 'Constraints, Opportunities and Choices'.
23. *Bulletin of the European Communities* 1-1970, p. 12.
24. Clive Archer and Fiona Butler, *The European Community: Structure and Process*, 2nd ed. (London: Pinter, 1996), p. 214.
25. Wallace, 'Foreign and Security Policy'.
26. *Bulletin of the European Communities* 11-1981, and supplement 3-1981.
27. Piening, *Global Europe*, p. 35.
28. Ibid., p. 39.
29. Michael Smith, 'What's Wrong with the CFSP? The Politics of Institutional Reform', in Pierre-Henri Laurent and Marc Maresceau (eds), *The State of the European Union, Vol. 4* (Boulder, CO: Lynne Rienner, 1998).
30. Wallace, 'Foreign and Security Policy'.
31. David P. Calleo, 'Power, Wealth and Wisdom: The United States and Europe After Iraq', in *The National Interest*, Summer 2003.
32. Leonard, *Why Europe Will Run the 21st Century*, p. 16.
33. See Espen Barth Eide, 'Introduction: The Role of the EU in Fostering "Effective Multilateralism"', in Barth Eide (ed.), *Global Europe Report 1: 'Effective Multilateralism': Europe, Regional Security and a Revitalized UN* (London: Foreign Policy Centre, 2004).
34. Karen E. Smith, *European Union Foreign Policy in a Changing World* (Cambridge: Polity, 2003).
35. Smith, 'The Instruments of European Union Foreign Policy'.
36. R. James Woolsey, 'Appeasement Will Only Encourage Iran', in *Survival* 38:4, Winter 1996–97. See also Russell A. Berman, 'The Psychology of Appeasement', in *Hoover Digest* 3, Summer 2004.
37. 'US "appeasement" warning to Spain', in BBC News Online, 18 March 2004, http://news.bbc.co.uk.
38. Quoted in *Christian Science Monitor*, 29 March 2004.
39. Václav Havel, 'Appeasement Revisited', in *Project Syndicate*, January 2005, www.project-syndicate.org/commentary/havel24.
40. European Commission, *Eurobarometer* 63, Spring 2005, pp. 68–9.
41. Worldviews survey undertaken by the Chicago Council on Foreign Relations and the German Marshall Fund, 2002. Taken in six European states (Germany, Britain, France, Italy, Poland, and the Netherlands).
42. Larry Diamond, 'Patching Things Up', in *Hoover Digest* 3, Summer 2003.
43. Noam Chomsky, *Rogue States: The Rule of Force in World Affairs* (London: Pluto Press, 2000), pp. 1–2.
44. See Attali, 'A View from Europe (II)', and Rupert Pennant-Rea, 'A View from Europe (III)', in *Foreign Policy* 109, Winter 1997/98, pp. 54–8 and 62–5.
45. Geoffrey Wiseman, 'Pax Americana: Bumping into Diplomatic Culture', in *International Studies Perspectives* 6:4, November 2005, pp. 409–30.
46. For an outline of US objections, see Jennifer Elsea, 'US Policy Regarding the International Criminal Court', Congressional Research Service/Library of Congress, 3 September 2002.

47. For more details, see 'Q&A: International Criminal Court', in BBC News Online, 13 July 2002; 'US Warning over Court', in BBC News Online, 10 June 2003, http://news.bbc.co.uk, and website of the International Criminal Court, www.icc-cpi.int.

48. Richard Haass, *The Opportunity: America's Moment to Alter History's Course* (New York: Public Affairs, 2005), p 198.

49. Clyde Prestowitz, *Rogue Nation: American Unilateralism and the Failure of Good Intentions* (New York: Basic Books, 2003); T. D. Allman, *Rogue State: America at War With the World* (New York: Nation Books, 2004).

50. Patrick E. Tyler, 'A New Power in the Streets', in *New York Times*, 17 February 2003.

51. Minxin Pei, 'The Paradoxes of American Nationalism', in *Foreign Policy* 136, May/June 2003, pp. 30–7.

52. 'Europe and America: Weathering the Storm', in *The Economist*, 9 September 2000.

53. Henry Kissinger, 'A Global Order in Flux', in *Washington Post*, 9 July 2004.

54. Quoted in Daniel S. Papp, Loch K. Johnson and John E. Endicott, *American Foreign Policy: History, Politics and Policy* (New York: Longman, 2005), p. 204.

55. For a discussion of this, see Dennis H. Wrong, 'Problems in Defining Power', in Marvin E. Olsen and Martin N. Marger (eds), *Power in Modern Societies* (Boulder, CO: Westview, 1993).

56. Richard Rosecrance, 'Mergers and Acquisitions', in *The National Interest* 80, Summer 2005, pp. 65–73.

57. Adrian van den Hoven, 'The European Union as an International Economic Actor', in Neill Nugent (ed.), *European Union Enlargement* (Basingstoke: Palgrave Macmillan, 2004).

58. Commission of the European Communities, *Report on the Regional Problems of the Enlarged Community* (the Thomson Report), COM(73)550 (Luxembourg: Office of Official Publications of the European Communities, 1979).

59. José da Silva Lopes, *Portugal and EC Membership Evaluated* (London: Pinter, 1993), pp. 2–3.

60. Panos Kazakos and P. C. Ioakimidis (eds), *Greece and EC Membership Evaluated* (London: Pinter, 1994), pp. 297–8.

61. OECD, *Economic Survey of Greece 2005*, OECD website, http://www.oecd.org.

62. See OECD, *Economic Survey: Ireland 2003* (Paris: OECD, 2004).

63. World Bank figures, World Bank website, http://www.worldbank.org/data. Using purchasing power parity calculations makes Ireland the fifth most productive country in the world, and the second most productive in the EU after Luxembourg.

64. Benjamin Powell, 'Economic Freedom and Growth: The Case of the Celtic Tiger', in *Cato Journal* 22:3, Winter 2003, pp. 431–48.

65. See discussion in Jan Zielonka, 'Policies Without Strategy: The EU's Record in Eastern Europe', in Zielonka, *Paradoxes of European Foreign Policy*. See

also Alan Mayhew, 'The European Union's Policy Toward Central Europe: Design or Drift?', in Rhodes, *The European Union in the World Community*.

66. See, for example, discussion in Fraser Cameron, 'The European Union and the Challenge of Enlargement', in Marc Maresceau (ed.), *Enlarging the European Union: Relations Between the EU and Central and Eastern Europe* (London: Longman, 1997). See also Roy H. Ginsberg, 'The Impact of Enlargement on the Role of the European Union in the World', in John Redmond and Glenda G. Rosenthal (eds), *The Expanding European Union: Past, Present, and Future* (Boulder, CO: Lynne Rienner, 1998).

67. Requirements are laid down in the Copenhagen conditions, agreed at the Copenhagen European Council in June 1993.

68. Leonard, *Why Europe Will Run the 21st Century*, pp. 53–5 and 145–6.

69. Roberto Aliboni, 'The Geopolitical Implications of the European Neighbourhood Policy', in *European Foreign Affairs Review* 10:1, Spring 2005, pp 1–16.

70. For data and discussion, see David Roodman and Scott Standley, 'Tax Policies to Promote Private Charitable Giving in DAC Countries', Working Paper 82, Center for Global Development, Washington, DC, January 2006.

71. Olufemi Babarinde, 'The European Union's Relations with the South: A Commitment to Development?', in Rhodes, *The European Union in the World Community*.

72. Karin Arts and Anna K. Dickson (eds), *EU Development Cooperation: From Model to Symbol* (Manchester: Manchester University Press, 2004), pp. 2–3.

73. Oxfam, *Europe's Double Standards: How the EU Should Reform its Trade Policies With the Developing World*, Briefing Paper (London: Oxfam International 2002).

74. Pew Global Attitudes Project, quoted in 'Still not Loved. Now not Envied', *The Economist*, 25 June 2005.

75. Figures from UNHCR website (2006), www.unhcr.org.

76. The ten new members, together with prospective members and neighbouring states.

77. Quoted by Walter LaFeber, *Inevitable Revolutions: The United States in Central America*, 2nd ed. (New York: Norton, 1993).

78. Don M. Coerver and Linda B. Hall, *Tangled Destinies: Latin America and the United States* (Albuquerque, NM: University of New Mexico Press, 1999), p. 18.

79. Lars Schoultz, *Beneath the United States: A History of US Policy Toward Latin America* (Cambridge, MA: Harvard University Press, 1998), pp. xv–xvi.

80. Peter H. Smith, *Talons of the Eagle: Dynamics of US–Latin American Relations*, 2nd ed. (New York: Oxford University Press, 2000), Chapter 8.

81. See Abraham F. Lowenthal (ed.), *Exporting Democracy: The United States and Latin America* (Baltimore, MD: Johns Hopkins University Press, 1991).

82. Abraham F. Lowenthal, 'The United States and Latin American Democracy: Learning from History', in Lowenthal, *Exporting Democracy*, pp. 399–400.

83. Smith, *Talons of the Eagle*, Chapter 12.

84. Latinobarómetro poll, 2005, quoted in 'Bush Heads into Bandit Country', in *The Times*, 3 November 2005.

85. Peter Hakim, 'Is Washington Losing Latin America?', in *Foreign Affairs* 85:1, January/February 2006, pp. 39–53.

86. Carolyn Rhodes, 'Introduction', in Rhodes, *The European Union in the World Community*, p. 8.

87. Rosecrance, 'The European Union: A New Type of International Actor'.

88. See William A. Orme, *Understanding NAFTA: Mexico, Free Trade and the New North America* (Austin, TX: University of Texas Press, 1996), pp. 30–9.

89. Sidney Weintraub, 'The North American Free Trade Agreement', in Ali M. El-Agraa (ed.), *Economic Integration Worldwide* (New York: St Martin's Press, 1997).

90. Robert A. Pastor, *Toward a North American Community: Lessons from the Old World for the New* (Washington, DC: Institute for International Economics, 2001), p. 172. See also pp. 8–14, 59–62.

91. See Timothy Murithi, *The African Union: Pan-Africanism, Peacebuilding and Development* (Aldershot: Ashgate, 2005).

Chapter 6

1. David Rothkopf, 'In Praise of Cultural Imperialism?', in *Foreign Policy* 107, Summer 1997, pp. 38–53.

2. Samuel P. Huntington, *The Clash of Civilizations and the Remaking of the World Order* (New York: Simon and Schuster, 1996).

3. For a survey, see Barry Rubin and Judith Colp Rubin, *Hating America: A History* (New York: Oxford University Press, 2004).

4. See John J. Miller and Mark Molesky, *Our Oldest Enemy: A History of America's Disastrous Relationship with France* (New York: Doubleday, 2004).

5. For example, see Paul Hollander, *Anti-Americanism: Irrational and Rational* (New Brunswick, NJ: Transaction, 1995); Andrew Ross and Kristin Ross (eds), *Anti-Americanism* (New York: New York University Press, 2004); Kishore Mahbubani, *Beyond the Age of Innocence: Rebuilding Trust Between America and the World* (New York: Public Affairs, 2005); Tony Judt and Denis Lacorne (eds), *With Us or Against Us: Studies in Global Anti-Americanism* (New York: Palgrave Macmillan, 2005); Richard Crockatt, *America Embattled: 9/11, Anti-Americanism and the Global Order* (London: Routledge, 2003); Brendan O'Connor and Martin Griffiths (eds), *The Rise of Anti-Americanism* (London: Routledge, 2005).

6. See, for example, Bush's speech to Congress on 21 September 2001.

7. Larry Diamond, 'Patching Things Up', in *Hoover Digest* 3, Summer 2003.

8. Paul Johnson, 'Anti-Americanism is Racist Envy', in *Forbes.com*, 21 July 2003, www.forbes.com/global.

9. Minxin Pei, 'The Paradoxes of American Nationalism', in *Foreign Policy* 136, May/June 2003, pp. 30–7.

10. Jean-François Revel, *Anti-Americanism* (New York: Encounter, 2004).

11. Chalmers Johnson, *Blowback: The Costs and Consequences of American Empire* (New York: Metropolitan, 2000).

12. Rubin and Rubin, *Hating America*.

13. Ziauddin Sardar and Merryl Wynn Davies, *Why Do People Hate America?* (New York, NY: Disinformation, 2003), pp. 194–203. See also discussion in Mark Hertsgaard, *The Eagle's Shadow: Why America Fascinates and Infuriates the World* (New York: Farrar, Strauss and Giroux, 2002).

14. Speech prepared upon receiving the Nobel Prize for Literature, 2005.

15. 'Anti-Americanism', in *The Economist*, 17 February 2005.

16. 'US Image up Slightly but Still Negative', Pew Global Attitudes Project press release, Washington, DC, 23 June 2005.

17. Review quoted on dust jacket of Hollander, *Anti-Americanism*.

18. It was down from 71 per cent to 59 per cent in Canada, from 83 per cent to 55 per cent in Britain, from 62 per cent to 43 per cent in France, from 78 per cent to 41 per cent in Germany, from 75 per cent to 38 per cent in Indonesia, and from 52 per cent to 23 per cent in Turkey.

19. Andrew Kohut, 'Anti-Americanism: Causes and Characteristics', Pew Research Center Commentary, 10 December 2003, http://people-press.org/commentary. See also 'Still not Loved. Now not Envied', *The Economist*, 25 June 2005.

20. A search on Google in May 2006 provided an unscientific indication of how anti-Americanism compares to anti-Europeanism; the former resulted in more than four million hits, while the latter resulted in 31,000.

21. See Timothy Garton Ash, 'Anti-Europeanism in America', in *New York Review of Books* 50:2, 13 February 2003.

22. Robert S. Leiken, 'Europe's Angry Muslims', in *Foreign Affairs* 84:4, July/August 2005, pp. 120–35.

23. Christopher Booker and Richard North, *The Great Deception: A Secret History of the European Union* (London: Continuum, 2003), Chapter 20.

24. John Redwood, *Stars and Strife: The Coming Conflicts Between the USA and the European Union* (Basingstoke: Palgrave Macmillan 2001), p. 182.

25. Franck Petiteville, 'Exporting "Values"? EU External Cooperation as a 'Soft Diplomacy', in Michèle Knodt and Sebastiaan Princen (eds), *Understanding the European Union's External Relations* (London: Routledge, 2003).

26. Quoted in Andrew J. Bacevich and Lawrence E. Kaplan, "Battle Wary', in *New Republic*, 25 May 1998, p. 20.

27. Rothkopf, 'In Praise of Cultural Imperialism?'.

28. Pew Global Attitudes Project, 'Views of a Changing World' (Washington, DC: Pew Research Center for the People and the Press, June 2003), p. T59.

29. See discussion in Minxin Pei, 'The Paradoxes of American Nationalism'.

30. Anatol Lieven, *America Right or Wrong: An Anatomy of American Nationalism* (New York: Oxford University Press, 2004), p. 2.

31. HarrisInteractive, 24 June 2004, www.harrisinteractive.com/news. US figure is for 2002, all other figures are for 2004.

32. All results from European Commission, *Eurobarometer* 63, Spring 2005, pp. 43–6 and 111, and 64, Autumn 2005.

33. European Commission, *Eurobarometer* 63, Spring 2005, pp. 50–4.

34. Mark Leonard, *Why Europe Will Run the 21st Century* (London: Fourth Estate, 2005), p. 13.

35. Eric Schlosser, *Fast Food Nation: The Dark Side of the All-American Meal* (New York: Harper Perennial, 2002).

36. Rothkopf, 'In Praise of Cultural Imperialism?'.

37. Not everyone is agreed on the degree or the significance of secularization in Europe. See, for example, Andrew M. Greeley, *Religion in Europe at the End of the Second Millennium: A Sociological Profile* (New Brunswick, NJ: Transaction, 2003).

38. George Weigel, *The Cube and the Cathedral: Europe, America, and Politics Without God* (New York: Basic Books, 2005).

39. Crouch, Colin, 'The Quiet Continent: Religion and Politics in Europe', in *Political Quarterly* 71: Supplement 1, August 2000, pp. 90–103.

40. Grace Davie, *Religion in Britain Since 1945: Believing Without Belonging* (Oxford: Blackwell, 1994) and *Religion in Modern Europe: A Memory Mutates* (Oxford: Oxford University Press, 2000).

41. Gerda Hamberg, *Studies in the Prevalence of Religious Beliefs and Religious Practices in Contemporary Sweden* (Uppsala: Uppsala Academy of Sciences, 1990).

42. J. Christopher Soper and Joel Fetzer, 'Religion and Politics in a Secular Europe: Cutting Against the Grain', in Ted G. Jelen and Clyde Wilcox (eds), *Religion and Politics in Comparative Perspective: The One, the Few, and the Many* (Cambridge: Cambridge University Press, 2002).

43. For discussion, see Carole Tonge, 'A Christian Union?', in *New Humanist* 18:2, 1 June 2003.

44. Patrick Buchanan, *The Death of the West: How Dying Populations and Immigrant Invasions Imperil Our Country and Civilization* (New York: Thomas Dunne, 2002).

45. Clyde Wilcox and Ted G. Jelen, 'Religion and Politics in an Open Market: Religious Mobilization in the United States', in Jelen and Wilcox, *Religion and Politics in Comparative Perspective*, pp. 294–5.

46. Gallup International, Gallup International Millennium Survey. Results at www.gallup-international.com.

47. Associated Press/Ipsos poll, 6 June 2005, www.ipsos-na.com.

48. Pew Global Attitudes Project, 'Views of a Changing World', p. T64.

49. Ibid., p. T58.

50. Will Hutton, *The World We're In* (London: Abacus, 2003), pp. 57–8.

51. CBS News/*New York Times* poll, November 2004, quoted in *New York Times Magazine*, 20 February 2005, p. 15.

52. '"Creationist" Schools Attacked', in BBC News Online, 28 April 2003, http://news.bbc.co.uk.

53. July 2005 poll by Pew Forum on Religion and Public Life and Pew Research Center for the People and the Press, quoted in *International Herald Tribune*, 1 September 2005.

54. See Allen Hertzke, *Freeing God's Children: The Unlikely Alliance for Global Human Rights* (Lanham, MD: Rowman and Littlefield, 2004).

55. John B. Judis, 'The Chosen Nation: The Influence of Religion on US Foreign Policy', Carnegie Endowment for International Peace, Policy Brief 37, March 2005.

56. 'Rice Presses Karzai on Convert's Life', 24 March 2006, www.washingtonpost.com.

57. See discussion in Kenneth D. Wald, *Religion and Politics in the United States*, 4th ed. (Lanham, MD: Rowman and Littlefield, 2003), pp. 151–3.

58. R. Laurence Moore, 'American Religion as Cultural Imperialism', in R. Laurence Moore and Maurizio Vaudagna (eds), *The American Century in Europe* (Ithaca, NY: Cornell University Press, 2003).

59. See discussion in Wald, *Religion and Politics in the United States*, Chapter 9.

60. The figures were 58 per cent of Americans, 39 per cent of Germans, 36 per cent of the French, 33 per cent of Britons, 31 per cent of Poles, 24 per cent of Italians, and 22 per cent of Russians. Pew Global Attitudes Project, 'Views of a Changing World', p. T42.

61. The figures were 95 per cent of Britons and Russians, 94 per cent of Poles, 90 per cent of Germans, 89 per cent of Italians, and 87 per cent of the French. Pew Global Attitudes Project, 'Views of a Changing World', p. T55.

62. The figures were 32 per cent of Americans, 35 per cent of Canadians, 48 per cent of Britons, 54 per cent of the French, 63 per cent of Poles, 66 per cent of Italians, and 68 per cent of Germans. Pew Global Attitudes Project, 'Views of a Changing World', p. T7.

63. Amnesty International figures quoted in CNN report, 'US One of a Few Nations with Juvenile Death Laws', 26 January 2004, www.cnn.com.

64. The figures were 83 per cent of Germans, 77 per cent of French, 74 per cent of Britons, 72 per cent of Italians, and 51 per cent of Americans. Pew Global Attitudes Project, 'Views of a Changing World', p. T65.

65. For a discussion of the issues involved, see Evan Gerstmann, *Same-Sex Marriage and the Constitution* (New York: Cambridge University Press, 2003); Ellen Andersen, *Out of the Closets and into the Courts* (Ann Arbor, MI: University of Michigan Press, 2005).

66. Different polls in recent years have found either slightly more than half opposing same-sex marriage or slightly more than half expressing support.

67. For more details see John McCormick, *The Global Environmental Movement*, 2nd ed. (Chichester: Wiley, 1995), Chapter 1.

68. Pew Global Attitudes Project, 'Views of a Changing World', p. T105.
69. World Commission on Environment and Development, *Our Common Future* (Oxford: Oxford University Press, 1987), p. 8.
70. See Susan Baker and John McCormick, 'Sustainable Development: Comparative Understandings and Responses', in Norman J. Vig and Michael G. Faure (eds), *Green Giants: Environmental Policy of the United States and the European Union* (Cambridge, MA: MIT Press, 2004).
71. For an overview of the climate change issue, see Robert Lempert, 'Finding Transatlantic Common Ground on Climate Change?', in *International Spectator* 36:2, April–June 2001.
72. For details, see McCormick, *Environmental Policy in the European Union*, pp. 280–90.
73. See Jonathan Golub, *New Instruments for Environmental Policy in the EU* (London: Routledge, 1998).
74. For discussion, see chapters in Vig and Faure, *Green Giants?*.

Chapter 7

1. For discussion, see Geoffrey Edwards, 'The Problems and Possible Future Development of a European Identity in the European Union', in Peter J. Anderson, Georg Wiessala and Christopher Williams (eds), *New Europe in Transition* (London: Continuum, 2000), and David Dunkerley, Lesley Hodgson, Stanislaw Konopacki, Tony Spybey and Andrew Thompson, *Changing Europe: Identities, Nations and Citizens* (London: Routledge, 2002).
2. See results of Eurobarometer surveys on the Europa web site at http://europa.eu.int/comm/public_opinion.
3. Václav Havel, address to the European Parliament, Strasbourg, 16 February 2000.
4. Roger Scruton, *A Dictionary of Political Thought*, 2nd ed. (London: Macmillan (now Palgrave Macmillan), 1996), p. 180.
5. Dominique Strauss-Kahn, quoted in *Le Monde*, 26 February 2003.
6. Jürgen Habermas and Jacques Derrida, 'February 15, or What Binds Europe Together: Plea for a Common Foreign Policy, Beginning in Core Europe', in *Frankfurter Allgemeine Zeitung*, 31 May 2003. Reproduced in Daniel Levy, Max Pensky and John Torpey (eds), *Old Europe, New Europe, Core Europe* (London: Verso, 2005).
7. Will Hutton, *The World We're In* (London: Abacus, 2003), pp. 54–8.
8. See Lars Rensmann, 'Europeanism and Americanism in the Age of Globalization', in *European Journal of Political Theory* 5:2, 2006, pp. 139–70.
9. Timothy Garton Ash, *Free World* (New York: Random House, 2004), Chapter 2.
10. See discussion in Philip H. Gordon and Jeremy Shapiro, *Allies at War: America, Europe, and the Crisis Over Iraq* (New York: McGraw-Hill, 2004), pp. 189–93.

11.　Joseph Nye, *Bound to Lead: The Changing Nature of American Power* (New York: Basic Books, 1990); and *Soft Power: The Means to Success in World Politics* (New York: Public Affairs, 2004).

12.　Alfred van Staden, 'The Case for Complementarity', speech to conference organized by the German Council on Foreign Relations, Berlin, June 2003, reproduced on Tech Central Station website, ww.techcentralstation.be.

13.　Francis Fukuyama, comments at Brookings Institution seminar 'What's Next for the United States and Europe?', 10 November 2004, www.brookings.edu.

14.　Clyde Prestowitz, *Rogue Nation: American Unilateralism and the Failure of Good Intentions* (New York: Basic Books, 2003), pp. 236–7.

15.　Jeremy Rifkin, *The European Dream: How Europe's Vision of the Future is Quietly Eclipsing the American Dream* (New York: Jeremy Tarcher/Penguin, 2004)

16.　'Ducking Change, the European Way', in *The Economist*, 22 April 2006.

17.　Owen Harries, 'The Collapse of "the West"', in *Foreign Affairs* 72:4, September/October 1993, pp. 41–53.

18.　Charles A. Kupchan, 'The End of the West', in *Atlantic Monthly* 290:4, November 2002, pp. 42–4. See also Anatol Lieven, 'The End of the West?', in *Prospect* 78, September 2002, and David Calleo, 'The Broken West', in *Survival* 46:3, September 2004, pp. 29–38.

19.　Dominique Moïsi, 'Reinventing the West', in *Foreign Affairs* 82:6, November/December 2003, pp. 67–73.

20.　Michael Mastundano, 'Preserving the Unipolar Moment: Realist Theories and US Grand Strategy After the Cold War', in *International Security* 21:4, Spring 1997, pp. 49–88.

21.　Richard Lambert, 'Misunderstanding Each Other', in *Foreign Affairs* 82:2, March/April 2003, pp. 62–74.

22.　G. John Ikenberry, 'Liberal Hegemony or Empire? American Power in the Age of Unipolarity', in David Held and Mathias Koenig-Archibugi (eds), *American Power in the 21st Century* (Cambridge: Polity, 2004).

23.　Philip H. Gordon and Jeremy Shapiro, *Allies at War: America, Europe, and the Crisis Over Iraq* (New York: McGraw-Hill, 2004), pp. 185–6.

24.　Geir Lundestad, *The United States and Western Europe Since 1945: From 'Empire' by Invitation to Transatlantic Drift* (Oxford: Oxford University Press, 2003), pp. 3–5.

25.　Elizabeth Pond, *Friendly Fire: The Near-Death of the Transatlantic Alliance* (Pittsburgh, PA: European Union Studies Association, 2004), p. x.

26.　Thomas S. Mowle, *Allies at Odds? The United States and the European Union* (New York: Palgrave Macmillan, 2004), pp. 147, 159–68.

27.　Gerald A. Dorfman, 'Why We Need Europe', in *Hoover Digest* 1, Winter 2005.

28.　Doug Bereuter and John Lis, 'Broadening the Transatlantic Relationship', in *Washington Quarterly* 27:1, Winter 2003–04, pp. 147–62.

29.　Samuel P. Huntington, 'The Lonely Superpower', in *Foreign Affairs* 78:2, March/April 1999, pp. 35–49.

Index